# MAN
# BUSINESS ANALYSTS

### Edited by Rick Clare, CBAP, OCP, PMP

http://iiba.org

# MANAGING BUSINESS ANALYSTS

International Institute of Business Analysis, Toronto, Ontario, Canada.

ISBN-13: 978-0-9811292-7-3 (print)
ISBN-13: 978-0-9811292-8-0 (ebook/PDF)

Managing Editor: Rick Clare, CBAP, OCP, PMP
Editor-in-Chief: Kevin Brennan, CBAP, PMP
Editor: Tracey Peer
Graphic Design: Adam Jury

http://iiba.org

# SPECIAL THANKS

A special thank you to our reviewers who checked the book's content and lent us their expertise. Your feedback, suggestions, and wealth of experience helped to shape and define how to successfully manage a Business Analyst.

- Patrick van Abbema, CBAP, PMP, CSP
- Ken Alexander, CBAP, CBA
- Jennifer Battan, CBAP
- Laura Brandenburg, CBAP
- Bart den Dulk
- Lisa Campbell, CBAP
- Cj Cummings, PMP, ITIL, CSM
- Steve Erlank
- Linda Erzah, CBAP
- Roel de Graaf, MBA/MBI
- Kathleen B. (Kitty) Hass, PMP
- Alain Henry
- Ola Ifidon, CBAP, PMP
- Tammy Jones, CBAP
- Aminah Nailor, CBAP
- Laura Paton, MBA, CBAP, PMP, CSM
- Joy Toney, MBA, CBAP

# TABLE OF CONTENTS

# INTRODUCTION: MANAGING BUSINESS ANALYSTS

By Rick Clare, OCP, PMP, CBAP

Managing Business Analysts is easy. All you have to do is understand their capabilities thoroughly, provide for their training as they continuously grow, adjust your processes to include the added flood of communications activities that will accompany them, cater to their need to analyze everything to the bitter end, lead the effort to establish a Business Analysis Centre of Excellence, produce excellent corporate document templates (or be prepared to substantially change the existing ones), modify your management strategy to maximize collaboration and minimize the authoritarian approach (and be prepared to politely discuss almost every decision), join the process of changing your company's Project Management strategy, become a champion of an expanded business analysis career path, have a thorough understanding of any off-shore impacts on your team, and seriously look into gaining the Certified Business Analysis Professional™ (CBAP®) credential yourself. See? Nothing to it!

## What is Business Analysis?

Business analysis is the art of helping business people and solution people understand one another. Usually when we refer to business analysis, we are talking about Information Technology (IT), although it must be stressed that the skills of a good Business Analyst are useful in just about any industry. In the training world, we are starting to see construction and engineering people show up in our Business Analysis classes, but the vast majority of students are still IT. This makes sense since business analysis began in the IT world.

Business analysis is essentially translation work and it was born of hard necessity. To a business team, software programs are tools that are just supposed to work. The job of the business team is to increase the revenue of the company so they employ marketing and sales techniques, coming up with new ideas and looking for ways to implement those ideas as quickly as possible. They know that software helps them but they have little concept of how software is designed or built. They do not really understand the limitations under which IT operates, nor should they since *this is not their job*.

Software developers, on the other hand, *do* understand how computers think and work. They know the various computer languages and how they can be used to build the applications that are needed. What they do not really understand is *why* these applications are needed and the ultimate goal of the project. To them, the software itself is the goal, with the code they write and the testing they do aimed simply at producing a working program. They are not thinking about the deep business objectives that drive the work, nor should they since *this is not their job*.

As explained above, the business team and software developers are two disparate groups, each lost in their own way of thinking. What is needed is a bridge between the groups, and business analysis is that bridge. Business Analysts need to understand business perspectives without being sales or marketing personnel. They also need to comprehend the developer's viewpoint even though they aren't Java or Oracle coders. Thus, Business Analysts are the glue that holds these two worlds together, and this book is about how to manage them while they do that.

# What is a Business Analyst?

The Business Analyst (BA) that we are talking about managing in this book is the *new* BA, the one defined, codified, and certified by International Institute of Business Analysis™ (IIBA). Many companies still do not have BAs in place or at best have another profession using that title. In fact, one of the problems with business analysis is the title itself because it sounds like someone who analyzes businesses, perhaps an efficiency expert or a stockbroker. Many companies use the term BA when in fact they mean a Subject Matter Expert (SME), and many of us have encountered these SMEs in BA clothing. It can be a frustrating experience for both sides because often expectations are not met anywhere. The SME, confident and comfortable in their role as a holder of knowledge, is confused and angered by the additional and confusing requirements workload, and the manager is frustrated with someone who cannot get the true BA job done. In actuality, the manager is looking for the professional who is defined clearly in *A Guide to the Business Analysis Body of Knowledge*® (*BABOK*® *Guide*): the facilitator or bridge between the business units and the solution team.

The BA profession had its inception during the software crisis of the 1960s and 1970s. In the very early days of computing, the programs that could be created were very simple, usually just tallying large sets of numbers. As computers evolved and the human/machine interfaces become more sophisticated, it became possible to write more complex programs and users started demanding more. The problem was that the only people who knew anything at all about the computers were the programmers, and it proved to be very difficult for the business teams to communicate with these "techies". This communication breakdown resulted in software that met no one's needs.

The solution was a new job—Systems Analyst (SA). An SA was someone who knew enough about the technical nature of the machines and the programmers to understand their limitations and capabilities, but at the same time possessed the ability to translate these facts into something that the business people could understand. The modern BA profession has its roots in this job and the term is still used today, often as a synonym for BA.

The Developers of the late 1980s also served as a source for the BA profession. In its early use, the term Developer was intended to describe someone who was not just a computer programmer but who also possessed the skills to design and analyze the system prior to its actual construction. Developers could use cool new tools like Entity Relationship Diagrams and Process Maps, and they usually had to be adept at communicating with the users of the system to understand what exactly was needed. If this job description sounds eerily like a BA, your intuition is serving you well! Today the term Developer is often used in a simpler sense and can often represent a pure programmer, but the term still envokes analysis and design rather than simply coding. Except for the actual coding skills, all of the skills that were used earlier by Developers apply to the modern BA.

What characteristics or traits does this professional display? What skills does a modern BA, as defined by the IIBA®, possess? The BA:

- Is an excellent communicator, in all meanings of the word
- Is capable of guiding groups of people through difficult events
- Is an excellent documenter and researcher
- Is able to use many software tools in pursuit of the truth
- Can acquire business knowledge quickly
- Can acquire technical knowledge, or whatever else is needed for an understanding of any potential solution, quickly
- Approaches each problem with an open, analytical mind
- Is unsatisfied with mediocrity
- Is a champion of the customer
- Is trained and experienced in many elicitation techniques
- Loves diagrams and models as expressions of information as well as analysis techniques
- Uses collaboration and detective work to get the requirements right
- Is not afraid of change (shouldn't be, anyway!)
- Knows more about project management than they want to admit!
- Knows more about quality assurance than they think!
- Wants bigger and better things—they are ambitious for themselves and for their profession

# What is Management?

At one time, management was easy to define, at least on paper. A Manager was a person who was in charge of other people. The world has become more sophisticated since the early 20th century, when this simplistic definition held sway, and the term Manager is used in many ways now. For example, a Project Manager may not be in charge of anybody at all. This fact adds greatly to the challenge of the task of Project Management, when that person is tasked with completing a job while being given no direct control over the project personnel. Many of us have been in this position and we find ourselves asking rather than ordering, a situation at which a Manager of the 1920s would scoff.

The workplace has changed as well. As education levels have climbed through the years, the dynamics of command have changed and very few civilian environments today will tolerate the level of authority that a military structure displays. The IT industry especially has become a place where persuasion and education are the primary management methods. Those of us who have managed in an IT environment know very well that if we push too hard, they will walk. Even in a recession, IT work can be found elsewhere. One of the criteria used by senior management in the IT world to evaluate managers is turnover rate. If you are losing too many people, there is something wrong with your management style.

So, what has management become? These days, it is more about accomplishing the goal than being the boss. Your project results and how your people learn are the measures of success. It is not about distributing orders in all directions; it is about collaboration and teamwork. At the same time, if you are responsible for other people's actions, you do have to *manage* them by knowing what they are doing and guiding them as necessary. It has become fashionable in some circles to speak of empowerment and to denounce actual interaction as "micro-management". This approach only succeeds if you are redundant. If this is your management method, and it is working well for you, consider retirement!

# What Can This Book Offer Me?

This book is full of advice and guidance on how to take on the management of BAs, written from many perspectives. Here you will read about how BAs manage themselves and how they might manage other BAs. You will also encounter information on how Project Managers (PMs) can best make use of the BAs on their teams and on how Senior Management can adapt corporate processes to take advantage of the skills that BAs bring to the table. How will off-shoring affect the use of BAs? How do they fit into the corporate organization charts? What kind of specialized training will they require? This book can help with these questions, and provide expert-level guidance from people who have been there and done that. Here are just some of the subjects addressed in this book:

- How do PMs manage BAs?
- How do BAs manage BAs?
- How do BAs manage when they find themselves responsible for projects?
- How do functional or line managers manage BAs?
- How should we train our BAs?
- What does the career ladder for BAs look like?
- How should BAs be organized in my company?
- How do I persuade my senior management that BAs bring great value?

This book is a collaborative effort, consisting of the views and contributions of a wide variety of experts in the BA arena. The contributing authors include two Vice-Presidents of the IIBA®, the Presidents of training and consulting companies, well-known international authors, working BA Managers, Trainers, Project Managers, and a number of international contributors. This group's wide range of backgrounds and subject matter expertise provide a perfect blend of theory and real-world experience, and this book should become an excellent resource for you as you manage your way through the world of business a nalysis.

# THE NEW BUSINESS ANALYST

By Kevin Brennan, CBAP, PMP

Business analysis is often referred to as a "new" profession but, in fact, it's been around for decades. Business Analysts (BAs) have worked for years in many large companies, performing management consulting, developing Requirements for software systems, identifying and improving business processes, and helping to manage change as it affects the people, processes, and technology in an organization.

Nevertheless, the profession of business analysis is changing, as shown by the existence of and interest in this book.

First, there's a growing tendency in organizations to see IT as something woven into everything they do, rather than as a thing in and of itself. Recent innovations, including adoption of business process management (BPM) systems and business rules engines, cloud computing, and ERP (enterprise resource planning) platforms, as well as new methodologies such as agile software development, are pushing the profession away from the traditional lengthy Requirements document.

Similarly, these technologies are forcing the traditional management consultant to become much more "IT savvy" and understand the role technology plays in the business. Where Business Analysts once may have seen themselves as bridging the gap between business and IT, we now have to think of IT as one of a number of ways we can help to create value for our stakeholders.

In the past, many organizations viewed their Business Analysts as technical writers or scribes, who were primarily responsible for documenting the needs of users so that everyone could agree on what those users wanted. A similar complaint is common about management consultants—I've heard a consultant defined as "someone who borrows your watch and then tells you what time it is". Those traditional skills are still needed but today that skill-set is only enough for a relatively junior BA.

To be truly effective in the role, Business Analysts must understand a wide range of analysis techniques, knowing when and how to apply them, and to provide stakeholders with useful guidance in understanding what solutions will be effective for their business. Effective Business Analysts need as much education and training, and need to put as much time and effort into honing their skills, as good Project Managers (PMs) or good developers. If you're a manager responsible for leading a team of Business Analysts, you need to understand how the role is evolving and what you can do to help your Business Analysts do it better.

# What Does a BA Do?

First of all, let's make sure we are all working from the a common set of assumptions about the role. Many organizations use the "Business Analyst" title to describe someone who can fill multiple roles on a team (a sort of utility player, with Requirements Analysis, project management, development, and testing skills) or a junior PM. In reality, business analysis is a distinct profession. Version 2 of *A Guide to the Business Analysis Body of Knowledge*® (*BABOK*® *Guide)* defines business analysis as:

*... the set of tasks and techniques used to work as a liaison among stakeholders in order to understand the structure, policies, and operations of an organization, and to recommend solutions that enable the organization to achieve its goals.*

First of all, this recognizes that business analysis is needed most when we have to work in a liaison role among a group of stakeholders. That's not to say that a person can't perform business analysis on their own but rather that we perform analysis to reduce a complex question to a manageable level of simplicity. As the number of stakeholders affected by a solution increases, so too does the complexity of the problem.

If you have a single customer for a product or service, you may be able to simply ask that person what he or she wants and then give that to them. That person may still do business analysis but probably has some operational or management responsibility as well (and that is probably their "real" job). When you are dealing with large numbers of stakeholders, they are likely to have conflicting and often confusing requirements. The conflicts arise naturally because each stakeholder has a different perspective on the problems faced by the organization and different priorities regarding the solution.

While it would be nice to imagine that we can solve these problems simply by pointing everyone to the organization's strategy, that rarely works in practice. Many organizations don't have a clearly articulated strategy or make decisions in ways that directly contradict their stated objectives. Often, different operational groups will have strategies of their own. Even if the executives think they have a clear strategy, and they all agree on what it is, that strategy may be intentionally or unintentionally kept secret from the employees. And then, even if there is general agreement and understanding of the strategy, people may legitimately disagree on the tactics used to accomplish it.

Complex problems force us to break down the issue to understand the organization and how its various components, groups, and processes interact. In fact, that's one of the key meanings of the term "analysis" (it also can refer to psychoanalysis, which is another big part of the BA role). We analyze businesses in order to understand, and to help others understand, how the organization is structured, how work is performed, and what systems and functionality is needed to support that work.

**How Executives Think
Their Strategies Work**

**How the Strategy
is Actually Executed**

That's the first essential role of the Business Analyst: to bring clarity to business decisions and assist participants in understanding the role they play in the larger objectives. Certainly, the additional insight given by business analysis into those decisions doesn't guarantee that the organization's strategy will be effective, but without that objective analysis, all you can do is hope that the requirements your stakeholders come up with will actually benefit the organization. The Business Analyst must be prepared to act as a facilitator to help stakeholders overcome this challenge.

When acting as a facilitator, a Business Analyst focuses primarily on helping people understand and articulate their own goals, objectives, and solutions. A good facilitator uses their experience as a tool to help ask probing questions designed to uncover potential issues but ultimately responsibility for finding the right answer lies with the business stakeholders. The outcomes are theirs.

A good facilitator is not a passive participant in the discussion and is most certainly not simply an order taker. Effective facilitation is hard work; you have to be effective at ensuring that conflicts are exposed and resolved in a productive fashion, that all stakeholders have a chance to express their opinion, and that decisions are made in the best interests of the organization and not just based on the opinion of the strongest or most senior person.

Business Analysts must typically take the facilitator role upon entering the profession because they lack the business knowledge and experience to consider taking on the other roles. However, that doesn't mean that more experienced BAs abandon that role. Many remain facilitators for their entire career and often advocate this face as the only one Business Analysts should adopt.

Ultimately, though, the role of the facilitator is a support role, and Business Analysts seeking to increase their authority and influence must learn to act as a consultant as well. We don't perform analysis simply to explain the organization, we perform it so that we can then use that information to figure out what changes to the organization are needed so that the organization can accomplish goals and objectives that have been set within it, and to deliver value to its stakeholders. In short, we also have to synthesize a solution to the problem faced by the organization.

Consultants are expected to have an in-depth knowledge of a particular business domain, solution type, or software application, and to bring that knowledge into their work as a Business Analyst. They will still engage in the usual business analysis activities but will do so with a different goal in mind. They are expected to contribute to the design of the solution or may even be responsible for that design. They work with stakeholders to understand the current situation and to create buy-in for their proposed resolution.

Consultants must use their facilitation skills in order to be effective. You need to listen in order to understand what the real needs of the organization are because if you propose something that doesn't meet those needs, you will fail in this role.

Some Business Analysts will move beyond facilitating and consulting to take on the responsibilities of an owner. Owners are responsible for the successful implementation and ongoing operation of a solution. An owner is unlikely to do business analysis full-time and may not even think of himself or herself as a BA.

As an owner, the Business Analyst will likely focus heavily on enterprise analysis work and may be supported by other BAs taking on the other roles. Analysis becomes more ad-hoc and intended largely to support decisions you make as an owner, rather than detailed instructions for someone else to implement. However, the challenges of business analysis in the owner role lie outside the scope of this work.

# Why is the Role Important?

In most organizations, the cost associated with poor processes, poor communication, and unnecessary development due to poor requirements is staggeringly high. Many of these problems can be traced back to ineffective business analysis practices.

The easiest cost to measure, and the one we have the most industry data on, is the cost from rework associated with poor quality or incorrect requirements[1]. The advantage of this metric is that it's one that most companies can actually measure without too much difficulty. That's not to say that it's the best one, or the most important, but it represents a significant cost to most companies. Now, factor in the lost value from late delivery of projects (because the revenue or savings are implemented later) and you typically have a substantial case for change right there.

A number of studies have shown that 40% or more of defects in a typical software development project stem from requirements. Certainly, not all of

---

1   Are requirements inherently unknowable, as some people attest? This is a debate that's gone on for decades, and it's not one that can be resolved because there are a lot of hidden assumptions that go into the discussion. In most organizations, though, we're not building a completely new, unprecedented application from scratch. Most often, we're replacing and improving something that the organization already has. Under these circumstances, most requirements should be (and in my experience are) knowable in advance of implementation. On the other hand, if your company is entering (or creating) a new market, this may well not be the case. Even within a project, requirements may have differing levels of stability—for instance, requirements which relate to meeting legislation or regulations may be much more knowable than an ideal User Interface.

these defects are fixed but bugs that originate in requirements are likely to be more serious and so are more likely to require fixing. How much could your organization save by eliminating 40% of bug fixes? For most companies, that's a substantial sum of money, generally considerably more than they actually spend on business analysis work. Plus there are other, equally expensive, consequences to that wasted effort.

First, late projects don't just lower the value that the project delivers. They also produce a significant opportunity cost. Opportunity cost is the value of the things you could have done if you weren't doing something else. Let's say that your team was supposed to deliver release 5 of the NAS application on December 31 of last year, and instead the project runs six months overdue as a result of avoidable changes to the requirements. Not only do you lose the revenue that would have been generated in that time by the release, but you've also lost whatever other benefits your team could have delivered in that six-month period.

Those delays don't just stem from bug fixing. Poor business analysis also leads to poor estimation because critical elements of the problem are overlooked or the solution ends up being more complex than it really needs to be.

Poor business analysis skills also mean that it's less likely that you will be able to capture the value projects were intended to deliver in the first place. Without effective enterprise analysis, project requirements can devolve into a wish list from various stakeholders. Yes, your stakeholders may individually be happy if they get what they want but there's no guarantee that what they want is what the organization needs.

Uncoordinated changes made without analysis can cause us to make one unit's work easier and another group's harder. They can cause the organization to violate regulations or make unwise decisions. They can save money but make it harder for the organization to accomplish its objectives. It's the Business Analyst's job to make sure that the bigger picture is understood and that the requirements are in line with that larger objective.

# Why is Business Analysis So Hard?

Given how much most organizations struggle with requirements, it may seem a little surprising that more attention hasn't been given to improving them. We've seen a lot of attention being paid to making Project Managers and developers more effective, and even some for testing, but business analysis seems to be almost ignored by comparison.

The reasons for this vary from organization to organization, and in some cases may be rooted in organizational dysfunction—a truly effective Business Analyst will force managers to question the rationale behind their decisions, something many are uncomfortable with. For our purposes here, though, let's assume that you have a reasonably healthy organizational culture and are simply asking how you can better support your Business Analysts. If so, you'll find a lot of advice on how to do that in this book but there's one thing you should understand about the context of BA work as you set out to improve it.

Business Analysts, like most of the people they work with, are *knowledge workers*. That term gets thrown about a lot, so it's probably useful to talk a little about what it actually means. In practical terms, it really has two critical elements. One is that the job requires knowledge to perform, the second is that the job produces knowledge.

The knowledge that Business Analysts need to perform their job is set out in detail in *A Guide to the Business Analysis Body of Knowledge*®, and further supported through IIBA® *Business Analysis Competency Model* and our Certification of Competency in Business Analysis™ (CCBA™) and Certified Business Analysis Professional (CBAP®) certification programs. Understanding how they produce knowledge, and what that knowledge needs to look like, is more challenging.

Business analysis processes are incapable of being easily defined and modeled. The *BABOK*® *Guide* provides a framework for business analysis processes but no more. The reason it's a framework is that business analysis work is essentially improvisational—we can set goals for it, define deliverables and outcomes, but we should not expect to be able to define exactly how that work will progress in advance. This is true no matter **what** methodology you follow: agile, iterative, or waterfall; change-driven or plan-driven; BPR or continuous improvement.

The problem is that external events shape every business analysis effort. For example, during any requirements analysis process, we may:

- Identify an overlooked stakeholder
- Experience a change in organizational priorities
- Experience a change in the executive sponsor (who sets a new direction)
- Have to respond to changes in the marketplace
- Have to respond to changes in legislation

Each of these events can force us to redo much of our pre-existing business analysis work. Even without an external event, we may find ourselves having to step back in the process just because we have realized that the problem-solving approach we're using isn't a good fit for the problem—for instance, we're working on developing requirements for a software application only to come to the realization that the problem fundamentally lies in the business process that the application was supposed to support.

So how do you improve an improvisational, exploratory process? It may sound impossible but just because a task has unpredictable elements doesn't mean you can't get better at doing it. In fact, many of the tasks you perform every day have unpredictable elements, like driving to work. A skilled BA will need to get better at anticipating and responding to changes in the environment, or learning to investigate a clue that a problem may exist that hasn't been clearly understood.

The key is to remember that business analysis work is usually performed to support a larger initiative, such as process reengineering, software development, strategic planning, or other changes. That means that we can define an end state that we're working toward. The product of business analysis work is rarely valuable in its own right so the first question you need to ask is what problems are the people using that analysis facing? And what can your business analysis team do to help them? In short, BAs are working to reduce the risk that the implementation of change in the organization will go wrong.

The question for you is where does that risk lie? Is it different stakeholders with different views of reality? Is it that the developers won't consider enough unexpected circumstances when developing their code? Is it that the legislation you operate under is complex and has a lot of specific cases that you have to include? Your Business Aanalysts should focus on the uncertainty your organization faces and ensure that it is effectively assessed and addressed.

Another key skill for effectively estimating and managing business analysis work is, believe it or not, analysis. Business Analysts need to be able to break a problem down into its component parts and understand how they fit together. If you can do that, and if those parts are kept small enough for you to figure out the work involved in a reliable way, you can do a pretty good job of managing the process. For instance, I know from years of experience that I can create a fully detailed use case, including alternative flows, in about 1–2 days of work effort. Once I know how many use cases will be needed to support a business area, I can give a fairly reliable estimate of how long it will take to complete the requirements, assuming I have reasonable access to key stakeholders. My first step in any business analysis effort is to decompose the problem into its constituent parts for this very reason. Certainly, this initial analysis will need to be revised but it's usually a good basis for predicting the work involved. If it turns out to be off-base, that's also a sign that you've run into a problem that's much harder to solve than was likely anticipated in the business case itself.

A common complaint from Business Analysts is that they don't have enough time to do their analysis work. As a manager, you should be alert to these complaints. Certainly, it's possible that this is the cry of a perfectionist unwilling to let something go—but it's at least as likely that your Business Analysts are concerned about real risks to the organization because of conflicts that they know are there but haven't been surfaced, or key requirements that are still ambiguous, or that critical implementation details haven't been considered. If they're bad at articulating these problems, help them to get better at it because they will need to do so in order to become better Business Analysts.

# Who Makes a Good BA?

The qualities that make for a good Business Analyst are set out in chapter eight of the *BABOK® Guide:*

***Analytical Thinking and Problem Solving*** *supports effective identification of business problems, assessment of proposed solutions to those problems, and understanding of the needs of stakeholders. Analytical thinking and problem solving involves assessing a situation, understanding it as fully as possible, and making judgments about possible solutions to a problem.*

***Behavioral Characteristics*** *support the development of effective working relationships with stakeholders and include qualities such as ethics, trustworthiness, and personal organization.*

***Business Knowledge*** *supports understanding of the environment in which business analysis is performed and knowledge of general business principles and available solutions.*

***Communication Skills*** *support Business Analysts in eliciting and communicating Requirements among stakeholders. Communication skills address the need to listen to and understand the audience, understanding how an audience perceives the Business Analyst, understanding of the communications objective(s), the message itself, and the most appropriate media and format for communication.*

***Interaction Skills*** *support the Business Analyst when working with large numbers of stakeholders, and involve both the ability to work as part of a larger team and to help that team reach decisions. While most of the work of business analysis involves identifying and describing a desired future state, the Business Analyst must also be able to help the organization reach agreement that the future state in question is desired through a combination of leadership and facilitation.*

***Software Applications*** *are used to facilitate the collaborative development, recording and distribution of Requirements to stakeholders. Business Analysts should be skilled users of the tools used in their organization and must understand the strengths and weaknesses of each.*

One of the most critical traits I would look for in any prospective Business Analyst is a genuine interest in learning about new ideas and new skills. I suspect that this one trait is the most important indicator as to whether someone will be successful in a business analysis career.

I think a good argument can be made that business analysis, at its core, is about learning and teaching. We work with stakeholders to understand what it is they do and what they need, and we then have to teach others—project teams, managers, and often the stakeholders themselves—what we have learned. To do that we need to be able to absorb a lot of new information and structure it in a useful fashion.

However, this trait is one that affects you in other ways as well. A BA should always be seeking out new ideas. Are other organizations coming up with new methods of customer service? Are there new approaches I should be learning to deal with problems? How will new technology better support the needs of my stakeholders? Look for people who are willing to learn on their own time—not because you want to save on training but because those are the people who are really interested in getting better at their jobs.

# What Skills Should BAs Learn and Improve?

The *BABOK® Guide* lists thirty-two tasks and over forty techniques that Business Analysts should be able to perform, and that number can increase for BAs working in specific areas. That's a lot, so what should you really look for in hiring a BA or helping your BAs improve?

To be honest, I don't think it's unreasonable to expect your senior Business Analysts to be able to use all of those techniques when the situation arises, and that's one of the reasons we do include all of them. A broad mental toolkit is a real asset for a BA. While a smaller set of skills will probably get you through most of the work you have to do, I can remember a number of occasions in my BA career where a problem that had seemed completely intractable proved easy to solve when I tried a different approach or used a different analysis technique.

While circumstances may vary, though, I would want most BAs in most organizations to have strong skills in all of the following areas. (You may also want to take a look at IIBA® *Business Analysis Competency Model* for additional guidance based on specialisation and job level). I'm not suggesting that these are the only things a Business Analyst should be able to do but I do think that skill with these techniques are needed to succeed in about 80% of the situations a Business Analyst is likely to face.

First of all, every, and I mean *every,* Business Analyst should be able to build business cases. If your organization only engages Business Analysts after the business case is developed, you're only hurting yourself. If your BAs don't have this skill, then they need to develop it. The reason is simple: your Business Analysts are the ones working with stakeholders to define their requirements, and if they can't write a business case, they don't have the skills they need to recognize when a proposed requirement will help your business and when it won't. A Business Analyst must be able to figure out when a requirement really is needed by the organization and be able to help set the priorities of various requirements, and you can't do that if you can't write a business case.

The other important thing to understand is that the business case shouldn't be a document written to justify the project and then never referred to again. In reality, the business case is the most important tool your organization has to control project scope creep. Without a solid and current business case for a project, the scope is just an arbitrary set of things your teams have promised to deliver. Business cases explain *why* that scope was selected, and how a solution built to that scope delivers value to the organization[2]. It sets out the goals and objectives of an initiative. If an addition to the work done by the team is needed to support those goals and objectives, then it makes sense as part of the project. If it doesn't, then it shouldn't be included in this project, even if it may belong in another. The point here is that even if a Business Analyst on a project didn't write the original business case, they need to understand it and regularly revisit it to make sure that the assumptions in it are still valid.

A closely related skill is prioritization. This skill has become increasingly important as organizations have moved away from the more traditional, waterfall-style project approach (where prioritization could be reduced to a question of whether a requirement was in or out of scope) to iterative and agile approaches (where "do it later" becomes an increasingly valid option, and where Business Analysts must manage relationships between and dependencies among requirements).

Effective prioritization of requirements involves two critical and distinct skills: the ability to properly assess the value delivered to stakeholders when a requirement is implemented, and the ability to help the various stakeholders reach a consensus on the importance and order in which Requirements are delivered. These are by no means the same thing and in practice it's pretty common to see people focus primarily on the latter and assume that the outcome will reflect the former. Again, BAs must be able to tie this back to the business case that justifies the initiative, as well as work with the Project Manager and team to define and understand necessary dependencies between these changes.

The need for business analysis doesn't end when the solution goes into construction and delivery. Business Analysts need to be able to help assess whether a solution is a fit for the business need and whether it will be successful in production. A critical skill here is the ability to identify and evaluate a solution against acceptance and performance criteria. These criteria set out how the organization can actually understand if the solution is meeting the business needs. They are useful both for the initial testing of a proposed solution and for gathering information on how well a solution performs over time.

---

2    If you're using agile methods, user stories capture much of the information required in a traditional business case—in fact, I think they're closer in purpose to a business case than they are to stakeholder or solution requirements.

Finally, the BA plays a critical role in the benefits realization process. In a lot of organizations, solutions get built and deployed without any real assurance that the goals of the original business case are fulfilled. It's rare that the solution benefits the organization simply because it's been implemented. Usually, there's a need for ongoing organizational, process, or behavioural changes. Part of the solution development process (along with the business case and defining the acceptance criteria) should be to develop the metrics and key performance indicators that will be used to measure its ongoing performance and allow people to correct problems when they occur.

And finally, there are the "traditional" BA skills, the ones related to requirements[3] analysis. These are being discussed last not because they're unimportant, but because many people think that they're all that a BA does, and I wanted them to be put in a broader perspective.

I run into a surprising number of Business Analysts (well, at least surprising to me) who seem to think that use cases are the only analysis technique they need to master. In fact, I would recommend that Business Analysts, whether IT or business focused, need to master several different analysis methods. For a generalist, I would recommend learning the following:

- **Business Rules:** Be able to state policies in a simple, logical, easy to follow fashion. While many business rules can be stated in simple English, a little understanding of concepts like decision trees and tables will help analysts deal with more complex situations and manage ambiguity.
- **Data Dictionaries and Data Models:** Again, Business Analysts need to know what information the business captures and how that information will be stored and used. A good glossary of terms can go a long way towards exposing and resolving discrepancies between the different ways departments use information. While only the more IT-focused analysts will need to be able to go all the way to developing a normalized data model, a logical model can be very useful to clarify relationships between important business concepts.
- **Process Analysis:** Business processes describe how people and groups within organizations collaborate to get work done. Business Analysts must be able to define and understand these processes to find improvements, in order to ensure that all stakeholders agree on what the process actually is, and that software applications that are in place effectively support that work. While process improvement is most likely to be the responsibility of business-focused Business Analysts (or BAs who specialize in process analysis),

---

3    There is a ongoing debate in the BA and software development community regarding the "line" between requirements and design, a distinction often (badly) described as being one between "what" needs to be done and "how" it gets done. The problem with that distinction is that whether something constitutes "what" or "how" is really a matter of perspective—your "what" is your manager or customer's "how". From the perspective of the *BABOK® Guide* and IIBA®, business analysis encompasses any decision that affects the value a stakeholder derives from a solution.

all BAs need to understand the ways in which technological change will affect them.

- **Metrics and Reporting:** BAs need to understand what information managers need to run the day-to-day operations of the organization, how that information is used, what decisions it influences, and how to improve the quality of those decisions.
- **Non-functional Requirements:** These describe the performance and overall quality of the system. They are often very difficult for stakeholders to articulate until and unless the solution fails to meet them. Is it OK if your website is closed down for maintenance one day a month? Do you need to manage 10,000 or 10,000,000 users? This kind of information is likely to have a significant impact on the time and cost for implementation.
- **Use Cases:** Use cases tell you how a person in a particular role will use a system to fulfill a need. They should be written as a relatively short narrative flow—I've seen a certain degree of backlash against them from people who either try to cram too much information into a use case or mistake them for the entirety of the requirements, but when done properly they do an excellent job of scoping the essential functions of an application and ensuring that each function is clearly linked to some kind of stakeholder value.
- **Stakeholder Analysis:** Who will be affected by the solution? What interests of theirs will it affect? How are those stakeholders related to others? Business Analysts should be able to understand what their stakeholders really want and how that may affect the success of a solution.
- **State Transition Diagrams:** I had to add this one to the list even though our research shows it's not that widely used, because it really should be a lot more common. A state transition diagram shows the lifecycle of anything you need to track—from employees, to customers, to products, and how and when that lifecycle progresses. I have had to create at least one of these on every project I've ever worked on and it's always exposed some real business issues.

# What Next?

Business analysis is still maturing as a profession so there's still a lot of variation in what Business Analysts do from organization to organization. Your BA team may or may not have the skills I've described here. If not, you need to start planning your next steps because they're not adding the value to your organization that they should be capable of. Change is always difficult for people and it can be especially difficult when you're challenged to master an entirely new set of skills after having done the same job for years.

Another challenge you may face as a manager is that after years of seeing BAs perform a limited role, your peers within the organization may be reluctant to allow them to take on a greater role in shaping its direction. As a manager of BAs, you have to start thinking of yourself as leader of a consulting practice. Your job, in many ways, is to help the various functional managers look good. You can do that by helping your BAs become effective internal consultants, by giving them the tools they need to do that job, and by helping them influence their co-workers in ways that bring work being done within your organization in line with its strategic goals. To manage Business Analysts effectively, you yourself will have to take on a leadership role in your organization, even if it's a quiet one.

## About the Author

Kevin Brennan, CBAP®, PMP®, is IIBA® Chief Business Analyst and EVP. In this role, he is responsible for IIBA's strategy and alignment of organizational change initiatives, advancing the BA profession through standards development and research, and development of the global community of practice through local chapters and social networks. He led the development of version 2.0 of the BABOK® Guide and served on the IIBA Board of Directors from 2006 to 2009. Prior to his involvement with IIBA®, Kevin worked as a Business Analyst for organizations in several different industries for over a decade.

He can be reached at kevin.brennan@iiba.org.

# BA MANAGEMENT FOR THE LEAD BUSINESS ANALYST

By Janina Buldrini, CBAP

## Introduction

As a Business Analyst (BA) moves forward through his or her career development, at some point the BA will be asked to take the lead on a project. This can mean the Lead BA will work autonomously or by leading one or more Business Analyst practitioners. To become a Lead BA indicates that you've developed the discipline to motivate yourself. The question now becomes how do you lead and motivate others?

Sometimes the BA, Quality Assurance (QA), and Developer teams report to different managers. Sometimes one or more BAs may report to different managers. The communication and reporting up through management and across teams is crucial in keeping everyone on the same page.

Although you are drawing on your prior BA work experiences to be successful, as a Lead BA your communication style becomes the link between you, the BA practitioners, and other project resources. As a Lead BA, you most likely are not creating the requirements analysis deliverables. You are now leading others to create them.

A Lead BA must also coordinate activities and communicate regularly with the Project Manager (PM). The PM and the Lead BA must agree on which tasks, techniques, and work deliverables will be used for requirements analysis.

A Lead BA should be familiar with the BA practitioners they are working with. They should be familiar with each BA practitioner's skill set, strengths, and weaknesses, and be able to account for these when assigning the Requirements analysis tasks.

A Lead BA must keep track of the requirements analysis activities and their progress. If they don't know what's going on, how can they lead others? The Lead BA must be clear on the project scope, project plan, and timing of requirements analysis deliverables.

The problems that a BA may encounter across organizations and projects are common. A Lead BA may have the benefit of prior experience with the organization, culture, management, and organizational project artifacts. A Lead BA may also have knowledge and experience utilizing business analysis methodologies. Regardless, they should be able to communicate what needs to be done, how it needs to be done, when it needs to be done, and what obstacles may be encountered along with how to overcome them. A Lead BA can testify to what works and what doesn't work. A BA practitioner will be more successful, both in the short and long term, with the mentorship of a Lead BA.

# Challenges for the Lead Business Analyst

A Lead BA may encounter one or more of the following challenges:

- The Lead BA may not have managerial or supervisory experience. They may have been "one-of-the-gang" and now are required to set direction and provide leadership.
- Often the Lead BA has been appointed the Lead based on their subject knowledge as well as their prior experience of getting a quality job done. They may not be a natural teacher or may perceive the transition of knowledge as a threat. Also, it could be difficult for them to lead another BA and allow them to do the work while they oversee and fulfill a mentorship role.
- A Lead BA may be assigned to a project in order to strengthen the weaknesses (perceived or real) in a BA practitioner.
- There may be separate teams for BA, QA, and Developers. The BAs themselves may be split across multiple teams. Some of these teams may be geographically dispersed, such as in an outsourcing model.
- The project may require the Lead BA to work with BA practitioners and other project resources that do not have the business or system knowledge. One example of this is an external BA consultant who is engaged to meet the resource demands of a project.
- Sometimes managers and BA practitioners act as if the direct manager is the only one who has the right or authority to set direction, assign work, or rate performance. This can create conflicting loyalties.

## Leading Your Peers

Imagine that you have worked side by side with a peer. You've learned, struggled, and succeeded together. There may even have been times when you failed together. Now you are the Lead BA on a project working with that same peer. How should you proceed? Perhaps you have been brought in as the Lead BA on a project with individuals you have not worked with before. You may be walking into unfamiliar group dynamics.

In order to succeed as a Lead BA it is important to recognize that you are still one of the team, only now your success relies (even more) on the success of others. It is up to you to foster an atmosphere of collaboration and creativity.

As the Lead BA you should take responsibility for the process. Do not be afraid to BE a leader and facilitate. There will be times when you must control the direction. You can do this by having everyone take a step back and rethink the solution, or by steering the group towards a new solution. Do not be afraid to say any of the following or something like it in the spirit of facilitation. Do not be afraid to bring things back to the most basic level as a strategy for refocusing the group.

- "I would like us to take a step back and ........."
- "Have we asked the question why can't it be done?"
- "Have we asked the question why it needs to work this way?"
- "Is there a legal statute or compliance rule that dictates a specific approach?"

Sometimes in a conversation there will be silence. There are some who do not like silence and will fill it by rambling. Try your best not to do this. One approach to jump start the conversation is to ask the team what they think. If you're trying to engage a particular person within the team then ask the question of that person. For example, ask "How would you approach this problem or situation?" People are more inclined to feel they are contributing something and will contribute more if interest in their thought process and experience is expressed.

Draw on your prior experience. Remember what has worked well in the past, what hasn't, and why. Share that with the BA practitioner and the group.

## Resistance—Why *Should* the BA Practitioner Listen to the Lead BA and Why *Should* Others Listen to the Lead BA?

Sometimes BA practitioners resist when one of their peers is assigned as their mentor. Reasons can include loyalty to the direct manager, previous differences with the Lead BA, the feeling that they should have been given the Lead role because they are more senior or have been with the organization or team longer, or that the Lead BA was assigned due to favoritism.

So why have YOU been appointed the Lead BA? Is it based on your domain knowledge? Is it based on your skills? Play to those strengths. Focus on how those strengths give you an advantage and use those advantages to teach others.

Often the BA role is one where the value is not readily perceived. A BA must focus on value creation. Demonstrating skills such as communication, leadership, conflict management, negotiation, and effectively interacting with management will demonstrate the value added role that a BA can be. A Lead BA must be able to display these skills for the practitioners so that the practitioners can learn by example.

For example, if the developers are circumventing the BA and going to the business for direction, then the value of the BA role has not been established. BAs are NOT glorified secretaries although there are some that do think so. BAs are distinguished by the art of elicitation, analysis, and documentation. It is very important to use these skills effectively to demonstrate your value to the project, to the team, and to the organization.

*Figure 1. The following is an example of where the Business Requirement Deliverables do not match the Developer and Quality Assurance Deliverables:*

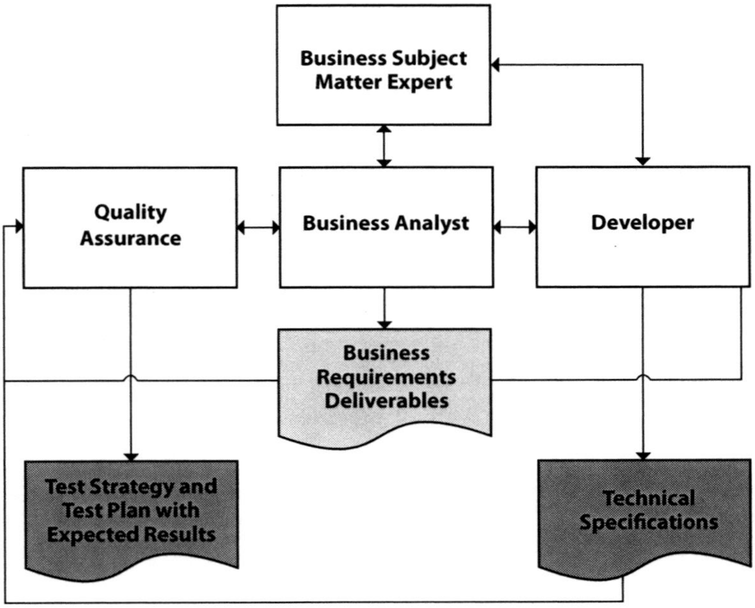

One way to insert the BA role back into the process is to share the requirements management plan with the business, QA, and the Developers. Communicate the techniques that will be used, the timelines for each set of tasks, and the format for the deliverables. Revise the plan based on the feedback received from everyone. This way each component of the team is invested in the requirements analysis process.

*Figure 2. The following is an example of where the Business Requirement Deliverables are in sync with the Developer and Quality Assurance Deliverables:*

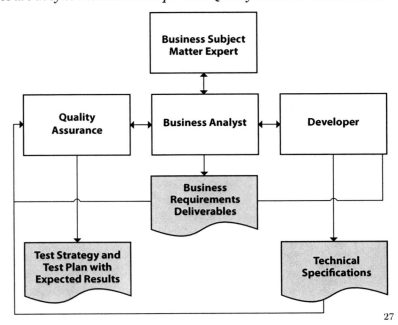

## Confidence—I Could Do a Better Job...

The BA practitioner may feel that they could do a better job than the Lead BA. The practitioner may believe they have the experience to do the role but were not given a chance. They may feel that they have more technical BA experience or subject matter expertise. You can leverage this mindset to assign tasks and enforce accountability. If a practitioner has more technical BA experience, such as data mapping, then assign that practitioner to the technical tasks. If a practitioner has more subject matter expertise, then assign them the elicitation tasks. Develop the practitioners by partnering them up based on their complementary strengths and weaknesses. For example, a practitioner wants to develop their technical experience and another practitioner has the technical experience. Partner them up and assign them the technical tasks of a project. Identify and utilize each practitioner's strengths and weaknesses to assign tasks and provide development opportunities. This can create synergy between peers.

*Figure 3. Example of Synergy Between Peers:*

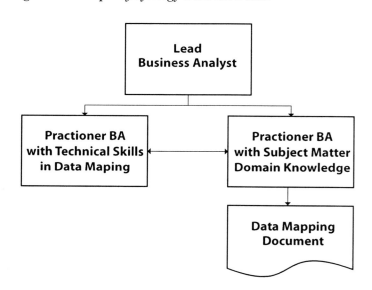

## Management Skills and Experience

Often organizations promote or assign people to supervisory roles based on the expertise they have demonstrated in their work but do not give them additional training or support in people or project management. Often the expectation is that the Lead BA should have no trouble handling the people and project management aspects of the new responsibilities.

A Lead BA most likely became the lead because of their skills and performance in business analysis. Now is the time to build your people skills. Learning more about facilitation would be helpful.

Wikipedia defines *facilitation* as "Any activity which makes tasks for others easy. A facilitator is used in a variety of group settings, including business and other organizations, to describe someone whose role it is to work with group processes to ensure meetings run well and achieve a high degree of consensus."

Wikipedia offers three definitions for *facilitator*[1]:

- "An individual who enables groups and organizations to work more effectively; to collaborate and achieve synergy. She or he is a 'content neutral' party who by not taking sides or expressing or advocating a point of view during the meeting, can advocate for fair, open, and inclusive procedures to accomplish the group's work." (Michael Doyle, quoted in Kaner, et al.)[2]
- "One who contributes *structure* and *process* to interactions so groups are able to function effectively and make high-quality decisions. A helper and enabler whose goal is to support others as they achieve exceptional performance." (Ingrid Bens).[3]
- "The facilitator's job is to *support everyone to do their best thinking and practice*. To do this, the facilitator encourages full participation, promotes mutual understanding and cultivates shared responsibility. By supporting everyone to do their best thinking, a facilitator enables group members to search for inclusive solutions and build sustainable agreements." (Sam Kaner et al).[4]

Learning more about project management will help as well. Align yourself with the PM on the project and solicit their guidance and input. You could work with them to create the Requirements Management Plan. Or solicit their feedback prior to sharing it with everyone else. Let the PM share their knowledge and guidance just as you are willing to share your knowledge and guidance with the BA practitioners.

## Trust—Will You Support Me?

The BA practitioner may have established a good working relationship with his or her manager. This relationship most likely was built over time. The BA practitioner knows what is expected and has learned what is important to the manager.

The new Lead BA has not yet built up this trust with the practitioner. There may be uncertainty as to how the Lead BA may react, especially when the practitioner is questioned by the stakeholders or business regarding the quality of their work.

Whenever leading someone you have never worked with, it's probably better to tread softly. People usually work better when what is expected of them is clear.

---

1    Original Source: http://en.wikipedia.org/wiki/Facilitator.
2    Original Source: Kaner, Sam, Lenny Lind, Catherine Toldi, Sarah Fisk and Duane Berger, *Facilitator's Guide to Participatory Decision-Making* Jossey-Bass, (2007), xiii.
3    Original Source: Bens, Ingrid, *Facilitating With Ease!: A Step-by-Step Guidebook with Customizable Worksheets on CD-ROM*, (Jossey-Bass, 2000), 5.
4    Original Source: Kaner, Sam, Lenny Lind, Catherine Toldi, Sarah Fisk and Duane Berger, *Facilitator's Guide to Participatory Decision-Making* Jossey-Bass, (2007), 32.

**Strategies to Level Set Expecations**

- 1:1 Meetings
- Meet with all impacted parties
- Revise timeline as a collaborative effort
- Identify risks as a collaborative and communication to the Project Manager
- Work with the Project Manager and Practioner BA on creating a Risk Mitigation Strategy and communicate the plan to all impacted parties

Work with the practitioners on assigning the BA tasks. Solicit their feedback as part of the assignment process. Schedule regular 1:1 meetings to enforce the understanding of what tasks are expected to be completed by when and hold the practitioner accountable to what was agreed upon. If something has come up that causes the timeline to be pushed out, then revise the timeline as part of this meeting so that both parties are in agreement. These 1:1 meetings can also identify issues that can be documented and communicated to the PM as risks. The Lead BA should work with the practitioner on creating a risk mitigation strategy. Perhaps loop the practitioner into communicating the risk and its mitigation strategy to the PM.

## Letting Go

Not everyone is a natural teacher. Not everyone is comfortable sharing his or her knowledge. However, as Business Analysts, we must be successful at listening to our business partners and reiterating what we have heard. Teaching others what you know can help you mentally organize the information and link concepts together. Teachers have to understand the big picture in order to be able to answer questions. And if they don't know the answer, they have to be prepared to own the question and do the necessary research to find the answer and relay back the information.

Explain things the way you understand them. It is not necessary to rely on the way someone explained something to you. Draw pictures whenever possible. Pictures are valuable, especially when you are working with someone whose primary language is not the same as yours.

Sharing knowledge can feel threatening if one perceives it as a loss of control. So much of what a BA does is elicitation. A BA requires others to share their knowledge so passing your knowledge on to a BA practitioner will assist the BA practitioner in successfully accomplishing the tasks they have been assigned.

A Lead BA must allow others to accomplish the tasks that they have been assigned. So much of business analysis is about knowledge and control. It is a strong temptation not to assign tasks but to complete them yourself or do them on behalf of others. A Lead BA must let go enough for the BA practitioner to have the room and creativity to grow. A Lead BA must not tell a BA practitioner exactly how to do something. Instead they should give the BA practitioner enough information to move forward, check on their progress, and give them the necessary knowledge to successfully complete their tasks. In other words, mentor the BA practitioner. The word mentor (according to Microsoft® Word's English Thesaurus) means to guide, counsel, tutor, and teach. Not do.

## Assignment of Tasks and Accountability

With a Requirements Management Plan and a joint effort with the practitioners, assign tasks. The Lead BA should ensure that each BA assigned to a task is fully aware of the expectations for the assigned task(s), has the skill set and resources required to complete the assigned task(s), and is accountable. One way to enforce accountability is to schedule regular 1:1 meetings.

If the assigned practitioner is not completing the tasks, the Lead BA should identify the obstacles. The root cause could be lack of experience, skills, and/ or resources. A lack of experience or skills could be remedied by either reassigning the task (which would remove the obstacle to accomplishing the task but do little for developing the practitioner) or partner the practitioner with someone who has the necessary experience and skills.

## No Direct Reporting Relationship

When the Lead BA is not the direct manager, there can be conflicts based on the priorities of the direct manager versus the Lead BA. This is mitigated when the Lead BA reports directly to the same manager as the practitioners he or she are leading. If the Lead BA and the practitioners do not report to the same manager, however, then the practitioner may have the added pressure of assigned work from their manager in addition to or instead of the project work the Lead BA has assigned to them.

*Figure 4. Sample Status Report*

# Status Report

| Tasks Completed | When Completed |
|---|---|
| 1. | |
| 2. | |
| 3. | |

| Tasks in Progress | Due Date |
|---|---|
| 1. | |
| 2. | |
| 3. | |

| Task Not Yet Started | Target Date to Begin |
|---|---|
| 1. | |
| 2. | |
| 3. | |

Frequent status reports can identify these conflicts. The status report may list the tasks that have been completed and when, the tasks that are in progress and when they are due, and what tasks have not yet been started and the dates that they are projected to start and complete. A status report can also include any concerns and issues that the practitioner wants to bring to the Lead BA's attention. The Lead BA can compile this information and forward to the practitioner's direct manager so that there is a shared understanding of resource requirements.

## Transition

If the project has been inadequately defined, there is scope creep and change management has not been followed, or the project date has moved, the resource requirements for a project may change. It is important to raise the new resource needs as soon as possible so that the Lead BA can escalate that need to management.

There may be times when a particular practitioner's knowledge and/or skills may be better used on another effort and they are pulled as a resource. This puts a twist in any well-planned organization since this is becoming the "Norm" rather than the exception.

Transition to a new BA practitioner takes time. It is important to have all project documentation in one central location so the new practitioner can be brought up-to-date on the project. A new practitioner should attend as many project meetings as possible in the beginning, even if it is not necessary to the tasks they are taking over, just to provide them with background information on how their piece fits in with the other pieces.

## Crossing Team Boundaries

A project will usually have BAs, QAs, and Developers. Sometimes these roles are on separate teams. The BAs may be split across multiple BA teams and members of the project may be geographically dispersed.

*Figure 5. A Model of Where Roles Reside on Separate Teams:*

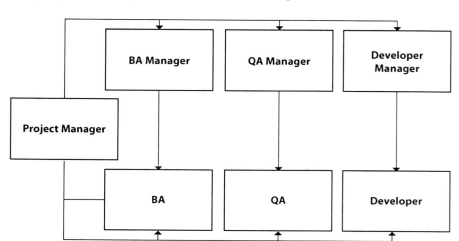

All project team members must understand the Requirements Management Plan. It should identify all the project artifacts necessary to complete the business analysis effort. The documentation must be sufficient and accurate so that:

- The developers can design and build
- QA can test
- Other BAs on the project will understand the delineation of tasks. The last thing you want to hear is, "I thought you were going to do that." or have a developer ask you, after completing the requirements document, "Where is…".

If an email chain is more than 3 responses deep, schedule a meeting. Do not let the email chain continue. Obviously there is misunderstanding and dialogue is needed. If it's just a back and forth with one person over email, then call them, as long as they aren't located in an off-hours time zone.

For those situations where time zone is an issue, wait until the proper time to reach out. In an outsourcing model, the time difference may be too great. You can wait until it's late at night or early in the morning to reach out. Or you can explain to the onshore resource and have them explain to the offshore resource. Usually the onshore resource will be of similar cultural and language background, and can help you understand where the gap in understanding lies.

## Relying on BA Skills Versus Domain Knowledge

As a Lead BA, you may be assigned to a project where you know little, if anything, of the business processes and/or systems. You have no choice BUT to rely on your business analysis skills. Or the organization may have engaged an external BA consultant in order to meet a temporary resource need and they are the one walking in with little or no knowledge of the business processes and systems.

Whether it is you or someone else, review all documentation. Documentation related to past projects, training, and the current project will provide background information. Perhaps job shadow a business subject matter expert who can show you how the day-to-day work is accomplished. Where the documentation is not sufficient or not understood, ask questions of the other BAs who have the knowledge and document their responses so that you can refer back to them.

If the organization has a Centre of Excellence and/or a common repository of organizational project templates, familiarize yourself with them. This will help you understand the outputs required from your business analysis activities.

## Leading by Example

A good Lead BA leads by example. Don't just be someone assigning the work. Roll up your sleeves to help the team out. Lead requirements elicitation sessions and have the practitioner observe. Meet with the stakeholders and have the practitioner attend. These are several ways to mentor less experienced BAs. Perhaps begin by doing the "driving" and then hand off the "driving" to the practitioner. Show them how it can be done and then give them an opportunity to do it. Model the behavior you want them to emulate.

Observe the practitioner at work. At first, attend all meetings with them. After each meeting coach them with suggestions. Teach them what works well for you and why, then give them the time and space to pick and choose what works well for them. Over time, attend fewer meetings. One test of progress will be when fewer and fewer questions come back to you and the feedback from others on the practitioner's performance becomes increasingly positive.

Meet with the Project Manager for feedback on the practitioner's performance. Integrate that feedback into further opportunities for development and mentorship. Frame everything in a positive manner and express concepts with a value-added approach.

Always remember that each person internalizes new lessons at his or her own pace. Be patient and supportive. Cheer the small victories.

## Enhancing Teamwork

A resistant mindset can be difficult to combat. One place to start is to identify the root cause of the resistance. Often the root cause has nothing to do with the Lead BA, it's most likely based on prior experiences and prejudices. If you have worked with this practitioner before, then you may already be acquainted with their negativity and the source of it. If not, meet with the practitioner's direct manager and ask them for their input on a strategy for handling the practitioner. Then meet with the practitioner. Stress with them that they are part of the solution and that problems are solved when people work together. Explain to the practitioner how their assigned tasks are important to the project and how important those tasks are to the ultimate outcome. By making the practitioner part of the solution and holding them, at least partially, accountable for the success of that solution, you can demonstrate how their efforts directly impact their peers and the success of the project. This can engage the resistant BA.

## Building Consensus

The art of facilitation can be a powerful tool towards building consensus. It is vitally important for each member of the team, regardless of their role, to feel that they have an opportunity to provide feedback and input. Everyone must be heard. When people are polled for their ideas and proposed solutions to a problem, one person's idea can lead to another person coming up with an idea. This creates a synergy within the team, which can be a powerful problem-solving tool. For any action items or tasks that are created as part of the discussion, ask for volunteers. This will encourage shared responsibility among the participants.

### No Micromanaging!

Micromanaging is dangerous. It can suck the life out of you and distract you from seeing the big picture. There needs to be trust and confidence in the practitioner's capabilities. Provide enough space to the practitioner to succeed on his or her own merit and not yours. It is important to give people the space and chance to fail, while at the same time supporting them so that they cannot fail. Keep a close eye on the practitioner. Review their work but do not, under any circumstances, do the work for them.

Coach them on what has worked best for you in the past. This must be a dialogue where you solicit the practitioner's experiences on what has worked well for them, and if possible, integrate the two. Everyone has strengths; use those strengths and do your best to strengthen weaknesses without allowing the practitioner to fail.

### People and Project Management

A Lead BA can benefit from taking courses on management, whether through their company or through a college or university. Project Management in particular would be most beneficial since being a Lead BA draws on many of those strengths. A BA must use their analysis, planning, and execution skills in order to be a successful. Leading and coaching others to do the same is what distinguishes a Lead BA from a practitioner.

### Software Tools

A Lead BA should be familiar with business requirement management tools, especially the ones employed in the organization for which they are working. There are several tools in the marketplace that can facilitate requirements management and traceability. These tools can assist not only with creating and storing requirements but also facilitate the transition to system testing and user acceptance testing by providing electronic storage of requirements and traceability to test cases and execution results. Software tools assist in the transition of requirements from one phase to another.

### Process and Procedures

Expertise in the organization's defined processes, procedures, and methodologies is important. Often failures occur because a process is not followed. Process and methodologies exist for a reason. While we are often tempted to take short cuts, it is important to recognize that those short cuts usually have consequences. Sometimes that consequence is acceptable in the face of the benefits to be gained, sometimes it is not. Process and the appropriate methodology and techniques are what separate a successful effort from an unsuccessful one (although there are many flavours in between). Pick your battles. Sometimes in order to move the project forward a compromise is necessary. But be sure, regardless of the compromise, that the succeeding processes have what is necessary to move to the next phase and that the outputs created from business analysis are accurate and sufficient for the next phase to accomplish its goals successfully.

# Conclusion

To be a successful, the Lead BA has to relate and communicate well with people from all areas of the organization. A Lead BA must lead by example. Modeling of the appropriate and successful behavior is extremely important because often people do not hear what you say but rather focus on what you do. That is the legacy that will last the longest. A Lead BA should be empathetic and patient. Never forget what it was like to be a new BA. We were all ignorant at some point in our careers and it is through the development and sharing of knowledge that we all grow. Do not be afraid to share your knowledge for it is by the sharing that often we learn the most.

# About the Author

Janina Buldrini's career started at Aetna Financial Services as a Customer Service Representative. Finding through various project assignments that she had an aptitude for system development, she became a Business Analyst. She spent a period of time as a Senior Software Developer, a background she often draws on in her business analysis work. Currently, Janina is a Senior Business Analyst at ING. She has served as Secretary of the IIBA Hartford, CT Chapter, Inc where she worked on the governance aspects of the Chapter's Affiliation Agreement and Attestation and the resulting Chapter Bylaw changes. She has a B.S. in Business Administration with a Concentration in Management and a Minor in Accounting.

# BA MANAGEMENT FOR THE PM
## PROJECT MANAGEMENT PERSPECTIVE

By Rochelle Tan, MBA, CBAP, PMP

# Introduction

More and more organizations recognize the value of business analysis to the success of projects. Complementing each other, the Business Analyst (BA) and the Project Manager (PM) collaborate on the requirements management to get the project off to a good start.

## What is a Project?

*A Guide to the Project Management Body of Knowledge* (*PMBOK® Guide*) defines a project as a temporary endeavor undertaken to fulfill a definite purpose, to create a unique product, service, or result within a defined period. It is an activity that has a definite beginning and definite end[1]. This is distinct from operational or functional activities that involve ongoing work within an organization but may also be called as 'projects'.

## Who are the Project Stakeholders?

In projects where a BA has been identified as part of the project team, the BA serves as the liaison between the business users and the implementation team. The BA translates business requirements into viable solutions to address a business need, problem, or opportunity. The PM, on the other hand, is responsible for managing the implementation of the defined solution within the stated project cost, scope, and time.

The project involves more stakeholders than the BA and the PM but this article focuses primarily on the relationship between the BA and PM. The intention is to provide practical guidelines on how the PM can work with the BA throughout the life of the project, in a way that ensures the success of the latter and ultimately, of the project.

## Application of BABOK® Guide and PMBOK® Guide

Teaching the *PMBOK® Guide* and *A Guide to the Business Analysis Body of Knowledge (BABOK® Guide)* is beyond the scope of this chapter. The reader is assumed to have a basic understanding or knowledge of *PMBOK® Guide* concepts (Project Management Process Groups, Knowledge Areas, among others) and BABOK® concepts (Knowledge Areas, Underlying Competencies and Techniques, among others).

---

1    Project Management Institute, *A Guide to the Project Management Body of Knowledge (PMBOK® Guide) – Fourth Edition*, (2008), 5.

The goal of this chapter is to teach PMs and BAs how to apply the theories to practice. The guidelines used are based on the application of processes and knowledge areas defined in *PMBOK° Guide*, and relating them with the business analysis tasks, tools, and techniques defined in *BABOK° Guide*.

# Project Management Essentials

## Collaboration and Communication

In a project, the PM is tasked to be the main driver who steers project activities in the right direction. On top of that, the PM needs to balance his or her time to efficiently manage the project variables: project plan, scope, stakeholder expectations, project progress, and constraints.

The BA is responsible for gathering and managing the requirements and ensuring that the agreed solution and the stakeholders' expectations are aligned with the requirements, among others. Note that this definition refers specifically to Project BAs, rather than their senior cousins the Strategic BAs, although the ideas are the same.

The PM needs to recognize that the effective management of the project variables is highly dependent on information that other stakeholders, especially the BA, provide. At different stages of the project, the BA passes information to the PM to enhance the quality of the processes managed by the PM. Conversely, the BA needs project management information and the PM's support to fulfill the business analysis tasks, ensuring their alignment with the project plan.

By following the simple steps below, the PM is able to collaborate and establish open communication with the BA to make more informed decisions and effectively manage the overall project:

*Figure 1. The Balance Between Steps 1 to 3*

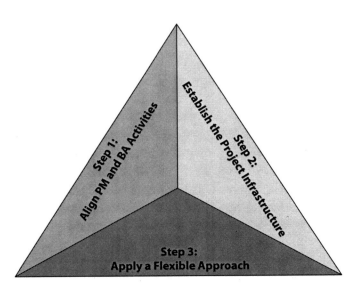

# Step 1: Align the BA and PM Activities

The PM needs to ensure that the BA is engaged in the project from the start and understands how information will be managed. Communicating the right amount of information at the right level and through the correct medium is critical in making the information useful. For instance, developing detailed requirements for the project charter is counterproductive to the purpose of a project charter. On the other hand, when a change request is introduced into the project, the PM will require the BA to provide all the details pertinent to the change. This will help the PM work with the project decision maker(s) in making informed decisions on whether to accommodate the change request.

The next section presents the overlap and interdependence between project management and business analysis activities. For simplicity, the project management tasks are arranged based on the 5 Project Management Process Groups: Initiating, Planning, Executing, Controlling and Monitoring, and Closing[2]. These process groups are related to *BABOK® Guide* knowledge areas and tasks. This mapping shows the information that the PM and BA need to have at their dispersal at various points of the project. This mapping aids the PM in aligning the activities of the BA and the other project stakeholders.

## Initiating Process

In the initiating process, the PM identifies the project stakeholders and develops the project charter. The BA helps by identifying stakeholders who will assist in defining the requirements and conducts high-level requirements elicitation to gather the content needed for the project charter's high-level scope definition.

The PM must be aware that there are business analysis activities that happen prior to the initiation process, such as Enterprise Analysis (EA). The enterprise architecture, initial solution scope, and the business case, are outputs of the EA Business Analysis Knowledge Area. The PM can use these artifacts to develop the project charter and plan. Note that this is the work of the Strategic BA, mentioned earlier.

## Planning Process

In the planning process, the PM and the BA work to integrate and verify the compatibility of the business analysis plan with the project plan, and the compatibility of the business approach with the project activities. They collaborate to identify specific tasks that the project team members should accomplish, based on the project scope.

The BA may also provide organization information and requirements prioritization from requirements analysis. This information is integrated into the overall project plan. The defined priority and organization of the requirements influence the schedule of the project activities. The information from

---

2    Project Management Institute, *A Guide to the Project Management Body of Knowledge (PMBOK® Guide) – Fourth Edition*, (2008), 43.

the BA is useful in developing various project documents that will be used to monitor and control the project: communication plan, project plan, project stakeholder list, and risk register, among others.

## Executing Process

In the executing process, the PM manages the plan to ensure that the tasks within the project scope are completed.

During this process, the BA is tasked to elicit, analyze, and document requirements, as well as determine the most suitable solutions for the business needs. These tasks require consultation with various stakeholders and depend on the availability of resources.

Furthermore, the BA helps the PM manage the stakeholders' expectations, ensures that the solution is within the expressed business need, and provides business analysis work progress and other relevant information that may affect the project scope, schedule, and cost.

The PM's job is to provide the necessary support for the BA. The PM ensures that resources are available for requirement elicitation and validation, evaluates the solution's relevance to the project scope, and evaluates the feasibility of the solution work plan. The PM also works with the BA to validate any changes that may be introduced into the project.

## Controlling & Monitoring Process

The controlling and monitoring process is an iterative process necessary to validate the alignment of stakeholders' project activities, manage required changes with the project plan, and monitor the status of identified project constraints. This process occurs throughout the project.

- During this process, the BA is responsible for the requirements with the overall goal of making sure they are tracked and traced properly, consistently relevant to the business needs, and properly implemented. This involves monitoring the progress of the business analysis performance, validating the quality of the requirements, and reviewing assumptions and constraints. The BA reports all information to the PM who, in turn, records the progress of the whole project and determines any possible risks or issues that may affect the schedule and output.
- The PM should encourage the BA to be as objective as possible during the reporting process. For example, in a software development project, the percentage completion of the application under development is hard to gauge. One approach is for the BA to group requirements into packages based on priority, easy wins or any other criteria, so as to measure completeness.

## Closing Process

During the closing process, the PM and the BA are responsible for assessing the project's success or failure. It is important to determine whether the project was able to achieve its original goals and fulfill its deliverables, as stated in the project charter. Part of this exercise requires the validation of the metrics defined by the PM (on a project level) and the BA (requirements level). The PM is also responsible for any administrative closing events such as contract closure and the release of resources, and may require the BA's help with these tasks.

The project must be set up to have an evaluation system, from the start of the project, to determine the project's success during the closing process. This includes the evaluation of the delivered solution, to determine its effectiveness based on the project goals and stakeholder feedback. The project team is also evaluated, to determine which areas they performed well in and which areas need improvement. Information gathered from these assessments must be stored, submitted to the business owner, and may be forwarded to management, for future reference. This post-implementation review, a form of lessons learned, is vital and is not done often enough.

# Step 2: Establish the Project Infrastructure

Project infrastructure and resources are essential tools to foster collaboration and communication. At every stage of the project, the PM uses these resources to share information and exchange ideas with the BA and vice versa. They are composed of project templates, standard processes, project management information system, and meeting rooms, among others. These resources may already exist within the organization sponsoring the project or can be created if time and budget permits.

Examples of project infrastructure that the PM can employ for the project, to facilitate collaboration and open communication between the PM and the BA:

TABLE 1. EXAMPLES OF PROJECT INFRASTRUCTURE

| Infrastructure Module | Sample | Function | Benefits |
|---|---|---|---|
| Project management information systems | Central repository area | • Provide storage for project artifacts (i.e., Project Charter, Status Reports, Business Requirements Documents, Meeting Minutes, etc.)<br>• Provide tools and data to evaluate team productivity | • High data accessibility for easier monitoring<br>• High data availability for more efficient collaboration<br>• Security<br>• Backups |

## TABLE 1. EXAMPLES OF PROJECT INFRASTRUCTURE

| Infrastructure Module | Sample | Function | Benefits |
|---|---|---|---|
| Facilities and equipment | Meeting areas, video and teleconference equipment, facilitation kits (e.g., white boards, pens, flip charts, eraser, etc. ) | • Enable teams to hold meetings of varying purposes (e.g., ad hoc, brainstorming, Requirements analysis, etc.) | • Eliminate or minimize distance constraints if team members are not in the same geographical location<br>• Faster discussion and analysis, as opposed to using email, for example. |
| Project standard operations | • Use of project templates<br>• Defined reporting process | • Allows for PM and BA to track deliverables, resources, and issues | • Organized and up-to-date reports<br>• Close monitoring of progress and constraints |
| Emergency channels | Team contact information list, issue escalation procedure(s) | • Allows for the BA to address critical situations and raise issues outside the normal reporting process. | • Faster and more efficient emergency response rate<br>• Can be tailor-made by the PM and the BA into a process that is best for the team |

Many organizations have useful project resources in place but have not taken the time to educate project stakeholders in their availability and use. The PM should correct that.

# Step 3: Adapt a Flexible Approach

There is no single template or methodology that fits all projects. Even organizations with established Project Management Offices (PMO) with recognized standards, acknowledge the need to provide flexibility to accommodate projects based on various factors: rigor, business need, organizational culture, geographical, and cultural differences, among others. *PMBOK® Guide* refers to this as "tailoring the approach." These variations affect the overall project approach but. regardless of the project variation, collaborative planning and communication are staple elements that will facilitate the PM's tasks in effectively managing the BA and the whole project team to successfully achieve the project's objective(s).

There is no such thing as an issue-free project. The more variables introduced into the project during its lifetime, the bigger the challenge will be. The PM must remember to take a flexible approach in managing the project to adjust to the situation and to mitigate, if not avoid, any issues that may arise. This is possible with the PM working closely with the BA throughout the project lifecycle. In general, projects succeed because of good communication and nowhere is this clearer than in the BA/PM relationship.

## Real World Case Studies

This section presents three real-life cases of project interactions between the PM and BA. These are actual situations that provide a realistic view of problems that PMs have experienced in managing their BAs, and they also show how these problems were addressed by applying flexibility and good project management practices. Take note that these cases are not all encompassing nor are the resolutions necessarily the best or the only approach. These are merely real-world examples of the approaches that have worked in the past, to show that conflicts and problems are common on projects. Just keep in mind that even problems that may appear too big or too complicated can often be solved by proper communication and collaboration.

All the names in the examples have been altered to maintain the anonymity of the companies and people involved, and to protect the guilty!

---

## Case Study #1:

I'll Be There: How to Enable the BA to Succeed

### Problem

Julio Aurelio was managing two projects. Each project was assigned its own BA. Project Alpha was a process improvement project and its BA was Leila Li, a new contractor working offsite. The other project, Project Finance, was a minor enhancement to the existing accounting system of the Finance Department and its BA was Raz Juwani, a senior analyst who had been with the organization for three years and had worked with Julio on several projects prior to this.

Both projects were on tight deadlines with limited resources. Julio was being pressured by management to complete both projects on time. According to his preliminary estimates, both projects had little room for delay or slippage. Within this environment, management required Julio to provide project status updates during the manager's bi-weekly meeting.

Julio found himself spending too much time trying to catch Leila and Raz at the right time to discuss project updates and ensuring their activities' alignment with the project plan. When contacting Leila, she did not always pick up the phone and took a while to answer emails. She usually sent her emails in bulk or would combine all her responses, from various emails, into one very long email. On the other hand, Raz preferred to provide verbal project updates during his spare time.

The organization had no formalized project management standards. Projects were managed based on the PM and team's preference.

How did Julio manage the two projects to ensure that the projects were completed successfully without spending too much time running around trying to track the BA's progress?

## Resolution

Julio realized the challenges his projects were facing and the importance of being able to have a process to monitor the activities of both projects. He needed to ensure that both projects were managed according to the individual needs.

Julio tasked Leila to create preliminary estimates of the amount of time she would need to conduct requirements gathering. Julio and Leila planned for Alpha's project activities: requirements elicitation, analysis, and requirements validation. This allowed Julio to plan upcoming project activities, like ensuring resource availability for Requirements elicitation and requirements validation. Julio collaborated with Leila to identify constraints that posed project risks. This list of constraints was reviewed by Julio and Leila on a regular basis to determine whether identified constraints were obsolete and whether there was a need to identify new ones. These regular touch point meetings also involved the re-evaluation of that project's plan, if recent changes in the project's status merited it. This process allowed Julio to track Leila's progress and provide the necessary support she needed to be successful in accomplishing her project tasks. It also allowed him to present regular status reports on the project to his supervisors.

With Project Finance, Julio took a different approach. Knowing that Raz had an excellent grasp on the amount of work and time his project required, Julio could afford a loose, agile approach. For project updates and risk management, they conducted five-minute Scrum meetings twice a week. Julio and Raz agreed that ad hoc meetings could be conducted at any time if an emergency called for it. Julio used this information to prepare his own status reports.

## Conclusion

While both projects still required planning and monitoring to ensure their proper completion, they required varying amounts of rigor.

Julio's task was to make sure both BAs understood that accomplishing their projects on time was of utmost importance, and at the same time Julio made them part of the decision-making process, at their level of competence and comfort. Julio still had the responsibility to manage the project plans and monitor the constraints but he was most effective when working with his BAs strengths.

---

## Case Study #2:
PM vs. BA: Who has the Right Perspective?

## Problem

In one of the projects that Asghar was working on, he had challenges in getting the project activities moving forward. He was trying to convince Kim, the BA assigned to the project, to advance with her requirements elicitation and analysis task. The project was already falling behind schedule due to delays in two of her requirements packages.

Requirements package four was to include the 'current' state diagrams and the detailed specification of each state. Kim said that she could not analyze and document the detailed specification without the mocked-up screens from the vendor, however, the vendor said that they could not provide those screens without the 'current' state diagrams from Kim.

For requirements package three, Kim had asked for an extension on this delivery that was already one week delayed. The package was missing the colours for the newsletter makeover and the Marketing Department was taking too long to translate the corporate colours into the newsletter's new design.

How did Asghar manage the project while allocating the appropriate amount of time for Kim to be effective in fulfilling her tasks?

## Resolution

Asghar sat down with Kim to discuss the problem he was facing. He stated that they are both working toward the same goal: the project's success. Asghar explained his concern that the project would be delayed should further slippage occur during requirements elicitation. He also gave Kim the opportunity to explain why she needed more details for requirements package three and what was holding her up.

Kim said that requirements package three was missing the required colours for the newsletter makeover. Given this is an important element to the requirement, Asghar approved allocating more time for Kim's task, agreeing with her on a new deadline for it. He also agreed to escalate these concerns to the Marketing Director, stressing that the delays were impacting corporate strategic initiatives.

Asghar and Kim met with the vendor to resolve the deadlock on requirements package four. The discussion provided closure on what Kim and the vendor were expecting from each other. Kim was to deliver the high-level 'current' state diagrams to the vendor but leave out the detailed specification for each state. The delivery of the state diagrams allowed the vendor to provide the mocked-up screens, which Kim needed to provide the detailed specifications. Both parties proceeded accordingly and Asghar made sure that they did not divert from the plan.

## Conclusion

Sometimes, the PM and the BA may have conflicting views because of their varied mandates. As there is no cookie-cutter solution that solves all types of PM and BA problems, Asghar analyzed the problem at hand and selected an appropriate approach to finding an agreeable solution for each of his problems.

He consulted with the concerned stakeholders to get first-hand information because he understood that the solution can only be fulfilled with the project stakeholders' active involvement. Furthermore, Asghar's approach showed that he recognized Kim's expertise and respected her request to delay requirements package three.

Despite Asghar's liberal approach of open communication and collaboration, he still made sure that the project was closely monitored to its successful completion. Many people think any management is micromanagement but Asghar knew better.

## Case Study #3:
Torn Between Two Managers: Who Will the BA Choose?

### Problem
Company ABC was an insurance company that followed a traditional functional organization. Based on the organizational structure of the IT department, Cary Smith, one of the senior BAs, reported to the Manager of the Business Solutions Team, Patricia Leung. Eric Beckham was a contractor hired by Company ABC to provide project management services.

Eric was assigned to work on one of the top-priority projects in the company. Cary was identified as a resource in the project because of her strong knowledge in the compliance business unit. The project began successfully but as they progressed, Cary, although very experienced, was having problems completing her tasks on time. Often, she was pulled out to provide operational support to the Sales Department, as the corporate standpoint was that production support trumped project work.

Eric was having challenges because Cary's task was on the critical path of the project. Cary had not yet completed business requirements elicitation. The delay of the requirement package was keeping the software architect from completing the architectural design. If left unresolved, this would directly impact the project finish date.

What did Eric do to solve the problem?

### Resolution
Eric realized that the interruptions had transformed from a risk to an issue. He talked to Cary and Patricia to express his concern about the problem. Patricia explained that Cary was the only person who could help the Sales Department when issues happen during operational hours, as she had the expertise in their Point of Sale (POS) application.

Given that the Sales Department needed Cary's services, the three came up with an alternative arrangement. They agreed to schedule the addressing of the Sales Department requests. Cary allocated two days a week for the Sales Department for operational support. This allowed Cary to have three days a week to concentrate on her project tasks. Furthermore, Patricia had one of the Sales Department's subject matter experts (SME) shadow Cary for a day or two to learn basic procedures so the SME could handle simple POS requests on his own.

### Conclusion

Many PMs in functional organizations face challenges in keeping their project resource(s) focused on tasks at hand because of commitments to functional managers. Eric recognized early that this was a problem. With regular monitoring of the project progress, Eric was able to identify the risk and when it materialized, acted on it before it got out of hand. To solve the problem, Eric collaborated with Patricia and Cary so they would understand the gravity of the situation. Both Patricia and Cary were able to contribute to the solution, which was a good tactic in getting their support.

Eric's collaborative approach allowed him to find a workable and creative solution, enabling his project to succeed.

## Conclusion

The PM faces various challenges in steering projects towards successful completion. There's no single methodology or formula that the PM can use to guarantee a positive outcome, however, the PM can apply the three simple steps to establish close collaboration and open communication with the project team members so they will be equipped to tackle any obstacle which may arise during the project lifecycle.

## About the Author

Rochelle Tan is a seasoned IT Consultant, providing Project Management and Business Analysis services. She has over 10 years of experience in various industries in North America and Asia, ranging from IT, Finance, Insurance, Government, and Software and Book Publishing. She graduated at the top of her class with a B.S. in Computer Science from Ateneo de Davao University (AdDU) in the Philippines and has an MBA from Ateneo Graduate School of Business (AGSB). She holds the CBAP® and PMP® designations and CELTA certificate in teaching English to adult learners. In her  free time, she takes care of her plants and baby girl.

# WHEN THE BA AND PM ARE THE SAME PERSON

By Robin F. Goldsmith, JD

Although *A Guide to the Business Analysis Body of Knowledge* (*BABOK* *Guide*) and *A Guide to the Project Management Body of Knowledge* (*PMBOK* *Guide*)[1] tend to imply that the Business Analyst (BA) and Project Manager (PM) functions are performed by separate individuals, more frequently than perhaps realized the same person acts as both BA and PM. This chapter describes the circumstances and considerations commonly connected with this special situation, which can occur regardless of whether the individual is explicitly designated as the PM, BA, both, or neither.

Projects depend on BAs and PMs applying different mindsets along with separate sets of skills and knowledge. When a single individual performs both roles, there is a good chance they are coming primarily from a strong background in one and consequently are likely to be weak in the other area. It is important however to realize that the dual role could indicate weaknesses (or probably less commonly, strengths) in both functions.

Conversely, when the PM and BA are separate individuals, they can complement and also check each other's performance; but there's no fallback on the other person when the same person plays both roles.

Additionally, other issues may afflict projects more than are recognized. Typically, BAs and PMs often follow unwise conventional wisdom, superstitiously apply ineffective behaviors, and are not aware of many important concepts and techniques. Such limiting factors affect projects with separate, specialized BAs and PMs. These limitations are even more likely when there's only a single individual since there's no double-checking and one or both skill sets may be weaker than with a dedicated specialist.

# Projects Need to Be Managed

## Relation of Business Analysis and Projects

Following a proven project management life cycle and having someone acting as a PM actively managing the project, even when a PM has not been assigned formally, markedly improve chances for the project's success. Every part of a project benefits from this discipline so a PM needs to be involved in a project throughout every life cycle phase.

In contrast, the BA role's primary purpose of defining requirements often means a BA is involved in only one or two early phases which typically are associated with requirements definition. This chapter mainly addresses PM and BA functions in the early phases related to defining requirements.

---

1    "PMI" and "PMBOK" are registered marks of Project Management Institute, Inc.

Some organizations take a broader view of the BA role that involves participating throughout later project phases as well. Recognizing that additional requirements continue to be identified throughout a project, some Business Analyst continued activity might consist entirely of defining and revising requirements. This could be occurring consciously, as when following the Rational Unified Process (RUP), which explicitly expects requirements definition activities to take place to varying degrees in each life cycle phase.

Perhaps more commonly, the BA's role may change in later phases, such as maintaining communications with users and monitoring system implementation. In such situations, the BA may still define requirements, somewhat implicitly and unconsciously, in order to deal with changing and later-identified requirements. Since both conscious and unconscious situations seem to be extensions of the earlier requirements definition activities, the BA/PM's issues here wouldn't differ appreciably from those encountered in the early phases.

In some instances, BA involvement in later project phases may include PM-like direction and control responsibilities for overseeing implementation of the requirements. The biggest challenge for either PM or BA can pertain to directing and controlling technical activities of which they are not especially knowledgeable. Since this is not a common BA role, this chapter will not discuss it further.

Some organizations make the BA also responsible for testing the developed system to confirm that it conforms to the requirements that the BA has defined. On the other hand, PMs seldom seem saddled with testing but could fall into this situation when the BA is also acting as PM. Managing testing as a project is a challenge in its own right for anyone doing the testing. It becomes all the more difficult when the testing is being done by a BA for whom testing is unlikely to be a primary skill or focus area. Since carrying out technical/development testing is not a typical BA role, this chapter will not discuss it further. However, BA/PM involvement in User Acceptance Testing is more common and is discussed below.

## Development and Project Management Life Cycles

A life cycle is a set of phases, stages, or major events that when followed have been found to lead to success in some endeavor. Following the life cycle increases chances for project success, whereas skipping phases or doing them out of sequence tends to reduce one's chances of success.

There are life cycles for many things. Figure 1 shows how two such life cycles, for project management and for system (or product) development, interrelate. The system development life cycle (SDLC) phases are depicted by the rectangles and represent the "work" of the project. The project management life cycle phases and key activities are listed on the left.

The bulk of the project work involves defining *detailed requirements*, designing a product/system to meet the requirements, and developing/testing the designed product/system. The bulk of project management work involves directing and controlling the execution of these work activities. While some projects perform each phase in its entirety before proceeding to the next phase, most projects (including many characterized as "waterfall") in fact break the project into a series of sub-project iterations within increments. Each iteration includes the sequence of phases for a portion of the project's detailed requirements and associated design, development, and testing. An increment usually consists of several iterations that together produce a deliverable piece of the project. BAs usually perform the requirements definition analysis phase(s), sometimes as a sub-project by itself, whereupon the BA also may have more explicit project management responsibilities.

After the developed product/system has been implemented, many organizations conduct a post-implementation review to identify lessons learned that could be applied to help improve subsequent project processes. All members of the project team, including PM and BAs, typically participate. Effective PMs and BAs continually analyze and improve their processes throughout a project, not just at the end. Except to the extent that it's always difficult for one to recognize his own shortcomings, I'm not aware of any special issues that arise with respect to project reviews due to the PM and BA being the same person.

*Figure 1. Project Management and System Development Life Cycles*

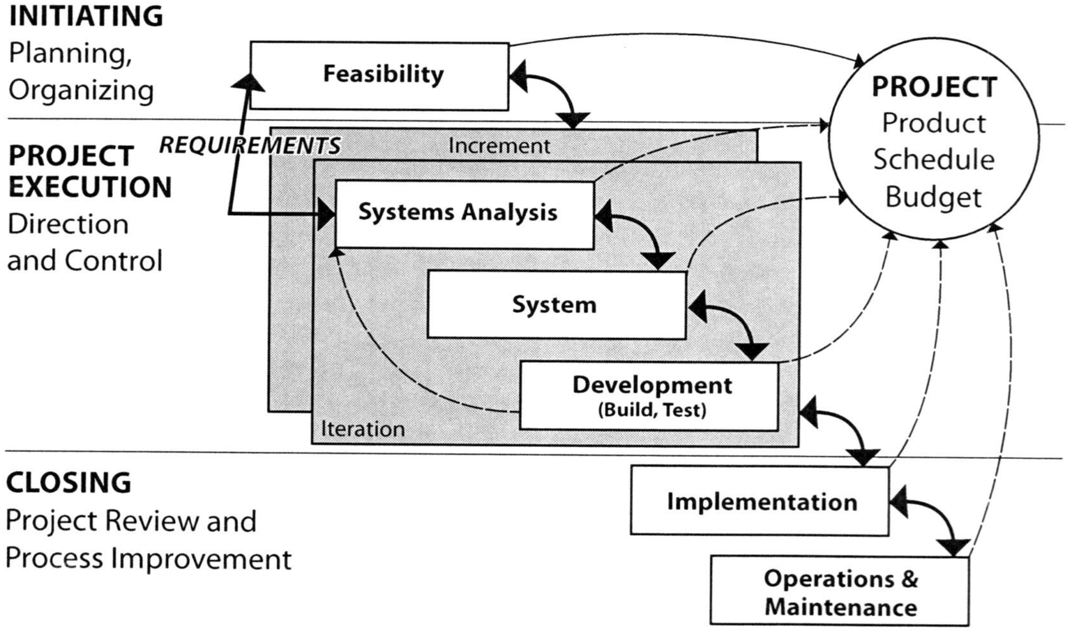

## Special Aspects of the Feasibility Analysis Phase

During the SDLC feasibility analysis phase, the project management Initiation phase occurs and includes planning and organizing the project. Even when the feasibility analysis phase is considered the first phase in the development project, as depicted in Figure 1, it often is performed as a separate project in its own right. Either a PM or a BA, though typically not both, could be assigned to carry out such a feasibility analysis phase/project.

On the other hand, many organizations (and *BABOK° Guide's* Enterprise Analysis knowledge area) treat feasibility analysis as a stand-alone activity. Each such stand-alone feasibility analysis ordinarily is considered its own project and typically is performed by a PM, possibly one of several PMs in a group that specializes in feasibility analyses. If the analysis deems the development feasible, it is initiated as a development project.

Regardless of whether the feasibility analysis is considered within or outside the development project, feasibility is based largely upon defining *top-level requirements*, which makes it appropriate for BAs to participate in project initiation. No doubt some organizations make BAs responsible for analyzing feasibility. My experience, however, is that many more organizations consider feasibility analysis to be a PM responsibility and often don't involve the BAs in this work, let alone make them responsible for it. *When there's no BA involved, the PM performing feasibility analysis must also do the business analysis tasks.*

## When the Feasibility Analysis Phase Seems Skipped

Of course, neither PM nor BA is likely to be involved when the feasibility analysis phase is not performed explicitly, which happens in perhaps the majority of projects. Realize that even when the feasibility analysis phase appears to take zero time, it always occurs because it's the feasibility analysis phase that defines the project deliverable, budget, and schedule.

*When the feasibility analysis phase is essentially skipped, the development project PM eventually gets saddled with a project that invariably is doomed to failure with an impossibly inadequate budget and a schedule that bears no responsible relation to the work actually needed to produce the project's product deliverable.*

Senior executives who initiate projects based on their positional authority very often perform the initiation work personally, typically informally. As such, they have both PM and BA role responsibilities but seldom consciously act in either capacity. Moreover, while they may have relevant PM skills, they frequently lack the relevant BA skills needed to define appropriately the top-level requirements upon which the project deliverable, budget, and schedule should be based. Nonetheless, they are very unlikely to enlist assistance from an experienced BA.

# Key Project Management Competencies

Following suitable life cycles is necessary but not sufficient. To improve project success, project management needs to involve several key competencies, which are unlikely to occur by themselves without the PM's conscious, informed efforts.

Classic project management recognizes key competencies in four of the project management life cycle phases: planning, organizing, directing, and controlling. While necessary, the four may not be sufficient for project success without a fifth, frequently unrecognized competency—administering.

*Typical BA role definitions and training ordinarily would not create awareness of, let alone provide competency in, these vital project success determinants.*

*Yet, a BA who also is functioning as a PM needs to develop and use these compe-*
*tencies. In fact, even a BA who is not also a PM nonetheless needs to enlist these*
*competencies to effectively and efficiently carry out the work of business analysis.*
*The need may be more apparent when multiple BAs are involved.*

## Planning

Unfortunately, planning has acquired somewhat of a bad name. In too many organizations, what is called "planning" is merely mindless, mandated, time-consuming bureaucratic generation of excessive and essentially useless paperwork. Agile methods arose largely as a reaction against excessive paper-work, which many agile projects equate to planning and therefore skip. Agile eXtreme Programming (XP) methodology actually does include planning but masks it as "the planning game."

Effective planning does involve writing, but no more than is helpful—and no less, either. The operative word is "helpful." Writing things down helps avoid forget-ting them and enables sharing, reusing, repeating, reviewing, and refining them.

There's an old cliché, "If you fail to plan, plan to fail." We plan in order to help us succeed. Planning serves three purposes that help both PMs and BAs succeed:

1. *Identify what to do.* This involves defining both top-level and detailed require-ments which is the province of business analysis and is what the BA mainly should be contributing to the project.
2. *Identify how to do it.* This is design, and many BAs do design, which is okay if designing how is in addition to identifying the requirements or what needs to be done. Too often designing the how is done instead of the identifying what to do.
3. *Identify what it will take.* This involves identifying resources, effort, and dura-tion for a suitable sequence of tasks.

Tasks need to be defined for the feasibility analysis (high-level requirements) and detailed requirements definition/analysis phases in which a BA is most likely to participate. Tasks also need to be defined for subsequent product/system design, development/test, and implementation phases. Tasks that are further out in time are less certain and can be defined and estimated at a higher level of granularity. Tasks that are nearer in time should be defined in sufficient detail to assure that all necessary work will be done.

Defining and estimating project tasks are perhaps the most fundamental PM responsibilities. Popular automated project management tools mainly deal with identifying the tasks needed to carry out the project and calculating project timeline schedules based upon the tasks' estimated effort and duration. The tools are only as good as the tasks and estimates the PM provides. Most projects are late and over-budget because necessary tasks were overlooked and because tasks that were identified were underestimated, often by a lot.

Effective estimating depends upon accurately understanding the task and sub-task work to be done and having reliable and relevant quantified historical data about similar work that already has been done. Those are big challenges that PMs often lack the personal skill and knowledge to meet. Effective PMs draw upon better-informed project participants, usually those that will be doing the particular tasks, to identify and estimate needed tasks.

Many PMs are not familiar with the tasks, and especially the sub-tasks, necessary to perform business analysis. BAs should, but frequently also don't, know what those tasks are. BAs are even less likely than PMs to know how to plan and estimate their work. When the BA and PM are the same person, these requirements definition task identification and estimating deficiencies can be compounded.

Some business analysis tasks that need to be planned and estimated include:

- Meet with management to understand the project and review status
- Research the subject area
- Gather data about the high-level business requirements
  - Plan, conduct, and document interviews
  - Arrange and conduct follow-up and other unplanned interviews
  - Review collected documents
  - Plan, conduct, and document requirements workshops (Joint Application Development—JAD), focus groups, and other facilitated group sessions
  - Prepare, distribute, collect, analyze, and follow-up on surveys and questionnaires
  - Observe operations
  - Learn to do the work
  - Prototype on paper and/or electronically
- Analyze and update the collected data
- Draft high-level business requirements
- Draft a high-level conceptual design for meeting the high-level business requirements
- Review high-level business requirements and conceptual design
- Finalize high-level business requirements and conceptual design
- Identify top-level product/system requirements and estimate resources, effort, duration, and Return on Investment (ROI) for alternative ways to accomplish the business Requirements
- Participate in reviewing and deciding among alternatives, including "no change"
- Participate in identifying one or more development projects to implement some or all of the high-level business requirements
- For each implementation project:
  - Gather relevant data for detailing the business requirements
  - Analyze the data
  - Draft detailed business requirements
  - Review and revise the detailed business requirements
  - Gather data, draft, and review user acceptance criteria
  - Define Requirements/specifications and use cases for a product/system that satisfies the detailed business requirements
  - Review and revise the product/system requirements/specifications and use case
- Update project plans based on current information

## Organizing

Organizing means identifying, obtaining, and assigning the (primarily human) resources with the capabilities necessary to carry out the project tasks at the times they need to be accomplished. Project management texts often depict project organizing as forming the project team by recruiting the most skilled workers to fit each defined project role.

In fact, many PMs have little control over selecting team members. Instead, it's common for the team to be assigned before the PM and/or before the project tasks and skills required for them have been defined. Thus, ordinarily, rather than picking the perfect team, the PM must transform whatever team is assigned to be as capable and focused as possible.

The challenge becomes even more daunting when there's no project budget or schedule for training team members in the skills and knowledge needed to perform the project, such as business analysis. Of course, some such training needs may be reduced when the PM is the one performing the business analysis and already has suitable skills. Conversely, difficulties arise when the PM lacks necessary BA skills and doesn't recognize it, which is especially likely when the same person is both PM and BA.

The BA/PM usually is assigned in one of the roles and performs the other by default, without conscious organizing that would identify required BA and/or PM skills, gaps, and needed training. Lack of such self-awareness can considerably diminish both BA and PM effectiveness, especially where neither role is explicitly assigned. Conscious project organizing, perhaps, is most likely to be skipped when the BA/PM is the *same* person and the *only* person assigned to the project at the time. Hopefully this chapter will help those in the BA/PM role become more aware of their need to self-organize and better assure they have the requisite skills and knowledge for both roles.

## Directing

Directing means ensuring that project participants know what to do, how to do it, and when to do it. It includes coaching, which combines training with encouragement. On smaller projects, directing is largely informal and even unconscious. While the need to direct others is usually apparent, self-directing can easily be overlooked.

Failing to recognize and carry out the need for self-direction seems most likely on one-person projects/phases where the PM also is the BA.

To-do lists are the simplest self-directing technique, and many PMs undoubtedly use them as second nature; but BAs may not even know to use such rudimentary tools. They should. It's a simple method to keep on track and avoid forgetting things.

As with organizing, the biggest issue with directing often is lack of sufficient awareness of required skills, one's own capabilities, and the need for self-directing.

## Controlling

Controlling involves monitoring what is actually happening as the project progresses, comparing actuals to what's expected, and making adjustments as appropriate to reduce undesirable variances and improve performance.

Effective planning is the secret to effective controlling. Thus, it's important to update plans periodically so that work which will be done in the next several weeks is broken down to a set of relatively small "work packet" tasks which each can be accomplished by a single resource in no more than one week. Experienced PMs often solicit informed input about necessary tasks from those who will be doing the work however a PM/BA who will be doing the business analysis work may not realize the need for—or have access to—assistance in defining and estimating those tasks from someone with greater BA knowledge.

By identifying an observable deliverable for each task, the project becomes a series of deliveries, culminating in completed delivery of the full project. Intermediate milestones should be identified indicating delivery of completed major project components. Effort and start/end dates should be estimated and scheduled on a project timeline so that all necessary work can be done to complete the milestones on time, which in turn results in completing the project on time.

As the project proceeds, each task's deliverables should be checked against standards and specifications to confirm that they are correct and of suitable quality. Actual effort, duration, and completions should be tracked task by task against expectations. Repeated overruns frequently can reveal trends and systemic errors.

Unplanned tasks which turn out to be necessary should be identified separately so that reasons for missing the tasks can be examined and corrected in upcoming parts of the project, and in future projects, which may be affected by the same issues.

The reasons for variances in effort, duration, and quality should be analyzed to determine whether they represent acceptable normal variation or are due to special causes that need to be addressed. Often variances identify tasks that must be added and/or estimates that must be adjusted. Sometimes the solution may involve getting additional or different resources.

Unclear, wrong, and missing requirements are the most common sources of errors affecting the PM's ability to deliver project quality on time and in budget. Consequently, it's extremely valuable for the PM to be able to switch to his/her BA hat in order to analyze and correct the processes producing such requirements problems.

One of the biggest challenges for the BA/PM is looking objectively at his/her own work. Because we ordinarily view things from our own perspectives, everything we do can seem fine. It can be hard to recognize our own shortcomings that need to be addressed. BA/PMs are less likely to recognize when they are the problem, inadequately defining requirements and/or inadequately managing the project. Effective PMs know they must look at results rather than intentions.

## Administering

Administering is a fifth key competency that classic project management does not recognize. Administering is doing the work of project management, such as holding the meetings, preparing the reports, and creating and updating project plans and tracking.

PMs are good at planning the work of other project team members but often neglect to plan time for doing their own administrative work. The likelihood of missing these critical administrative PM tasks increases even more when the PM is also the BA since doing the BA work may take up most of the PM's attention and the BA mindset is less attuned to the administrative part of PM work.

When tasks are not planned, they don't get done; and when the administering tasks of project management don't get done, the project ultimately will fail. The PM must provide time to do his/her own administering work, as must the BA.

# Classic Business Analyst/Project Manager Roles

### Project Manager

One of the central concepts in classic project management methodology is enforcing the distinction between managing the work and doing the work. There's a very important and legitimate basis for making the distinction and emphasizing that project management should be all about managing the work, as opposed to doing it.

Consider where most PMs come from: a *superworker* who gets promoted to *supervisor*, i.e., PM, charged with managing the work of their former worker-bee peers. When their project becomes stressed and up against impossible deadlines, as almost all projects eventually do, who does the PM turn to? They turn to the best worker, of course—the PM.

So while the PM is busy doing the work of several other members of the project team, what are those others doing? Who knows, but probably not much to help complete the project. And, who is doing the PM's work? Nobody! Projects that aren't managed generally fail; and PMs who don't manage their projects are *superfluous*.

That's why the classic project management model says the PM should only be managing the doing; and PM training should address only the managing but not the doing. Consequently, someone who is primarily a PM probably does not have the training and orientation needed to adequately also act as a BA defining requirements.

### Business Analyst

The title of Business Analyst has become much more common in the past decade. The emergence of the BA position probably largely reflects organizations' increasing awareness of the need to define requirements and, in turn, the need for some role responsible for doing it.

Such an orientation commonly characterizes business analysis in terms of its activities, such as requirements elicitation, analysis, writing, and management. Realize, though, that "requirements management" refers to the clerical/administrative activities involved in keeping track of requirements and changes to them.

That is, except for acknowledging the need to plan their requirements work by identifying sources for data gathering, the BA's role in managing the requirements definition work itself often receives scant attention within the BA community and BA training.

Consequently, a BA who also must act as a PM is unlikely to have the PM training and orientation to manage the requirements definition project/phases effectively.

# When There is No Business Analyst

Partly because the BA only recently became more widely-recognized as an important project role, many organizations don't have people with the BA title. Obviously, organizations without any BAs won't have BAs defining Requirements in their projects. Even in organizations that do have BAs, a BA is not always explicitly assigned to perform a project's requirements definition/analysis; and still fewer organizations have a BA participate in feasibility analysis.

In contrast, a project is much more likely to have an explicitly designated PM.

## But There is a Project Manager

### Project Manager is Expected to Do Business Analysis

Of course, in the, pardon the expression, "Real World," PM/BA distinctions are not quite so black and white. When I ask clients and students which role defines requirements in their organization, many say the PM. Expecting the PM to define requirements is understandable because often the PM is the project team member with the most work experience relevant to business analysis.

Moreover, small project teams don't have the need or luxury of a team member who only manages; and regardless, a dedicated full-time PM is impossible when the team consists of a single person, as is so common for the requirements portion of projects.

Consequently, on many projects, the PM very often may also be the individual responsible for performing business analysis. Even if not formally responsible, the PM needs to know the requirements to do the project and must act as BA if no one else does.

### Nobody Does Business Analysis

Sometimes when there is an explicitly designated PM but no designated BA, the PM should but often does not perform the needed requirements definition. Whether it's because the PM role is defined as managing but not doing, the PM doesn't take responsibility for results beyond his/her narrow job description activities, or the organization simply doesn't define requirements, the PM may be the BA by default but doesn't actually recognize the added role and doesn't consciously do business analysis.

I fear such business analysis vacuums are more common than may be recognized. They probably can persist without mechanisms for meaningful requirements discovery so long as the business continues to function in a relatively stable automatic-pilot manner, typically where other project team members have extensive personal familiarity with the project's products and systems. However, such vacuums are recipes for disaster when the organization is confronted with changing challenges.

# When There is No Project Manager Either

### Project Initiation that Destines Most Projects to Fail

Probably the most common situation requiring effective business analysis has neither an explicitly identified BA nor an explicitly designated PM. How could that be? It happens very often with respect to the feasibility analysis project initiation phase.

Most organizations rely on senior executives personally to formulate and fund projects. Some split the formulating and funding functions, such as through steering committees of key stakeholders, formal budgeting processes, or simply through the executive hierarchy authority structure.

It's the formulating, though, that's the issue. Typically, an individual senior executive acting alone formulates a project. The formulation may have some sort of deadline, such as being in time for a scheduled approval/funding meeting or, if the project is responding to a crisis, its deadline may be "ASAP" (as soon as possible).

Nonetheless, the project formulation activity is unlikely to be thought of as a project itself. Nor is it likely to be thought of as business analysis. Instead, it's just part of the senior executive's ongoing activity. The executive may manage the formulation as a project but, since the project formulation often is totally in the purview of the executive without visibility or accountability to others, the executive may not manage it with the mindset of a PM. So what?

The problem is that without a PM perspective, planning and organizing the formulation tends to be shortchanged. The executive is unlikely to appreciate that project formulation mainly involves business analysis. Therefore, the executive will not think of himself or herself as the BA either, let alone recognize his or her business analysis skill limitations. Consequently, this BA/PM situation almost never enlists more skilled BA assistance.

Instead the executive and the organization assume the executive's position alone enables him or her to make momentous and sound project formulation decisions. By relying solely on the executive's judgment, often without suitable data gathering and analysis, the formulated project can't help being ill-conceived. Frequently, the project is doing the wrong thing, or not doing the right thing, to provide the value the organization needs. Even if the project is appropriate, its budget and schedule almost always are set impossibly low.

Later, when the PM, BA, and other project team members are assigned to carry out such an ill-conceived development project, they can do little to avoid often inevitable failure. Yet, when such projects do indeed fail, it's usually the PM who is blamed, not the senior executive or the process whose inadequate business analysis destined the project to fail.

# When There is a Business Analyst

## But There is No Project Manager

Occasionally, the business analysis activity is assigned to a BA in one of several situations where no PM has been designated. For example, the BA is assigned to perform either formal initiation or requirements definition analysis as essentially stand-alone projects or separate phases within an overall project. In such instances, it should be evident that the BA must also act as the PM. The BA's challenge frequently is that they lack suitable PM awareness and training, which means the BA doesn't adequately know when, what, or how to perform PM responsibilities.

### Formal Initiation Treated as a Separate Project

When the project initiation (feasibility analysis) phase is considered pre-project, for deciding whether to initiate a subsequent development project, it's usually structured as a project by itself. Although defining top-level requirements should be the dominant aspect of feasibility analysis, BAs often are left out, in part perhaps because of the emphasis on financial analysis. Usually this phase is performed by a PM or consultant (who by the nature of a contractual relationship is very conscious of managing the project engagement as well as doing the involved business analysis).

However, because such separate feasibility analyses are considered pre-project, there may be no PM assigned; a BA may be charged with performing the feasibility analysis project, often as the only participant.

Although I think it's far less common, sometimes a BA is assigned (again, often alone) without a PM to perform a feasibility analysis, which is considered the first phase of the development project.

Whether considered part of a development project or its own pre-development project, BAs who are assigned alone to perform separately-identified feasibility analysis must also act as PM. Many factors should keep the BA abundantly aware of the PM role need. For instance, besides having a defined deadline, the results of the feasibility analysis typically are reported formally to management rather than to the development team.

In some ways, the separate project status can help the BA who is also acting as PM. Separate status may help create awareness of the need to gather data from diverse organizational areas and higher levels of management, which in turn necessitates greater attention to managing the project.

Separate pre-project feasibility analyses tend to put greater emphasis upon financial cost-benefit analysis and calculating Return on Investment (ROI), which can put a BA acting also as PM at considerable disadvantage. Not only can the emphasis on financial analysis divert attention from requirements definition, but also the BA may not be sufficiently versed in financial analysis since it's often not addressed in typical BA training.

## Requirements Definition/Analysis as a Project

Whereas it's somewhat less common for a BA to be involved in feasibility analysis, especially as the lead player who must also act as the PM, BAs are much more likely to be charged with defining detailed requirements in the requirements definition/analysis phase.

While certainly not the rule, surprisingly often the BA is left to carry out this phase's work without an explicit PM and thus must also act as PM. In some instances, such a phase is recognized at least implicitly as a project of its own, if only as a sub-project within the overall development project.

When performing detailed requirements definition, the BA who also acts as PM has many of the same types of challenges as when performing feasibility analysis. The BA again is likely to be impacted by lack of PM skills and orientation. Effectively managed projects perform updated financial analysis based on then current project knowledge at multiple key points throughout the project, sometimes referred to as phase or gate reviews, for management to make go or no go decisions. While most organizations perform financial analysis only once at the beginning of a project, those that also perform updated financial analysis based on the defined requirements could represent a challenge to a BA, who probably is not skilled in financial analysis.

A more common PM-type issue confronting a BA functioning without an identified PM in this phase would be political problems, such as difficulty gaining access to higher-ups and communicating through unfamiliar non-traditional channels. While typical PM training probably doesn't help much with politics, PMs may be more attuned to and experienced with organization politics than a typical BA might be.

## And There is a Project Manager

### Traditional Requirements Definition/Analysis

Even when there is an explicitly designated separate PM, a BA nonetheless often needs to act as a PM too. While this can happen in feasibility analysis, it's more likely to occur in the requirements definition/analysis phase, where BAs usually are involved. By the time the project gets to this point, most have a separate explicitly assigned PM. However, many PMs keep their distance from the requirements definition work and essentially delegate both doing and managing the bulk of the phase work to the BAs.

Consequently, even with a titular PM, effectively carrying out competent business analysis can mean at least the lead BA must plan, organize, direct, control, and administer the various BA activities for himself or herself and fellow BAs. Recognizing and carrying out such implicit PM responsibilities can be very hard for a BA trained only in business analysis, especially when there actually is someone else with the PM title for the project.

# Gaps Limiting All BAs and PMs

When the same person is both BA and PM, difficulties that tend to afflict any individual BA or PM can be magnified. Not only does the dual BA/PM not have someone else's knowledge and skill to fall back upon but also having to pay attention to both disciplines can reduce proficiency in each.

This section briefly describes some critically important project management-related requirements concepts and techniques with which even experienced trained BAs and PMs often are not sufficiently familiar. Additional information is available in my book, articles, and seminars.

### *REAL* Business Requirements

Most BAs and PMs, and their related training, use the term "requirements" to refer to the Requirements of the product, system, or software they intend to create. This conventional model considers "business Requirements" to be high-level, vague, objectives that the product must satisfy. Invariably this model causes creep, changes to the requirements after they've been agreed upon.

Conventional wisdom is that creep occurs because the product requirements are not sufficiently clear. In fact, much of creep occurs because the product requirements don't meet the REAL business requirements deliverable *whats* that provide value when met by the product *how*. REAL business requirements are not just high-level and vague. When driven down to detail, they map to product requirements. Scope defined in terms of high-level REAL business requirements deliverable *whats* don't creep so much. BAs should discover the REAL business requirements before they get into defining product requirements.

### Reviewing Requirements Content as Well as Format

Most requirements reviews use only one or two relatively weak techniques mainly focusing on clarity and testability, which are format issues and do not identify requirements that are wrong or overlooked. More effective reviews apply more than 21 techniques that catch many more requirements issues, including incorrect and overlooked requirements content. BAs can apply these methods during requirements discovery as well as in reviews.

### Determining Right, Reliable, and Responsible Return on Investment (ROI)

ROI calculations are usually unreliable because they fall prey to a number of common but seldom-recognized pitfalls. The most important pitfalls involve failing to recognize that value comes from satisfying REAL business requirements of all key stakeholders and both tangible and non-tangible costs and benefits must be quantified in dollars. BAs and PMs need to know to (and how to) identify and quantify value in order to provide reliable financial analysis upon which to base sound decisions.

### Acquiring and Outsourcing Systems and Software

Most software acquisitions and outsourcing encounter difficulties, largely because they are conducted prematurely during feasibility analysis and are based upon product/system Requirements. Effective acquisitions and outsourcing are based upon detailed REAL business requirements that the vendor's product/system design and implementation must satisfy with net financial benefit.

### Planning and Designing User Acceptance Testing (UAT)

UAT is usually costly and burdensome on users, yet largely ineffective at catching defects that continue to plague production. That's because most UAT is defined late in the life cycle from the perspective of the BA or QA to demonstrate the product is implemented as designed. Effective UAT is planned and designed in conjunction with defining REAL business requirements and includes both requirements-based tests that detect unclear/untestable requirements as well as tests based on less well-known but more powerful methods that expand the customer view and thus also can detect wrong and overlooked requirements.

### Identifying Master Test Planning Risk Reduction Strategy

Based on the high-level product/system/software design, BAs and PMs can participate productively in Master Test Planning to identify the big risks that the testing strategy should address. Many of these ordinarily overlooked risks represent design defects that, in turn, are mainly due to incorrect and missed Requirements. Catching and correcting these issues early prevents many of the problems that otherwise afflict delivered systems, especially showstoppers.

# About the Author

Robin F. Goldsmith has been President of Go Pro Management, Inc. consultancy since 1982. He works directly with and trains business and systems professionals in requirements analysis, quality and testing, software acquisition, project management and leadership, metrics, and process improvement. He partners with ProveIT. net in providing ROI Value Modeling™ tools, training, and advisory services.

Previously he was a developer, systems programmer/DBA/QA, and project leader with the City of Cleveland, leading financial institutions, and a "Big 4" consulting firm.

Author of the Proactive Testing™, REAL ROI™, and Beyond the Textbook™ Software Acquisition methodologies, numerous articles, and the recent Artech House book *Discovering REAL Business Requirements for Software Project Success*, and a frequent featured speaker at leading professional conferences, he was formerly International Vice President of the Association for Systems Management and Executive Editor of the *Journal of Systems Management*. He was Founding Chairman of the New England Center for Organizational Effectiveness. He is a Director of the Software Quality Group of New England, belongs to the Boston SPIN, and served on the Software Engineering Institute's SEPG'95 Planning and Program Committees.

Mr. Goldsmith held virtually all ASQ Boston Section leadership positions, and Chaired record attendance BOSCON 2000 and 2001 Annual Quality Conferences. He was a member of the ASQ Software Division Methods Committee and the IEEE Software Test Documentation Std. 829–2008 revision Committee. He is a member of Working Groups revising the IEEE Std. 730 on Software Quality Assurance and defining Enterprise Analysis for the International Institute of Business Analysis (IIBA) Business Analysis. He is a member of the International Institute of Software Testing and International Institute (IIST) for Software Process (IISP) Body of Knowledge Advisory Boards. He is a subject expert on requirements and testing for TechTarget SearchSoftwareQuality.com and a subject expert and reviewer for the IIBA Body of Knowledge (BABOK).

He holds the following degrees: Kenyon College, A.B. with Honors in Psychology; Pennsylvania State University, M.S. in Psychology; Suffolk University, J.D.; Boston University, LL.M. in Tax Law. Mr. Goldsmith is a member of the Massachusetts Bar and licensed to practice law in Massachusetts.

# BUSINESS ANALYST MANAGEMENT FOR THE FUNCTIONAL MANAGER

By Barbara A. Carkenord, MBA, CBAP, PMP

## Introduction

Managing Business Analysts (BAs) is similar to managing other employees. Fundamentally, they appreciate respect, open communication, direct feedback, and support in their career development. BAs, however, have unique characteristics that thrive under effective management support. This management support involves creating a productive work environment, making appropriate work assignments, overseeing planning at the beginning of each assignment, and conducting frequent checkpoints to monitor progress and provide coaching.

BAs are passionate about their work and as such need very little outside motivation. They are driven to solve problems and improve the way work gets done. They are naturally inquisitive and love to learn new things. As a functional manager, directing this passion and energy results in significant organizational improvements. This chapter will highlight a few key management techniques that will increase the productivity of Business Analysts. BA functional managers succeed by focusing on four main areas:

- Providing a conducive BA work environment with useful resources
- Making appropriate matches between work assignments and people
- Getting clear agreement and work plans at the beginning of each assignment
- Monitoring progress, coaching, encouraging, and assisting along the way

There are varying levels of competency within the business analysis profession. International Institute of Business Analysis™ (IIBA) has published *A Guide to the Business Analysis Body of Knowledge® (BABOK® Guide)* and *A Guide to the IIBA Business Analysis Competency Model™* with a set of levels and their related descriptions. These levels are called Novice, Advanced Beginner, Competent, Proficient, and Expert. These standards are used in this article to refer to business analysis tasks, techniques and the varying skill sets within business analysis.

## The Characteristics of a Business Analyst

Understanding the characteristics and motivations of people performing business analysis work will help functional managers better utilize their talents and skills. People interested in the BA field typically have a passion for learning, communicating, and solving complex problems. BAs are likely self-motivated and bring significant value to many assignments. The functional manager's role is to ensure clear work assignments channel a BA's energy in the best direction for the organization.

People who enjoy business analysis work come from different backgrounds, have different personalities, and work styles. They share a desire to solve problems and improve their organizations.

Some individuals are drawn to the business analysis profession because they value attention to detail and want to obtain a complete understanding of every problem they are asked to solve. These characteristics make BAs very valuable resources for analyzing and designing software systems because every function must be specified with exacting detail.

As with every positive characteristic, there can be a downside to this rigorous drive to detail. A BA may have difficulty letting go of an assignment before he or she feels it is perfect. This goal of perfection, while admirable, can hinder the success of a BA's work because there is rarely time for *perfect* when solving organization problems. Knowing when the analysis is "good enough" or the requirements have "just enough" detail is very difficult. Helping an analyst to know when to keep digging and when to stop is one of the most important challenges of the functional manager.

Other people move into business analysis work because of their excellent communication skills and desire to help business people solve problems. These individuals may focus more on relationships than requirements. They help teams stay positive and generate enthusiasm for the changes required to improve the business. Learning about each BA on the team allows more effective management and provides information needed when making assignments.

# Provide a Productive Work Environment

Business analysis work involves many different tasks requiring various resources. For a BA to be most productive and effective, their work environment should be conductive to the nature of the work and they need to have convenient, available resources which support the work. Table 1 describes the characteristics of the ideal BA work environment.

BAs are becoming more and more adept at virtual communications. This allows a BA to work remotely (from both their business stakeholders and their technical stakeholders if necessary). Since BAs need blocks of uninterrupted time for critical thinking and they can work remotely, a part-time, work-from-home arrangement may be helpful (if their home is a quiet place). Remote communication tools (i.e. high speed internet access, VOIP) must be available at all times. On the other hand, building strong, trusting relationships with stakeholders is more difficult from a distance. Ideally BAs will be able to meet each stakeholder in person at the beginning of an assignment to establish an effective working relationship.

### TABLE 1. BA TASKS AND THEIR IDEAL WORK ENVIRONMENT

| BA Tasks | Ideal Work Environment and Resources Needed |
| --- | --- |
| **Elicitation of Requirements**<br><br>(When stakeholders are remote, ideally travel will be approved for the project initiation workshops so the team can meet face-to-face and establish relationships.) | • Access to business domain and implementation stakeholders<br>• Background information on key stakeholders<br>• Interview space/ability to "close the door" to minimize interruptions<br>• Telephone<br>• Email, Instant Messaging (IM)<br>• Teleconference equipment<br>• Video conference equipment<br>• Collaborative workspaces (i.e. SharePoint, Wiki)<br>• Travel budget<br>• Focus group budget (when applicable) |
| **Analysis**<br><br>(Critical thinking, brainstorming, documenting requirements, preparing presentations, preparing for elicitation sessions) | • Quiet space (office with a door, conference room, offsite location)<br>• Access to another BA (as a mentor or by pairing assignments)<br>• Paper, sticky notes, pens, pencils, erasers<br>• Flip chart, whiteboards, markers<br>• Graphic, modeling software<br>• Word processor and spreadsheet<br>• Requirements templates and standards |
| **Research**<br><br>(Industry research, competitive analysis, vendor package comparison, learning new techniques, following industry best practices) | • Access to libraries, publications, articles, online forums<br>• Filing cabinet, disk storage, backups<br>• Access to social networking sites<br>• Budget for IIBA® and other professional organization membership dues<br>• Time for learning and development (if BAs formally report their hours, they need an account for learning and development time)<br>• Formal and informal training opportunities |
| **Presenting Requirements**<br><br>(Documenting and/or communicating requirements; getting confirmation on understanding, training users on upcoming changes) | • Graphics, word processing<br>• Desktop publishing support<br>• Presentation facilities<br>• Presentation software<br>• Project, microphone, podium<br>• Name tents<br>• Copying and printing access |

# Make Appropriate Assignments for BAs

Functional managers often have discretion when it comes to making work assignments. Carefully selecting the most qualified BA or group of BAs for each assignment increases the likelihood of success. There are many factors to consider when making these assignments. As with any employee work assignment, taking the time to select the most appropriate resource usually saves time in the long run. This section includes factors and recommendations for selecting the best BA for each assignment.

BAs have a spectrum of abilities and skills. Novice and advanced beginner level BAs are relatively inexperienced and will benefit by working with a more senior level BA. The development of a competent, proficient or expert BA comes from experience on different types of projects and working with different stakeholders. These more senior level BAs have enough experience in various environments to be able to step into any situation, assess the requirements and analysis needs, and choose the appropriate analysis techniques.

## Assign BAs Based on Project Characteristics

Important factors to consider when assigning a BA to a project are the characteristics of the project. If the project is in the initiation phase or not yet approved (as a funded project), a senior level BA is the best choice. Early project and pre-project work includes identification and definition of the business need. Often the business unit has a problem or opportunity that would benefit from analysis (i.e. root cause analysis) and assessment of the business case (see definition) before moving forward. These tasks are senior level tasks. Senior level BAs will assist the business sponsor to clarify the request and estimate the potential benefits to the business if the project is approved. If a Project Manager (PM) has not yet been assigned, the BA will consider possible solution approaches and develop high-level estimates for solution development.

Business case —
An assessment of the costs and benefits associated with a proposed initiative.
   – *BABOK° Guide*

When a PM is assigned to the project during this early stage, the PM and BA work together to form a well-defined scope and plan including a project charter, business case, project objectives, scope, and initial project management plan. The BA will create the business analysis plan as input to the overall project management plan. Figure 1 shows the business analysis plan as a part of the overall project management plan. Once the plan is complete, a less experienced BA may be selected to perform some or all of the work based on the recommendation of the senior level BA, leaving the senior level BA free to work on the more complex tasks and act as a mentor to the more junior BA(s).

*Figure 1. Project Management Plan Including the Business Analysis Plan*

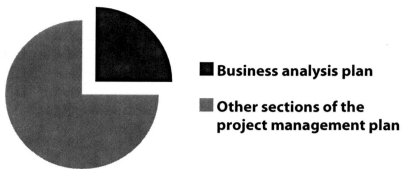

■ **Business analysis plan**

■ **Other sections of the project management plan**

Two other factors to consider when assigning a BA are project type and software development methodology or **approach**. The type of the project will help determine the appropriate BA by its complexity and size. Project types include business process improvement, software maintenance, vendor package selection, and implementation. The **BABOK® Guide** divides software development approaches into two categories: **plan-driven** and **change-driven**. Plan-driven approaches focus on minimizing uncertainty and controlling risk. They include traditional waterfall and iterative approaches. Change-driven approaches focus on rapid delivery in short iterations, accepting a higher degree of uncertainty. They include agile approaches. Table 2 recommends BA assignments based on project type and software development approach. The appropriate BA assignment will typically produce quality analysis and problem resolution, as well as lead to the most efficient use of time during a project.

## BA Pairing

When assigning BAs to projects the technique of **BA pairing** could greatly influence the analysis process. BAs are more productive when they work together discussing complex requirements and reviewing each other's models and analysis. BA pairing is very beneficial when the first BA of the pair brings different experience or knowledge than the second BA. For example, a BA who has a development or technology background paired with a BA who has deep business domain knowledge creates an analysis team that can easily bridge communication and requirements gaps. Pair a BA who possesses specific application knowledge with a BA who is new to the area. This pair will think outside the box while recommending changes that are feasible and consistent with current functionality. Pairing a competent, proficient, or expert BA with a novice or advanced beginner BA helps develop the skills of both because mentors often learn as much as those they teach.

Another pairing consideration is personality and work style. Some BAs are more outgoing and extroverted and really enjoy facilitation, elicitation, and team building. Pairing this extrovert with a more introverted BA who thrives on documenting details and solving complex analytical problems creates another example of a powerful team.

**TABLE 2. BA ASSIGNMENT RECOMMENDATIONS BY PROJECT TYPE AND APPROACH**

**Recommendations for BA Assignments**

| Project Type | Software Development Methodology | |
| --- | --- | --- |
| | **Plan Driven Approach** (e.g. traditional, waterfall, iterative) | **Change Driven Approach** (e.g. agile, scrum) |
| Bug fix (this may be too small to be called a "project") | When the organization has an established procedure for software development changes, any level BA may be assigned depending on the immediacy of the need. | Assign a BA familiar with the software application, he or she can easily work directly with a developer on the correction. |
| Small software enhancement | If the project has a project manager assigned, any level BA may be assigned. Without a PM, the BA must also have basic project management skills. | Assign a BA familiar with the software application who has access to business domain stakeholders. |
| Business process improvement | Any level BA can be assigned to study and document the AS IS business process. Pair a novice or advanced beginner BA with a more experienced BA to assist with the redesign and work with the business stakeholder to plan the changes needed for the transition. | Not applicable (Not normally run as a change driven project). |
| New product introduction | Assign a proficient or expert BA to work with the PM to plan and scope the analysis work. This experienced BA may be able to utilize the help of an advanced beginner BA but should oversee this work closely. | Assign a proficient or expert BA with strong facilitation skills to work with business stakeholders and the development team on the new design. |
| Large software change, application modernization, and systems with complex interfaces | Assign a proficient or expert BA to work with the PM to develop the business analysis plan. Assign multiple levels of BAs (pair technical and business specialists) to execute the analysis work. | Assign an expert BA with deep application knowledge. An advanced junior or competent BA as an assistant would provide support while also learning. |
| Infrastructure | Assign a proficient or expert BA to work with the PM to develop business analysis plan. Assign a BA with strong communication and marketing skills to help the business understand and embrace the change. | Not applicable (Not normally run as a change driven project) |

## Assigning BA Based on Stakeholder Relationships

Another consideration during assignment decisions is the stakeholders. Business domain stakeholders provide requirements and an understanding of the business needs. Implementation stakeholders work with the BA to design a solution and build the needed components. BA communication skills and relationships with stakeholders are very important. There are several considerations which may influence the assignments such as the number of stakeholders, number of different organizational units represented by the stakeholders, and level of commitment to the project. The more stakeholders or stakeholder groups involved, the more complex the elicitation work will be. Eliciting requirements from stakeholders who are not enthusiastic about the project necessitates a more highly skilled BA.

## Number of Concurrent Assignments

When assigning BAs to projects, be sure to review all existing assignments and responsibilities. Complex analysis work requires periods of intense concentration. To completely immerse himself or herself in a complex requirement, the BA needs ramp up time and blocks of quiet time (1–2 hours) in which to focus. BAs working on numerous projects, often in different application areas, will have difficulty carving out these blocks of "critical thinking" sessions. Interruptions and frequent meetings prevent thorough analysis often causing a BA to work evening or off hours to get the quiet time needed.

When a BA is only assigned to one or two major projects, or three or four projects within the same business domain, he or she stays focused on the problems and needs of the specific business area. He or she can often develop recommendations for one project, which are coordinated with other projects. Interacting with the same business stakeholders increases the opportunity to build trusting relationships and helps business people feel well-represented to IT team members.

## Assignments to Further BA Career Development

An excellent functional manager is always working to further develop his or her employees. BA skill development comes with practice and experience on various projects. Career development should also be considered when making assignments. A BA who is assigned to bug fixes and minor enhancements to the same application software, with the same business stakeholders year after year has little opportunity to develop additional business analysis skills. Although it is tempting to keep a BA on the same application because they become very efficient, his or her ability to perform analysis in other areas is severely limited. An excellent manager recognizes, and helps others in the organization understand, that assigning a BA to a different type of project or to a different area of the business stretches him or her to utilize more elicitation, relationship building, analysis, and requirements techniques. The BA functional manager may have to explain to a key stakeholder why a trusted

BA is being assigned to another group. Having experience on a variety of business domains develops a flexible, very valuable BA.

As BAs are assigned to work on different types of projects their strengths and interests will be exposed. Encouraging a BA to try something new gives them the opportunity to find new strengths and makes the organization aware of additional resource talents available. During a BA's annual review, discuss additional types of projects or analysis techniques he or she is interested in learning and practicing. With the BA, create a career development plan that includes these opportunities and outlines the criteria which will be used to evaluate performance.

# Business Analysis Planning

Business Analysts should always have a plan for their work. This plan may be formal or informal depending on the size and complexity of the assignment. Because requirements development and management can be time consuming, BAs must develop a work habit of planning and prioritizing their work. For every medium to large size project, the team should have a well-defined and documented business analysis plan. Senior level BAs are the best resource to create this plan during project initiation and in conjunction with the creation of the project management plan (typically created by the Project Manager).

A business analysis plan includes a description of the project, list of the stakeholders (called the Stakeholder Register in *A Guide to the Project Management Body of Knowledge* [*PMBOK® Guide*])[1], list of planned elicitation sessions, list of requirements deliverables, and time estimates for business analysis work completion. The plan will also include the BA approach describing how the work will be done. IIBA® *BABOK® Guide* has an entire knowledge area dedicated to business analysis planning.

# Monitor Progress and Coach to Successful Completion

## Time Management

With a good business analysis plan, the BA has clear tasks and structure around his or her work. He or she must be encouraged to schedule and manage time to ensure that tasks are completed as planned while ongoing responsibilities are still met. Functional managers can assist with time management by having frequent check-in points. It is important to coach novice and advanced beginner BAs on time management from the beginning of their career. A functional manager may suggest a daily stand up meeting to confirm the top 1–2 priorities of the day. BAs should report their progress on each assignment either verbally or via a status report.

---

1    "'PMI" and "PMBOK" are registered marks of Project Management Institute, Inc.

Most BAs have more work to do than time to do it. This requires diligent and constant re-prioritization of tasks. Functional managers should oversee prioritization to make sure the BA doesn't spend too much time on low priority tasks. There is a natural tendency to complete small, easy tasks first to "get them out of the way". BAs can find themselves putting off the big tasks until after all of the small ones are done. Remind BAs to focus on the high priority, critical path tasks. Help them break these big, complex tasks into smaller pieces that may be accomplished in a day. Encourage BAs to make these high priority tasks the first work of the day (or during their most productive hours); even doing them before checking emails and voice mails which will cause distractions. Staying focused on the high-risk critical requirements assures a higher likelihood of project success.

Time management is a major challenge for many BAs. Time management skills become more important as a BA's career develops. As his or her contribution to solving business problems is recognized, more and more business people will look to the BA for advice and assistance. The volume of assignments along with their complexity will increase. Constant re-prioritization and honest self-awareness of how much work can really be accomplished are key skills for senior level BAs.

## Requirements Reviews

There is significant value in documenting and reviewing analysis work. Writing down requirements confirms the analyst got it right. When eliciting requirements, a BA may listen and believe they understand but until that understanding is formally confirmed, the analysis work has not been evaluated for accuracy. On software development projects using a plan-driven approach, requirements deliverables will be packaged for review. When using the change-driven approach (i.e. agile) written requirements may be very informal (i.e. on a flip chart in the war room). Regardless of the approach, requirements should always be reviewed and approved by the business stakeholders.

BA functional managers must support requirements reviews. Having knowledgeable stakeholders review requirements confirms accuracy and agreement before building a solution. This review process results in quality improvements because missing and unclear requirements are identified and corrected. In addition to confirming accurate requirements, the review process educates team members on the complexity of the business and the importance of the solution. It provides clear agreement between the requestors of IT and the development team. It also provides valuable feedback to the BA on the success of his or her requirements elicitation work. These *lessons learned* improve the BA's process on their very next assignment.

Requirements reviews are often skipped or discounted creating unnecessary risk to the project. Functional and project managers must be disciplined in including these reviews in business analysis planning and making sure the reviews are held. This one simple act will improve the success of projects with very little cost. Make sure BAs and business stakeholders understand the importance of these reviews. Make sure business stakeholders are allowed time to review the requirements in detail and their concerns/findings are considered. Improving requirements is guaranteed to improve stakeholder satisfaction with project results.

## Coaching

The most important role of a BA functional manager is that of a coach. Sometimes the manager just needs to be a sounding board to help the BA think through complex ideas and get granularity on a solution.

An excellent functional manager will recognize the potential of BAs and will dedicate time to BA development. Excellent BAs can do many different types of work and are flexible enough to adapt to different situations. This means a competent, proficient, or expert BA can be assigned to a new type of project that has not been done before or is unclear. These senior level BAs willingly take on tough assignments. They will do research and learn about the business problem to help clarify the project needs.

Inexperienced BAs need more task-related support and may be overwhelmed by a new project or new business area. The novice or advanced beginner BA may feel he or she needs to learn everything about the business, the existing software application, the related departments, the interfaces, and the competitive environment. The learning curve may seem too steep and may frighten the BA as he or she also sees a timeline that appears too short. This initial feeling of intimidation is best alleviated by a plan. When the BA is given direction about how to get started, and when to let go, the fear subsides and the BA's natural curiosity and desire to learn takes over.

All BAs need frequent management status checks to maintain momentum, stay within scope, get help with obstacles, and report progress.

## The Importance of Listening

Developing BA competencies involves a functional manager's time on a regular basis. In addition to teaching time management as discussed above, managers help by listening and encouraging BAs as they analyze complex problems. Functional managers need to listen to descriptions of progress and help BAs get unstuck when necessary. *Talking out loud* is an analysis technique and many times a BA needs an interested listener to work through a problem. An outside listener asks naïve or off-target questions that often help crystallize the problem or allow the analyst to see it from a different perspective. For example, with modeling, the listener doesn't need to know the modeling technique or notations to listen to the BA explain it. Listening, asking for clarification, and noting areas of confusion often allow the analyst to improve the model.

During these discussions it is critical the functional manager maintain an attitude of curiosity and confidence in the BA. Complex analysis challenges will temporarily undermine the confidence of even the most senior BA. A supportive manager, who shows confidence in the BA's ability, releases the pressure that a BA may be applying to himself or herself. It may be this pressure, a fear of failure, which causes a block in the critical thinking process. Allowing an individual to talk through his challenges (and maybe even his fears) in a supportive, safe environment is the fastest road to success for both the BA and the project. Remind them of how much they already know and of their prior successes.

## Value of the BA Community

Novice and advanced beginner BAs also develop their skills by learning from other BAs. Encourage and financially support all BAs to join and participate in local professional groups such as International Institute of Business Analysis (IIBA®), Project Management Institute (PMI®),[2] Software Process Improvement Network (SPIN), communities of practice, and software user groups both inside and outside of the organization. Talking with other analysts reinforces confidence and gives BAs a forum to try new ideas. The small investment in time and money for BAs to participate in these groups will quickly reap huge benefits for the organization. They share solutions to common challenges and teach each other by telling stories of project situations. They get ideas for better communication skills, hear about other analysis techniques, are exposed to new technologies, and build a network of people to whom they can turn for help with future challenges. Give them time to read about new techniques and trends in industry publications. Encourage BAs to attend business analysis conferences and training courses.

---

2    "PMI" is a registered mark of Project Management Institute, Inc.

## About the Author

Barbara A. Carkenord, Director of the Business Analysis Practice at RMC Project Management, has over 25 years experience in business analysis, and is one of the original founders of the business analysis training industry. Barbara possesses an MBA from the University of Michigan, is a Certified Business Analysis Professional (CBAP®), and a certified Project Management Professional (PMP®). Barbara is the author of *Seven Steps to Mastering Business Analysis and is* a frequent speaker at industry events. Actively involved in the IIBA®, she was a core member of the IIBA® BABOK® creation committee. Barbara possesses detailed knowledge and experience in many analysis tools and techniques. She develops and delivers business analysis training using proven techniques and real-world experience. Barbara's other areas of expertise include software design, quality assurance, and project management. Her experience covers many industries including insurance, banking, and manufacturing. Barbara was named 2010 Small Business Woman of the Year by the Georgia Women in Technology association.

# IMPROVING BUSINESS ANALYSIS PROCESSES

By Shelley Cudly

## So You Think You Need Some Process Improvements?

When thinking about where to begin a discussion on requirements and business analysis improvement, I only had to look as far as my computer document folders. There I found handfuls of presentations created over the years to convince peers and/or management of the importance of requirements process improvement.

Most firms I have joined over the years have not had very advanced requirements processes. My experience is in keeping with general industry assessments: only 25% of companies operate at higher levels of requirements process maturity[1] The statistics regarding the reasons for project failure point to an overwhelming need for improvements in business analysis and requirements. At the same time, the poor maturity level indicates that organizations have not cracked the nut of business analysis process improvement.[2]

Better project outcomes are the concern of all involved in project work. Indeed, they should be the concern of the entire organization. Since every company is unique, it is difficult to come up with a handy checklist of things you can do to improve your processes. More than a list, process improvement is a mentality that, once embraced, will create an environment that is continually driving value and project success.

We will start this chapter by discussing the pain that is caused by poor requirements processes, look at software process improvement, and review a typical improvement cycle. I will detail steps and methods that have proven successful to moving an effort forward.

Through experience and research, I've discovered that meaningful and lasting Requirements and project improvement are not merely a result of solid processes but also of developing people and skill sets to support those processes.

### 1. Why Bother?

Why spend time focusing on requirements and the people and processes surrounding them? If you've done any reading in the requirements space,

---

1    Heembrock, P. *Hitting the Mark: The Impact of Requirements Maturity on Project Outcome.* IAG Consulting (2009): http://storage.pardot.com/464/56895/Hitting_The_Mark___The_Impact_of_Requirements_Maturity_on_Project_Outcomes.pdf

2    In fact, 70% of organizations recognize that requirements are important to project success but fail to take appropriate action. (Ellis, K. *Diagnosing Requirements Failure.* IAG Consulting. (2009): http://www.iag.biz/links/white-papers-and-articles/white-paper-diagnosing-requirements-failure.html).

you've undoubtedly run into dozens of articles that spell out the dismal state of technology projects. Documentation on technology failure is pervasive and there are many attempts to quantify the nature of that failure. While there have been some questions around how project failure is defined, the evidence does suggest an inability to reliably produce successful project outcomes.[3]

## 2. Improved Schedules and Planning

Better requirements lead to improved project schedules, cost estimates, and work breakdown structures.[4] Using established elicitation methods and good customer relationships leads to better understood requirements that require fewer changes throughout the lifecycle.

## 3. Less Waste/Lower Cost/Less Rework

Requirements rework slows down your project.[5] Requirements discovered late in the lifecycle lead to project, schedule, and cost overruns.[6] Conversely, projects with higher quality requirements have fewer changes, which results in less rework and lower costs.

## 4. Requirements Quality Drives Software Quality

Making code changes due to late requirements results in the deterioration of product quality. [7]

---

3    Many different studies define project failure as any deviation from the original project baseline, which arguably skews the results. The Standish Group's Chaos Report is a frequently cited reference but even its methods have come under scrutiny (Eveleens, J. L., & Verhoef, C. (2010). The Rise and Fall of the Chaos Report Figures. *IEEE Software* , 30–36.).

4    Poor requirements are one of the causes of poor project cost estimation (Davis, A. M. *201 Principles of Software Development.* New York: McGraw Hill, [995]). Average projects using poor requirements practices overran the amount of time expected of stakeholders for participation by 200% (Ellis, K. *5 Things You Need to Know About Requirements Planning.* IAG. (2010): http://www.iag.biz/resources/webinars/webcast-5-things-you-must-know-about-requirements-planning.html)..

5    "There is a 60% time and cost premium to be paid on projects with poor quality requirements." (Ellis, K. *Assessing the Impact of Poor Requirements on Companies.* IAG Consulting. (2009): http://www.iag.biz/links/white-papers-and-articles/white-paper-assessing-the-impact-of-poor-requirements-on-companies-quantifying-the-cost-of-poor-requirements.html).

6    Requirement problems comprise 40% of all errors within a project and the cost to fix those errors is very high, accounting for 70% to 80% of rework costs (Leffingwell, D. *Calculating your return on investment from more effective requirements management.* 26 February 2011 r., IBM. (3 December 2003): http://www.ibm.com/developerworks/rational/library/347.html ). The later in the lifecycle the error is discovered, the greater the cost to fix the mistake, costing up to 10 times more to correct during testing and over 100 times more once the system is in operation Grady, R. An Economic Decision Model: Insights into Software Project Management. *Proceedings of the Applications of Software Measurement Conference.* (Orange Park, FL: Software Quality Engineering, 1999), 227–239.). Getting Requirements correct early in your project can save you at a minimum one-third of your overall project budget Hooks, I., & Ferry, K. *Customer-Centered Products: Creating Successful Products Through Smart Requirements Management.* [New York., 2001].).

7    Missing and ambiguous requirements contribute to one-third of total delivered defects (Lauesen, S., & Vintner, O. Preventing Requirements Defects: An Experiment in Process Improvement. *Requirements Engineering Journal* (2001), 37–50. ). Requirements processes are the source of most (50% or more) serious quality problems ( Weinberg, G. M. *Quality Software Management: Anticipating Change.* [Dorset House Publishing Company, 1997)]).

# Other Signs You Might Be Right

If the research isn't enough to convince you that requirements process improvement is essential, you probably have your own experiences. These are some of mine:

## 1. Documentation Doesn't Match Up

When there is enough requirements documentation to support the testing effort, it often doesn't match the solution that is delivered by IT. Why? Because no one managed the requirements after they were initially submitted, or the requirements were insufficient and additional information was brought to the project outside of the requirements process. Frequently the other project processes are not very sound and there is no formal hand-off of the requirements or validation of the understanding of their content. Without proper requirements walkthroughs and validation, and subsequent requirements management, the activities of the developers don't always match what is represented in the document. Testers don't know who is right or what to test and don't have time to sort it all out so they make their best guess.

## 2. Lots of Defects Post-Production

As you can imagine, making your best guess as to the functionality of a module or piece of code generally assures that it will not be thoroughly tested and you will see many defects when that code is moved to production.

## 3. Business Needs are Not Met

Some of the defects may not be considered issues by the development team (the code was "designed" to do that) but they are considered defects by the users because the product is not delivering the business value that they need. The BA is left trying to determine why something was designed that didn't meet the business need and having to defend the IT organization, the faulty process, and the inadequate deliverable. Facing unhappy customers is never fun. Do it enough times and your IT group gets a bad reputation.

Every organization has its stories of project pain points and failed deliveries. Sound project processes lead to more successful projects, so the question really becomes, why would you NOT bother with process improvement?

# What is Process Improvement?

## A General Definition

Process improvement involves evaluating a process in order to change it to meet new needs or improve it in some way. The driving factors behind process improvement are the desire to drive out costs or raise quality by limiting errors (or both). There are many quality approaches that have sprung from the need to make business and manufacturing improvements.[8]

---

8    Many disciplines have arisen around business and production process improvements,

## Project Process Improvement

Even if you are not versed in the multitude of quality disciplines, as a Business Analyst it is your job to help business groups improve their processes. Depending on the maturity of your organization, you may use process maps, workflow diagrams, or other tools to understand an existing process and propose improvements. The requirements effort for a business process improvement project aims to define who does what in the current process, understand the information flows, look for inefficiencies, and present opportunities for automation.

We need to turn our skills inward and do some process analysis on our own activities. Project processes don't always fall so neatly into diagrams, although that doesn't mean we should abandon the effort altogether. For any type of technology project, the stages are generally similar to initiation, requirements, design, code, test, and deploy. How the stages overlap (or not) and the artifacts created in each are dependent on the type of process methodology you are using (plan-driven vs. activity-driven), but some permutation of each of these steps has to occur in some fashion. It could be that you don't end up getting your Requirements until after you deploy (a situation which is actually quite common, unfortunately) but the steps are there.

The requirements phase of a project can also be further broken down into process steps, although the steps are rarely very linear, nor are they often planned out. Various elicitation methods may be used, an attempt is made to document the requirements, and sometimes there is validation that the correct requirements were captured.

Once elicitation, validation, and the requirements phases are considered complete, the task moves to one of requirements management. As projects evolve and more information is learned, requirements inevitably change and the document (and more importantly, everyone's understanding of the requirements) must be updated. Improvement efforts may focus on the elicitation or management stages of requirements.

## Not Just Process Improvement

Process improvement by itself isn't enough. Only companies committed to achieving excellence in business requirements through improvement involving people, process, and documentation/information quality standards will be consistently, predictably successful[9].

---

originating from the need to reduce errors in manufacturing and raise quality of goods. Car manufacturing is the birthplace of many quality programs. The Japanese have been noted for the quality programs they initiated in the 1960s, which were the springboard for other efforts, such as Total Quality Management, sponsored by Ford Motor Company in the 1980s. Quality programs have continued to evolve, focusing on business and software processes. ISO, Six Sigma and business process engineering are only some of the models available.

9    The pay-off for those companies that have made pervasive change to their people and processes of requirements is quite substantial: Over 70% of companies in the upper third of requirements discovery capability reported having a successful project. Better than half of their projects (54%) are on time, on budget and on function, and as a group, these companies pay about 50% less for their applications. If your people and processes in business Requirements

An average analyst will have difficulty delivering on projects that have significant changes to business process or cost cutting as important goals. At the same time, higher-level Business Analysts will not perform as well in lower maturity environments as average Business Analysts will in higher-level maturity environments. You cannot focus on process to the exclusion of people and their skills if you want to make substantive change. You must consider both people and process. Effectively trained and competent Business Analysts are keys to your success.

## Assess Current State

As part of assessing your current state, look at your organizational environment and the challenges and support it may provide. Where you sit in the organization and your current relationship with business partners, IT, and other stakeholders can make a difference to your improvement plans. While a formal assessment isn't necessary, using organizational change management principles, understanding your place in the organization, thinking through organizational assets, finding allies, and obtaining management commitment are important elements to moving forward.

## Organizational Structure and Its Role

If you are a manager of Business Analysts, getting your direct reports on board to start an improvement effort can be considerably easier. However, there may be other Business Analysts not under you or your organization (which may point to the need for organizational alignment changes needed to support your efforts). Or you may be a senior BA or lead BA but don't really have the organizational title to easily sway people to do what you want. You have to rely on your communication and leadership skills to move the organization in the appropriate direction. Luckily, as a successful BA, you have most of those skills already.

Even if you can get all the BAs to support a new approach, the by-product of the BA effort (requirements documentation) is not something that exists on its own. It is the spine of any technology project (regardless of what the documentation looks like: sticky notes on a wall, a collection of use cases, a formal document). As the "keeper" of what the project is all about, an attempt to change almost any aspect of requirements usually have to be approved by people all along the entire project pipeline. So not only is there the organizational structure to consider but there is project structure also. You probably already have a sense of whom you can partner with in QA, IT, and the business. Using the skills you already have in cultivating relationships across the organization, spend time with your friends in development and testing to get an idea of where their pain points are and their readiness to adapt to change.

Knowledge of your organization will let you know if an improvement effort is something to take on yourself or if an external party may be necessary.

---

are only AVERAGE, rather than excellent, this lack of excellence will consume approximately 41.5% of the IT development budget for people (internal and external) and software on strategic projects (Ellis, K. *Getting Business Requirements Right.* IAG Consulting. (2009): http://www.iag.biz/links/white-papers-and-articles/white-paper-getting-business-requirements-right.html ).

There are many consulting firms out there that would love to come in and assess your requirements processes and the competencies of your individual analysts and give you a plan for improving both. If you have the backing and the budget to use such services, they can provide you with your improvement plan. I have never worked anywhere that had a budget for requirements consulting so I used whatever resources were available to work to become the in-house expert and then drove the process myself.

## Organizational Change Management

Although changes to requirements processes may not seem to be very large or have a significant organizational impact, it is valuable to understand organizational change management principles. As a manager or leader, you must take responsibility for change management and get the assistance needed to ensure your success. People are naturally resistant to change, no matter how good the idea might be. Previous changes may have been attempted and failed, or the current environment is introducing a great deal of change that makes people feel uneasy.

Ignoring the people impacted by change can result in higher turnover, loss of valued employees, reduced productivity, and delays in implementing your change (Hiatt, J., & Creasey, T. *Change Management.* [Prosci Research, 2003]). Expect some resistance and have a plan for handling it.

Making iterative and incremental change as part of your change management plan will give people more time to adapt to the changes. Your method of spreading the word about your plans and obtaining buy-in will also help to get people on board to assist the process.

## Management Commitment

In other software process improvement literature, I see comments about the importance of management commitment, and while I don't disagree, I have managed to bring about requirements process improvements without a huge steering committee, process group, or any formal assessments or much of a budget. A grass roots effort can be effective if managed correctly and frequently management commitment follows some small wins made informally.

As knowledgeable practitioners begin to make desired changes, leadership can adopt the language of change, speaking out about the implications of good requirements, and encouraging correct behaviors. To move toward your vision, having both business and IT leadership helping to blaze the path will greatly assist in the adoption of your changes.

## Current State Assessment

A current state assessment is a vital artifact to get you started on your process improvement effort. It will also help you begin to understand the metrics you will need, giving you a baseline to draw upon when determining whether or not your efforts have led to real improvements. Without such a baseline, it will be difficult to claim any success! The term "assessment" sounds very formal but there are some simple tools available that will help put together a general overview of your current state. [10] Then you can pinpoint some of the biggest areas of pain and focus your initial efforts on the areas of highest value.

## Skills Assessment

The International Institute of Business Analysis™ (IIBA) has introduced a competency model along with a self-assessment that is aimed at allowing individual BAs to assess their skills and help them create a plan for professional development, the Business Analysis Competency Model.[11] The assessment is based on *The Business Analysis Body of Knowledge (BABOK®)*, so it is hefty; you may want to trim it down and ask only about the areas currently most pertinent to your organization. Or, you may want to wait until you have a better understanding of what the critical capabilities are for your company.[12]

Combined results will also give you a picture of where your overall staff competency lies.

## Process Assets

What do you have in place already? Create an inventory of current assets including processes and templates and when they are used. Your process inventory will help you get an understanding of what services you currently provide to your organization. As you begin to compare your inventory to other best practices, you will begin to see improvement opportunities.

## Survey

Surveys can give you an idea of what people think about business analysis and requirements activities. You can gain a picture of the quality of the deliverables that are in your process inventory. A useful technique I have used is Start/Stop/Continue. Ask respondents to indicate activities they would like to see BAs start doing, stop doing, or continue doing. This method allows for feedback on what is working and gives suggestions for changes in a generally non-threatening way.

---

10    Karl has an assessment in his book you can use as a starting point (Wiegers, K. E. *Software Requirements Second Edition.* (Microsoft Press, 2003).

11    *Business Analysis Competency Model.* 25 March 2011 r., International Institute of Business Analysis. (2011): http://www.theiiba.org/Content/NavigationMenu/Learning/BusinessAnalysisCompetencyModel/default.htm

12    You may want to consider developing a competency model for your organization. There are other models available  Treasure, B., & Vaughan, M. *Business Analysis Competency Framework.* Core Consulting. (23 October 2008): http://www.google.com.br/url?sa=t&source=web&ct=res&cd=2&ved=0CA0QFjAB&url=http%3A%2F%2Fwww.abaa.org.au%2Fcms%2Ftiki-download_file.php%3FfileId%3D66&rct=j&q=business+analyst+competence+model&ei=pXRdS7u_AcWduAep_LTAAg&usg=AFQjCNEm1OGOD-k46jBUD3YxXszqhv7Y1g ), or you can develop one from scratch. See (Beal, A. 25 March 2011 r., Modern Analyst. (10 February 2010 r.): http://www.modernanalyst.com/Resources/Articles/tabid/115/articleType/ArticleView/articleId/1287/Developing-a-Competency-Model-for-Business-Analysts.aspx ) for ideas on developing your own competency model.

## Project Statistics

Sometimes organizations at lower project maturity levels do not have a lot of project statistics readily available. Work to put something in place immediately to help capture project information. The actual length of project phases and variance to the planned length, number of releases in a certain time period, number of issues arising from a release, and number of patches post-release are examples of data you can capture. As you move forward in your assessment and planning, you may discover other things you would like to measure to let you know if you have made an impact with your changes.

## Focus on the Pain[13]

People are more motivated to make a change if they know what is in it for them; and if what is in it reduces or alleviates pain they are currently feeling, you are likely to gain supporters fairly easily.

To get buy-in for your efforts, insight into the pains of upper management is very useful. What is the executive team hounding the CIO about? Are there issues that are being raised to the C-level that could be improved by better requirements processes?

# Planning

Similar to the work required to plan requirements elicitation activities and facilitated sessions, the planning effort for process improvement can be lengthy. There are many factors to consider before striking out on a path. There are numerous resources available to give you ideas on best practices and various approaches to implementing a process improvement effort. I wouldn't dream of launching any kind of change effort (even now, with a good amount of practical experience) without research and planning.

## Decide on a Guide (or Two)

Your current state assessment will give you a picture of where you are. To formalize your understanding of where you can go, review existing frameworks for requirements maturity. While you need not follow any particular model strictly, comparing your pain points with best practices will help you build your plan.

### 1. The Capability Maturity Model

The Capability Maturity Model was developed years ago by the Software Engineering Institute and is used as a general model to aid in improving both IT and business organizational processes (i.e. software engineering, system

---

13    Karl Wiegers Software Process Improvement Handbook makes this point. (Wiegers, K. E. *Software Process Improvement Handbook.* www.processimpact.com. (2005): www.proces-simpact.com)

engineering, project management, software maintenance). It is applicable to business analysis processes as well.[14]

You can have your organization formally assessed and assigned a level, and then have a plan put together for you that is designed to move you up the maturity ladder.

Compliance with the higher levels of CMM is deemed by some organizations to be more process than is necessary to get their work done. It is important that you understand the culture of your environment so that you don't push folks past the point of their process tolerance. The value added with the addition of more process must be worth the effort expended in working that process.

### 2. BABOK® Guide

*A Guide to the Business Analysis Body of Knowledge® (BABOK® Guide)* by International Institute of Business Analysis does not contain a maturity model per se but does give information on what a good Business Analyst needs to know and the processes she or he must follow. Using the standards developed by the professional organization for Business Analysts is helpful because it gives you a common language with other BAs and also helps your staff gain familiarity with *BABOK Guide®*, which standardizes industry best practices.

### 3. IAG

IAG has a useful requirements maturity model that is made up of five levels and six underlying capabilities.[15]

The levels are straightforward. The underlying capabilities give you other areas to look at aside from process alone: staff competency, tools, practices and techniques, organization (support and infrastructure around BAs and projects and how work is controlled, managed, and communicated), deliverables, and results. It is possible to be at different levels for each of the capabilities.

## Mind the Gap

As you get close to completing your organizational and requirements maturity assessments, the baseline that you create will tell you what you need to do to move forward. The gaps you see in your maturity, information on staff competence, the feedback from surveys, and your insights into your organization should give you a good idea of what you can do to start making improvements.

Having an idea of where you are and where you want to go is a good start. But what actions do you take to get to your desired destination? How will

---

14    See www.cmmilevels.com for more information. Many organizations operate somewhere between levels 1 and 2.

15    For further information, refer to Heembrock, P. *Gaining Momentum for Requirements Improvement.* IAG (2010): http://storage.pardot.com/464/56885/Gaining_Momentum_for_Requirements_Improvement.pdf

you know your actions got you there? Sometimes these questions can be a bit overwhelming and it is hard to know what the smartest first steps might be. Know that requirements improvement is not a one-shot effort; it is a mindset that you want to inculcate in your teams. Continual reevaluation of your projects and processes will have you making small adjustments to improve your project outcomes, in turn positively impacting organizational goals and your company's bottom line.

## The BA Off-Site Event

Even if your roadmap is clearly pointing to what changes need to occur, you are much more likely to succeed with your change effort if the group you are relying on to implement this change is totally behind you. While you can have regular meetings to discuss ideas and plans for moving forward, a more effective (and faster) approach may be an off-site event. An off-site gathering can be particularly effective if members of your group haven't yet decided that change is necessary. Having a teambuilding event to reaffirm the group's purpose and launch it into its next phase gives members the opportunity to express their concerns with where they are now and explore where they would like to go, while laying the groundwork for the improvements necessary to get there. The off-site event can be part of your change management plan; using the group to work through concerns and issues is a good way to gain buy-in for what you are doing.

Many BAs have the kind of experience in group facilitation and requirements workshops that will help with such an event. If you find the task daunting, however, look for other resources in your organization to help. Frequently facilitators can be found in training or human resources departments, and they can be recruited to assist in your efforts. Group work is a lot of fun but takes planning from skilled personnel.

### 1. Planning Your Event

You can use many of the same methods for planning collaborative requirements sessions to put together your BA event. I've found it helpful to engage other BAs in the planning process. You can assign people to help with certain parts, such as icebreakers/teambuilding activities, snacks, or meals. Having a small team (yourself and one or two other people) to help determine goals and outputs for your event is helpful because you add several perspectives. I have also found it helpful to include the folks who may be dissenters or be the slowest to adapt to change in these planning activities.

You may not want to label your event "Process Improvement Kickoff" but at the same time, you don't want to surprise anyone with the general content of the agenda. You can frame the session as a teambuilding and future planning event.

Planning the event is essential to achieving the outcomes you are looking for. Ellen Gottesdiener's *Requirements by Collaboration* is an excellent resource. Even though the book is geared toward requirements sessions, the tools and information are very transferrable to a BA working session. There are also additional session planning worksheets and resources on her website.

Define an agenda that brings to light what you have discovered as part of your current state assessment and pain point discoveries. You may not have completed all of your assessments prior to the event but having some information in the room creates an excellent springboard for discussion.

### 2. Time/Location

It is difficult to take BAs away as a group for any amount of time. I have had success with a few half days. If you are also trying to incorporate training, you will need more time. You may want to save training for follow up sessions and focus on using the team's time to help develop and buy into a go-forward plan. Note however that if you do not go off-site and have some ground rules about behaviors (no laptops, for example), you will be plagued by interruptions. Moving people out of their work environment ensures their participation and shows a dedication to the effort.

### 3. Homework for Participants

Helping participants get in the mindset to engage in the off-site activities will help you get off to a good start. The work you ask them to do depends on the content of your agenda but having them explore project frustrations and be ready to discuss them is helpful. You must plan for this feedback time and be prepared to channel it into improvement discussions. You may also want them to take a self-assessment on their own individual skills to get them thinking about their own personal development.

### 4. Homework for Planners

Put together an agenda and know what you want out of each item. Prepare good questions or activities that will orient the team to the real problems and get them focused. Know that the equivalent hours of planning are required to pull off an event that achieves its stated goals. Work with your sponsor to make sure your goals align and ask him or her to kick off the event. Coach your sponsor on what is important to say while focusing on the commitment needed to move the effort forward.

### 5. Example Agenda

Day 1

- Lunch
- Meeting Overview/Goals
- Ground Rules
- Teambuilding Activity
- Why Focus on Requirements?
- BA Evolution at Our Company
- Go Over "Homework" (Assessments)

- What are We Doing Well? (Incorporate survey results)
- What Do We Want to Do Better?
- Dinner and Activities

Day 2

- Recap of Day 1
- Organize Suggestions
- Plan for Moving Forward

### 6. Executing Your Event

Good planning and a skilled facilitator will ensure that your event goes smoothly. Be prepared for the venting of frustrations, especially if you have had significant process pains in the past. Keep these sessions productive by determining action items for the group (if the pain originates with them). If the frustration is with the activities of other groups, I have found it useful to use "request" language to take back to other parties. If the group feels as if the development team is misunderstanding the business need or not thoroughly reading the require-ments, request that they allow you to perform a validation step to go over the document and provide feedback. You may have requests to business partners to be more engaged in the requirements elicitation. Or you can request that the test team help you start preparing business acceptance cases earlier in the project. Documenting the requests targets a plan for dealing with frustrations with external groups that will need to be worked after the planning event is over.

### 7. The After-Party

Have some fun and relax. Invite your sponsor to join the group for some team-building fun.

## Create, Pilot, and Implement New Process

Reach out to express your gratitude to your sponsor for the budget expen-diture (no matter how small) and for allowing the team to be away from day-to-day responsibilities. Use this opportunity to let the sponsor know what was achieved.

Type up and distribute notes, remind participants of action items, and follow through on any commitments made during the off-site. Set up follow-up meetings to track status and keep folks on target. Also give them support if any roadblocks are discovered.

You may also want to present a "show and tell" for your sponsor, much like you would for a requirements elicitation workshop. What did the group discover and what are next steps, owners, and due dates?

Once you have your group on board and a plan to move forward, you can put your first change into effect. Make sure to communicate the change to affected parties. Be prepared to reward teams that quickly adapt and call out successes as they occur. Lead by example.

## What Works

Here are some ideas for changes you can start with, several of which are clearly derived from the pain points described at the beginning of the chapter.

### TABLE 1. POSSIBLE PROCESS CHANGES

| Suggested Action | Benefits |
| --- | --- |
| Stakeholder Analysis | Since lack of user involvement is one of the primary reasons for project failures, clearly all stakeholder groups must be represented when discussing the part of the project that impacts them. The activities are not difficult or particularly time-consuming, especially in comparison with the cost of omitting an important party. |
| Standardize Documentation | A standard template by itself will not likely fix anything but it makes the team appear organized and makes it clear what the expectations are for the deliverable. It is likely that additional training may be needed for certain folks to perform all of the activities needed to use the template to its fullest. |
| Requirements Change Management Process | Changes not communicated to the appropriate parties lead to missed functionality, missed test cases, and unmet expectations. Just having the process does not guarantee adherence to it. It takes time, constant monitoring, and a cultural shift to get everyone on board.[16] |
| Define What Sign-Off Means | Some organizations have the notion that requirements can be "locked down" or use sign-off is some sort of shackle (You can't complain! You signed off on these requirements!). Consider treating sign-off as an agreement that everyone understands the current deliverable and has enough information to move forward. Expecting changes and having a good plan for handling them is a more effective project approach than trying to lock down every detail up front. You may want to have stakeholder groups sign-off on smaller functional sections of the document instead of the whole thing, including appropriate diagrams, use cases, and data elements in the sign-off. |
| Document Reviews | Reviewing documentation at key intervals during the project is an important validation step to assure that you are building the right product. If one of the goals is to reduce the number of defects introduced and to find defects earlier, we need to focus our activities on what will drive these defects out sooner in the process. How can we tell we have done that? When are our defects introduced now? |

---

16   The greatest resisters to requirements change management efforts I've initiated have been IT folks, not business people. The process can be seen as an unnecessary layer. Make sure to educate all project members about the criticality of the improvement effort and be prepared for constant reminders.

### TABLE 1. POSSIBLE PROCESS CHANGES

| Suggested Action | Benefits |
|---|---|
| Train the Staff | Using the results of self-assessments and your understanding of where your team lines up on maturity, determine appropriate group or individual training needs. You can send folks away to training or if the need is great enough, bring in a professional to train on-site. |
| Requirements Planning Session | The elicitation phase is comprised of many different activities that vary for each project, depending on the skill of the individual BA and the nature of the project. Stakeholders perceive these differences as a lack of process.[17] A simple remedy is to have a requirements planning session to determine with the appropriate stakeholders which activities are to be performed for elicitation and requirements validation for the project at hand. You can bring in a more senior BA to help determine the activities and guide the group in their planning and implementation. You can use the planning session as a stepping stone toward creating a repeatable Requirements process. |

## Easy Wins

Sometimes you can do small things outside of a formal effort that may raise eyebrows but serve as the seeds of a change. At one point I joined an organization and immediately eschewed the hierarchical numbering scheme used in the requirements documentation, instead using unique numbering and distinct requirements. Folks knew I had a lot of experience from other companies so they tolerated my approach. When feedback started coming back from QA that my requirements were the easiest to understand and write test cases for, other analysts became curious and wanted to learn a new way of doing things. No meetings, no big plans, or organizational commitment. A change was born!

## Small and Steady

Depending on your organization, you may be able to put a whole new process or set of expectations into place at one time and be successful with appropriate training and support. I have found that focusing on smaller, iterative changes can move the group more quickly toward a desired end state than a huge overhaul. Scrapping everything and starting with a new process can be overwhelming. People tend to pick up bits and pieces (or more likely, nothing) and continue in the well-formed pathway of how they always did things. Some things may get better, some get worse, and since the change was so large, it

---

17    Studies have shown that even if a Business Analyst and his or her team believe they are following a methodology or process, the requirements phase of a project looks to the participants as if it is ad hoc (Ellis, 5 Things You Need to Know About Requirements Planning, 2010). Because each project and the requirements activities vary, those involved in the effort frequently do not perceive that there is any requirements process at all.

is difficult to assess what needs to be modified for continued improvement. Everyone is confused, the results are unclear, and the whole thing may be scrapped. Smaller improvements are easier to implement, as they are minor changes to existing protocol and not usually resisted the same way that large changes are. You can more readily attribute the results of smaller change to the change itself and you can make tweaks to your process before taking the next step.

Even though smaller changes have an advantage of being easier to implement, make sure to continually focus on meaningful activities that add value.[18]

## Evaluate Results

Part of planning of your change and the implementation of your pilot is the determination of success criteria: how do you know your change had the intended effect? A combination of many metrics is generally necessary to get a good view of your progress. Using the information captured during your assessment, you can compare simple items like milestone dates on similar projects to see if anything has changed. You can survey users to determine if their satisfaction with project results has improved.

While stories are useful and do point toward success, data seems to have a more lasting effect on institutional memory. Being able to clearly illustrate that your change had a positive impact on project outcomes will go a long way toward galvanizing support for your activities.

You can generally figure out your measurement by working backward from the problem that you want to solve. If you are trying to reduce the number of defects discovered post-implementation, you need to have an idea of how many defects are discovered today to see if that number gets reduced in the future. Look at standard project metrics (lifecycle stage durations, estimated versus actual delivery dates) to see if there is a place where your improvements could make a difference.

Remember, too, it is not always possible to isolate your efforts as the sole cause for the improvement. Different personnel, project complexity, and other factors also can contribute to your results—be careful not to claim success (or failure) until you have fully analyzed the scenario. But don't give up on measuring. Ensure that solid metrics have been identified, agreed upon, and are understood by all.

As your processes and measurements mature, you may want to consider trying to get a handle on how you measure quality Requirements and quality software. It's hard to know if you've improved the quality of anything if you don't have a baseline of what quality means to your organization.

---

18    If minor changes don't give you enough critical mass to have the effect you desire, you may need to re-think small and incremental and strive for a change that is more of an order of magnitude approach. There are times when a sponsor must require adherence to a new process or the adoption of certain methods to assure consistent usage while also reinforcing management commitment to the change.

Here are some Requirements-specific metrics you might consider implementing:

TABLE 2. HOW TO MEASURE REQUIREMENT IMPROVEMENT

| Metric | What to Look for |
|---|---|
| Defect Injection | It may be valuable to track at which stage in the lifecycle a defect is introduced. Lots of issues are coding errors but many are due to misunderstood, incomplete, or missing requirements. |
| Change Requests | When in a project are changes being introduced and what is their magnitude? (Being able to effectively track change requires a solid project change management process.) Large changes being requested late in the project likely point to some requirements or project process issue. |
| Estimation of Elicitation Effort | As the skill of the BAs in your organization matures, BAs should be getting better at estimating the requirements effort on a project. Tracking variation from estimates over time will show if planning and estimating activities have improved. |

## Important Note:
## Requirements Defect Does Not Equal BA Defect

While we have discussed the importance of addressing changes to process as well as growing individual BA skills, do not use project measurements for performance goals, at least at the beginning. Using measurements to determine professional development plans is smart, but again, it may make more sense to look at aggregate data and be wary of individual project results.

I have noticed that there is a lot of churn around the phrase: "missed requirement" and there can be a lot of arguing where a defect is injected into a project. No one wants a defect to have originated in his or her phase. Creating an environment where individuals can claim errors of misunderstanding and not be punished for missing skill sets is vital. The goal is to grow and improve processes and skills, not punish.

It's also important that as you introduce new measurements, you take time to understand the change in behaviors that are generated by the measurements. It is easy for tracking mechanisms to drive unintended consequences (rewarding on lines of code or defects found are classic examples) so starting with aggregate data and using it as an overall guide for improvement is wise. Use the measurements for process assessment, not individual assessment.

As your measurements and understanding mature, you can start using individual project results for more targeted actions.

Some personal anecdotal examples:

### TABLE 3: EXAMPLES OF CHANGE

| Sample Situation | End Result |
|---|---|
| Started in an environment where change was not well-managed, business people made requests to IT that got added to project and no one knew. | Ended in environment where business people still felt comfortable talking to developers directly but the developers brought in the BA and PM to ensure that the change was acceptable to the project team and properly documented. |
| Started in environment where design documentation and reviews did not even refer to the Requirements. | Ended in an environment where the design document actually referenced the Requirements by number. |
| Started in an environment where developers didn't feel like they knew exactly what to build until the product was in testing. | While this one didn't get to perfection, we moved toward an environment where the developers had a good understanding through requirements documentation and processes about what was required before beginning coding. |

# Set the Stage for Continual Improvement

## Follow Through on Commitments

When you originally developed your plan, you probably created a spreadsheet of items to do and indicated who was responsible. Follow through on the commitments that you make and hold your team members accountable for theirs. Allowing day-to-day work to get in the way of the process improvement efforts will prevent you from moving forward. Ensure your stakeholder agrees to continually push ahead even in the face of everyday work, and make process improvement an expected part of all project work.

You will want to continue meeting with your BA group to go over milestones and activities. You may want another off-site in 6–12 months to do another retrospective and plan again for your next goals.

Celebrate your wins! They will likely be small and sometimes they are so gradual that you miss them so keep your eyes peeled and be ready to reward your group for its efforts.

## Don't Forget Your Allies

Communicate! Keep up the conversations that you started at the beginning of your process improvement effort. The usefulness or influence of different individuals will vary over time; regardless, continue to communicate with your supporters.

## Starting a Centre of Excellence

As part of your process improvement activities, you may want to institute a Business Analysis Centre of Excellence (CoE) or Community of Practice (CoP).

Please refer to other chapters in this book as to which of these groups may make sense for your organization.

Companies pay dearly (and repeatedly) for poor requirements performance. As a manager or leader committed to the growth of your company and your people, it is imperative that you work toward more mature processes and developing business analysis competencies. Studies have repeatedly shown that sound requirements processes and skilled practitioners lead to better project outcomes. Going through the steps to assess your current state, build a plan for growth, and continually implementing and assessing will set you on the right path.

# Suggested Reading

Gottesdiener, E. *Requirements by Collaboration: Workshops for Defining Needs.* (Crawfordsville: Addison-Wesley Professional, 2002)

Hofmann, H. F., & Lehner, F. Requirements Engineering as a Success Factor in Software Projects. IEEE Software. (July/August 2001 r.): https://gul.gu.se/public/pp/public_courses/course41505/published/1293546982422/resourceId/16328933/content/ReqAsASuccessfactor.pdf

May, L. J. Major Causes of Software Project Failures. Crosstalk. (1998 May r.): http://crosstalkonline.org/storage/issue-archives/1998/199807/199807-May.pdf

Walker, B. Good Requir*ements Don't Come Easy.*
IAG: http://iag.biz/images/resources/good_requirements_dont_come_easy.jpg

## About the Author

Shelley Cudly has been working as a BA for the past 14 years (with a brief break to branch out as an Application Development Manager) primarily in the financial services and insurance industries. She served as one of the lead Business Analysts for a major on-line brokerage firm, performing traditional BA duties such as facilitating Requirements elicitation sessions for large and small projects, Requirements modeling, managing Requirements change, and coordinating user acceptance testing. She led the conversion of account demographic data for several large acquisitions. Shelley also developed successful BA hiring, training, and mentoring programs and drove continual Requirements process improvement changes. She has spoken at several Project World/World Congress for Business Analysis conferences. She is currently involved in an effort to evolve the role of the BA, driving it into business units, raising awareness of the enterprise business analysis role, and moving the IT organization into strategic partnership. Shelley is also involved with her local IIBA® chapter and is helping plan their annual development day.

# BUSINESS ANALYSIS TRAINING

By Rick Clare, OCP, PMP, CBAP

## Introduction

What is this chapter about?
How does training relate to management?
What kinds of managers and leaders are there?
How will this chapter examine training and learning?

This chapter concerns training, specifically the training of Business Analysts. Here we will examine the nature of training and trainers, what Business Analysts need to know, and how best to move that knowledge into their brains. This *book* is about management, however. What does training have to do with management?

My early working life was spent in the army, and the primary training focus of any military branch is not the specific skills of the soldier's chosen trade but rather leadership and its close relative, management. During my time in the army, three terms were used to describe the different kinds of leaders: the authority, the persuader, and the educator. The authority is that military stereotype most familiar to the world, the drill sergeant, who barks orders and expects instant obedience. The persuader is a leader who uses discussion and collaboration to achieve the goal. While the existence of a leader like this in the military might seem strange to someone who has never been in uniform, I can assure you that in reality most work gets done this way. The classic authority posture is a role that is only needed under certain circumstances. Note, by the way, that in our world Project Managers are usually persuaders in this fashion.

*Drill Sergeant—This is a type of leader/trainer but is it the one best suited to deal with Business Analysts?*

The last type of leader is the educator and in many ways this is the most valued type. The best leaders are the ones that lead by example, and what better example than an expert showing someone else how to do a specific job? The best trainers are always people who have made their living doing that very task Students can always tell the difference between a poser who merely talks the talk, and the real deal, someone who has walked the walk. As a manager, you must decide what training is needed and how best to conduct that training. If you are an expert and possess the necessary instructional skills, do the training yourself—this is a great bonding technique. If not, your job is to organize and supervise the training. Examined in this light, there can be no doubt that training *is* management.

This chapter will look at what professional training is and how people learn. We will examine trainers in the BA arena, the characteristics they should possess, and the pros and cons of the different training venues. We will look at the skills that should be targeted by Business Analyst training and the different ways of doing that training. While it is true that different companies need different things from their BAs, a certain core set of skills should always be present, conforming to International Institute of Business Analysis™ (IIBA) standards. Finally we will look at training from the BA's perspective, trying to figure out what they require and how training should be done for this special group.

# What is Training?

- How is adult learning different from other types of instruction?
- What characteristics must an instructor of adults possess?
  - Subject matter knowledge
  - The ability to run a classroom
  - Charisma
- What are the different learning venues in use for professional education?
  - Computer-based or online training
  - Virtual classroom
  - Face-to-face

## Adults and Education

Training is the art of imparting knowledge to someone so that they can make effective use of that knowledge afterwards. A human lifespan could be considered one long training session, as our species seems to have very few (possibly none) of the inherent behavior patterns that we call instincts in other animals. Everything that we humans do has to be learned so it is not surprising that much thought has been given to the mechanics of learning.

Learning for adults happens differently than it does for children. As we grow older, our ability to simply observe and absorb diminishes, until as adults, we simultaneously reach our slowest learning rate and our full growth. To teach a child a second language, all you have to do is speak that language in the presence of the child, while many of us know how painful that same process can be for grown-ups! Since it is expected that all the Business Analysts that you will be training will be adults, it is important to understand how adults learn.

*Figure 2. Two Models of Learning*

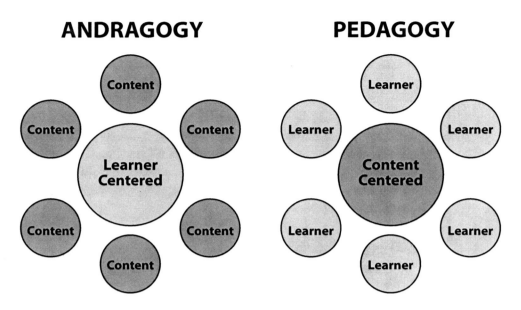

*These two styles of learning were originally developed by Malcolm Shepherd Knowles (1913–1997), who determined that adult learning differed from that of children in that adults should be the center of the learning process.[1]*

Adults are just that—adults, and they do not respond well to regimented or dictatorial teaching methods. They need to feel free and in control of the process and they function much better in a peer-to-peer environment with the teacher. Successful instructors at this level know that an adult classroom is best designed as a gathering of friends, where everyone has something to offer, not just the instructor. This works very well with Business Analysts. Discussions that allow all participants to share their experiences should form the core of most BA training.

## How Do Adults Learn?

Adults are goal-oriented and need to feel that the training has a purpose and an immediate applicability. Although learning is fun and many people take classes just for the joy of it, most of the students that a Business Analysis trainer will encounter are there for a specific purpose—to increase their worth. They know what they want, they know what they are expecting from the class and from the trainer, and they want the course content to be practical and to be taught within a context that is familiar to them. Why will these

---

1    (Original Diagram Source: University of South Alabama Online Learning Laboratory
     website, at
     http://southalabama.edu/oll/mobile/theory_workbook/adult_learning_theory.htm)

students attend this class? What motivates them to take this training? There are many reasons they will be in class:

- They have been required to obtain the training
- They are working towards personal enhancement
- Their job has changed and they need to understand the new direction
- They are exploring a new career
- They are taking the training just for fun (rare, but great when you can get them!)
- They are looking to add BA skills to their repertoire, even though they • are employed elsewhere (also rare but a growing segment)

Adult students respond to motivation and encouragement rather than force. They require respect, as do all students, but there can be no doubt that the respect pattern in an adult environment is very different than that in even the best high school classroom. Knowledge transfer must be geared towards the more methodical adult learning patterns and should emphasize repetition, retention, and association with the familiar. Adults usually want to know how well they are doing, and unlike high school students, they actively want to be tested! Adult educators have one advantage over child educators—they are not dealing with an alien species. To gauge the atmosphere in the classroom, all an adult trainer has to do is imagine himself or herself in the reverse position. It is no longer possible for most adults to do that in a classroom full of children.

## The Instructor

Now that we have thought about the students, let us turn our attention to the instructor. What traits should an adult educator possess, particularly a trainer of professionals like Business Analysts? One of the first things to remember is the equality issue that was discussed earlier. Adult students think of themselves as the equals of the teacher and there is little question of "authority". An important aspect of this is expectation—these students expect the teacher to do a good job and will have little tolerance for bad instruction. All professional education like this is subject to evaluation, and the students will have no problem making their opinions clear concerning the performance of the instructor. Most high school students would love to have this kind of power!

Here are the three primary traits that I believe must be held by any instructor of Business Analysts, and any professional group for that matter. Later I will provide additional details on these three traits, especially the last, which may be a bit controversial:

- Subject matter expertise, including current real-world experience
- Facilitation skills, including speaker confidence and poise
- Entertainment skills and personal charisma

*Figure 3. Instructor Traits*

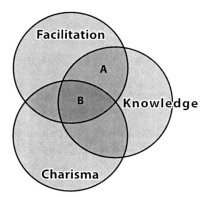

**A**—This is the minimum necessary for a professional instructor. This person may get the job done but they will win no prizes.

**B**—The very best instructors live here!

The first requirement is obvious although the second portion (real world experience) is often lacking, which can lead to problems. One of the difficulties in the professional training arena is that good instructors are often kept just in that job, and are no longer able to perform actual fieldwork. As the time span grows between the instructor's real experience and the teaching, the "war stories" that the instructor is able to share with the students become stale. The best arrangement is when the trainer divides time between fieldwork and training but not all trainers or training companies have the luxury of that arrangement. In any case, this remains true: whatever the employment model of the trainer, that person must be a subject matter expert with as much real world experience as possible. This practical familiarity and its transference is one of the most valuable tools of the professional training experience.

The facilitation abilities are also common sense. If the best subject matter expert in the world is tongue-tied and terrified in front of crowds of three or more, they are not going to work out as an instructor. Facilitation skill requirement goes deeper than that. The best facilitators are not only confident public speakers, they also listen well and are equipped to immediately detect and respond to a perceived lack of communication. They are great negotiators and they are prepared to resolve conflicts. They are guides through a difficult environment. In fact, from this perspective, many good instructors could come from the BA pool, and in my experience, this works very well. Look to your BAs for instructors and consider this instructional experience to be part of their own training.

The last item, concerning entertainment skills, might seem a little strangely placed here but most professional instructors will understand. In reality, this item could be considered part of facilitation skills, but with professional instruction of this level, the trait goes further than just ordinary facilitation. Adults in general and professionals in particular have a certain expectation from a training session like this—they want to be entertained. By this I mean that they expect the instructor to be personable, friendly, charming, and simply a pleasure to be with in the classroom. Boring is bad!

I have seen so many examples of this that it is difficult to choose one from among them. I have seen miserable courses, with poor lighting, food, and training material, nevertheless given excellent assessments because the instructor was not only knowledgeable and a good facilitator, but funny and charming. At the other end of the extreme, I have seen good rooms, good food, good subject matter expertise, and good facilitation skills receive bad assessments, all because the instructor never got a good laugh out of the group all day long. This is not just about student enjoyment, either. In every case where the results of the class were quantifiably measured, I have observed that the outcome was better in the presence of these "super instructors", even if all other things were equal. The problem is that these skills are very hard to acquire or transfer—the instructor is either charismatic or they are not. You cannot teach someone to be Jay Leno but I have noticed that the more relaxed the instructor is, the more likely it is that any natural tendencies like this will come out. Therefore the answer is to address the first two items, knowledge and facilitation skills, and then to get the instructor to teach so often that the last set of skills show up on their own. Practice makes perfect, and if the instructor is having fun, the students will also!

## Instructional Venues

How and where should this training be conducted? I am not talking so much about the room or the location so much as the style of training, and there are three primary modern delivery methods:

- Online or Computer Based Training
- Face-to-face instruction
- Virtual training

*Figure 4. Venue Comparisons*

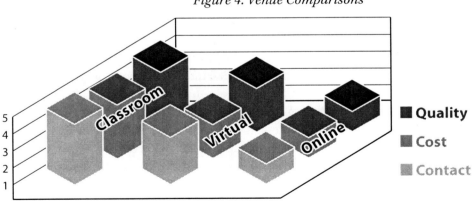

*The amount of direct human contact, the cost of the venue, and the overall quality all pretty much march in lockstep.*

Online training, or its elderly cousin Computer Based Training, occurs when students learn by guiding themselves through a computer program, either installed on their computer or available through a website. These programs can get quite fancy, with interactive games to play, self-assessment tools, and even places to post questions for an expert. In the end, however, the students are alone and the training is simply a guided tour of a book, with many features to enhance the experience. This kind of training has advantages, of course. The main one is its cost, which is very low compared to other kinds of instruction, and it is also great for location-challenged establishments. Online training has certainly come a long way from its infancy but, in the end, there is no real-time human interaction and this is always a problem for BAs.

Face-to-face instruction is the king of all styles of training, especially for BAs. Business Analysts are collaboration-focused and a large group gathered together in a room for training purposes fosters the kinds of discussion and information sharing that a BA prefers. This is the costliest form of training, however, even before factoring in any potential travel expenses. Consider, for instance, the company with two or three BAs each in a dozen cities. To have this kind of training make any sense at all, it should be at least a week long, and the cost of the airline tickets, hotels and meals for the out-of-town group are going to quickly add up. One week of such training could use a substantial amount of the department's yearly training budget! Hint: for something like this to be cost effective, you must get the very best instructor that money can rent. The training material is important, of course, but the instructor is more so.

I am sure that many of you are already well ahead of me concerning the cost associated with this last scenario, and have probably identified a solution—video conferencing. Set up video cameras in conference rooms in all of your cities and conduct the training in that manner. With this approach, you get the best of all worlds—the travel cost is removed and all of the advantages of face-to-face instruction are preserved! Right?

Unfortunately, it is not so simple. There are problems with video conferencing and virtual training which are not immediately apparent, and it takes knowledge of human communication to understand the problems. Essentially it boils down to one fact: anything short of true face-to-face interaction always degrades human communication. Most of these degradations are subtle, centered on things like territory or body language but everything counts. A good example of the less-than-perfect nature of video conferencing can be seen when you consider that usually the camera cannot be placed in the center of the TV screen. What does this mean? It means that when you are talking to someone during a video conference, you are not making eye contact. If you think this is not important, try a little experiment with your spouse sometime: have a complete five minute conversation with him or her without meeting their eyes once. Watch the irritation level rise and notice how the information flow is degraded. Imagine a whole day like this and think about how it would impact the communication level in your virtual classroom. Technology is advancing as we speak, however, and new features are being conceived to make the camera and TV sensitive to the position of the people in the room. These things are fine but they will never be more than a simulation of human presence, and therefore will always lack something.

To wrap this subject up, face-to-face training is best but it is also the most expensive. Despite the problems mentioned above with virtual training, it is the next best alternative and the cost savings can be dramatic. Finally we have online training, which offers the lowest costs of all but gives up any human contact. As with most important things in life, there are choices to make.

# What do BAs Need to Know?

- The IIBA® Standard
- The *BABOK® Guide* Knowledge Areas
- Human Communication Mastery
- Business and Solution-side Knowledge

## A Guide to the Business Analysis Body of Knowledge®

Where would we be without IIBA®? I know where we were *before* IIBA®—every company had its own vision of what BAs were and what they did. With a thousand different visions of a profession, you had a thousand different training plans. Now, even though not all companies use the IIBA® complete picture of what a BA is, at least there *is* a picture. Now we have a fixed point that can be used as a reference for all discussions about what business analysis is, and even if your company does not follow this path, I would strongly recommend that you familiarize your BAs with the *BABOK® Guide* and the six Knowledge Areas (KAs). If for no other reason, do this so that your team can be aware that there *are* other approaches. Who knows, maybe there is a good idea somewhere in there that you and your company have not considered.

*Figure 5. BABOK® Guide Knowledge Areas*

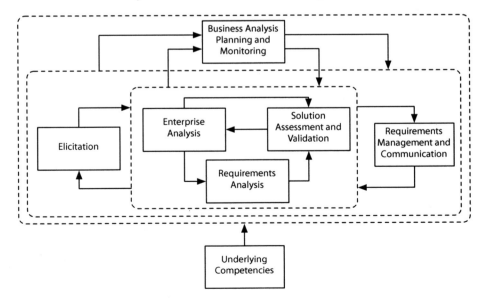

*This diagram shows the 6 BABOK® Guide Knowledge Areas, as well as the Underlying Competencies. Source: ©2009, International Institute of Business Analysis.*

I have no intention of discussing the KAs of the *BABOK® Guide* in detail here—if you do not already know them well, consider their study a homework assignment. I would like to talk about a couple of them from a training perspective though because there might be opportunities that you are not considering.

Business Analysis is not made up of skills that are completely esoteric—there are many overlaps with other professions in the KAs. Two come to mind: Project Management and Quality Assurance. IIBA® does not consider PM or QA activities when it is conferring the Certified Business Analysis Professional™ (CBAP®) certification. This may leave the impression that BA is somehow cut off from these professions. Nothing could be further from the truth and nowhere is this clearer than when we look at two KAs in particular: Business Analysis Planning and Monitoring, and Solution Assessment and Validation.

Business Analysis Planning and Monitoring is concerned with preparing for the requirements effort. Here we see tasks and activities such as Plan Business Analysis Approach, Plan Business Analysis Activities, Plan Business Analysis Communications, and Plan Requirements Management Process. In practice, BAs will find themselves doing all of the following activities during a project:

- Identifying requirements activities
- Estimating these activities
- Scheduling them
- Planning communications activities
- Documenting a process to control change to requirements
- Deciding on how the BA resources should be used (if there is more than one!)

If a Project Manager were to be given that list of activities, they would nod with complete familiarity. These are PM tasks! Therefore, why not consider PM training for your BAs? In my experience, this works really well, and in fact, the other direction works equally well—PMs getting BA training. I have always said that the best PMs are the ones that act like BAs and I personally attribute most of my PM successes to my BA skills. Note, by the way, that there may be some concerns when you propose this. I have spoken to many BAs who adamantly do not want to become PMs and you may encounter BAs that will resist getting PM training because they will think that you are trying to force them to change jobs. On the other hand, especially if you are employed by a company that thinks that BA is a stepping stone to PM, you may get resistance from your company. They may want to wait to provide that training until after a promotion. The solution to each of these concerns is the same—explain the new thinking and convince them of the advantages to this additional training.

Solution Assessment and Validation is concerned with ensuring that the solution meets the need. There was some controversy around this KA when it first came out in the old *BABOK® Guide* as it seemed to imply that a BA should not be involved in testing. I can recall many heated discussions about this with various BAs, and at some point someone would say something like this: "IIBA® is crazy! All BAs do testing!" Usually these discussions settled down when it became clear that what the IIBA® was trying to do was segregate the different professions for the purposes of certification—IIBA® has no interest in giving the CBAP® to a pure QA specialist. The wording in the new *BABOK® Guide* has cleared up any concern about IIBA® mindset towards the overlap between BA and QA. Given that, why not think about providing QA training for your BAs? This training would help in two major ways:

- Educating the BAs in the deep meaning of quality so that they can better understand and support the testing process.
- Starting the BAs down the path of Business Process Improvement. The skills that are used in this separate profession are useful to BAs, and include things like detailed process mapping, problem identification, and disconnect/enabler analysis. Training in the Quality disciplines such as Six Sigma and Lean Manufacturing fits very well here.

## Communication Skills

Several times now I have participated in one of the big panels at a BA conference where the question is this fundamental one: What is the top skill for a BA? There are always several candidates suggested such as business knowledge, problem solving or analytical skills, but in every case, one skill set has emerged as the victor—communications. We are speaking here of communications in its widest sense, which includes written and verbal communication, formal documentation, diagramming and modeling, and facilitation and elicitation.

*Figure 6. The Human Communication Loop*

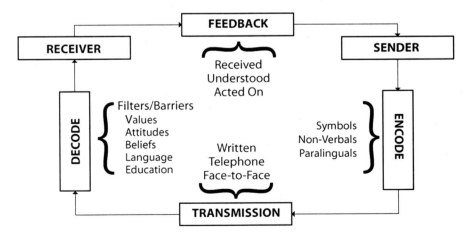

*All communication is encoded, even simple spoken language. The decoding happens through a variety of filters and only through feedback can success be determined. Source: Diagram is courtesy of PMCentersUSA, LLC.*

Many of these specifics can be addressed by standard BA training. You can go to a class to learn elicitation techniques and you can get better at documentation by attending a writing course. Diagramming and modeling can be taught both as ways of recording the results and further analyzing the information. These subjects are found in most standard BA curriculum.

The underlying human communication knowledge is a little harder to acquire. Whenever I am teaching elicitation, I always spend time on basic communications concepts, such as the encoding and decoding loop, cultural differences, and barriers to communications. I provide examples about body language, such as the true meaning of crossing your legs. Did you know that the standard female way of crossing legs (knee to knee) has little meaning but that when a man crosses his legs ankle to knee, this is a distancing gesture, essentially building a wall between the two parties? If this interests you, imagine how fascinated your students will be! Whenever I teach this subject to BAs, I always end by challenging them to become communications masters. I have found that if you get them interested, they will conduct research on their own, and if you stage regular sessions for discussion or presentation of findings, the overall understanding of communication will grow. Some suggestions for research:

- What does crossing the arms mean? (Research *all* body language)
- How does level of dress affect a meeting?
- Are there different levels of proper eye contact for different cultures?
- Are acronyms a good communications idea or a bad one?

## Business Knowledge

Business knowledge is vital for the performance of BA duties. This is clear to most people who work with BAs and I am not going to argue with this obvious fact. What I *am* going to do is to qualify it a little.

BAs are not just representatives of the Business. I know many companies that employ BAs in this manner—the BAs even report to the Business departments. The problem with this is that if it is taken to the logical extreme, the BA is soon considered worthless without years of business experience. These people are highly sought-after and are greatly prized, the only problem is that *they are not BAs*! They are Subject Matter Experts (SMEs), and if that is all they can do, the BA experience is going to be quite problematic. Recall that we rely on the BAs to elicit, analyze, and document requirements, not just to know about them. Many times I have seen a really good BA with no knowledge whatsoever of the subject matter, surround themselves with SMEs and elicit great requirements, but I have never seen a SME with no BA skills get the requirements right. Consider this the next time you are hiring—a good BA can *learn* that business knowledge as they go.

## Solution-Side Knowledge

BAs must understand both sides of the equation. This is one of my pet peeves—BAs that know the business but have no knowledge of the solution side. Most BAs work in IT, so it is simpler to say it in this manner: BAs that know nothing about the developer's world are doomed to fail.

I am not saying that a BA should be a programmer, although many excellent BAs come from the technical side. What I am saying is that BAs are a bridge between the two worlds, a translator/interpreter between the business and IT, and what kind of a translator only knows one of the two languages? The BA's job is to explain each side's position to the other, not just to understand and represent Business to IT. They must also be equipped to take technical issues back to the business teams and in order to do this properly, *they have to understand them.*

What level of knowledge is needed and in what specific areas? This depends on the environment. If you are in a Java shop, where all projects have an extensive web component, then the BA needs to understand how the web works, the basics of Object-Oriented Programming (OOP), and enough about programming to "get" loops and IF statements. You need to be able to speak with the developers using their own language. Here are some suggestions for training BAs to help them establish at least a basic technical knowledge level:

- Basic SQL training. (This skill is always useful, especially in testing.)
- Microsoft Access. (Get to a level where you can build a little application, with simple forms and reports. This is a great way to understand the Relational Database world.)
- Web history, nature and structure, and how the world moved from Mainframe to Client/Server and eventually to Three Tier.
- Software Configuration Management. (This is vital to understand of why you cannot put a simple change in two days before the Quarterly Release!)

*Figure 7. Bridge Between Two Worlds*

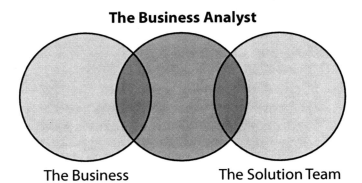

**The Business Analyst**

The Business          The Solution Team

*The Business Analyst is the connection between the Business Group and the Solution Team, and must understand both sides.*

# How Should Business Analysts Be Trained?

What should a professional education environment be like?
How should professional education be conducted?
What kind of planning needs to take place?

## The Classroom Environment

Business Analysts are curious, talkative, and analytical. They thrive in an environment where they get to meet often with other people and do not do well in dark, poorly lit spaces where the only company is their PC. In this they are decidedly different from most computer programmers, or at least the programmer's stereotype. As with all stereotypes, both for BAs and for programmers, the specific cases are often quite different, but as is sometimes true about stereotypes, there is enough truth to help guide your thinking. BAs are group animals and their nature, as well as their profession, drives them to interact with other people. Training for BAs should reflect this fact, and the optimal training environment for a BA should be a group setting. The smaller the group, the lower the dynamics, and the poorer the training experience will be. Technical instruction works just fine for smaller groups, as the instructor gets to spend more time with each student, but just the opposite is true for BAs. For BAs, the larger the group the more discussion there will be, and with discussion comes more cross-transference of knowledge.

## Training Process

Training should never be simple lectures. Participation is vital in any training activity that lasts more than an hour, and the exercises for a BA training session should consist mostly of group discussions. A perfect class size is 25 people. For your exercises, split this group into teams of five and give them something interesting to talk about for at least 30 minutes. For a class consisting of new BAs, especially people that are new to the working world, it will be a bit harder to find subjects for these exercises. In this situation, your topics can be pure imagination. Ask the groups to imagine themselves on a project, ask them to consider the training that they have received and how they might apply it to this imaginary project. Usually, thankfully, you will have at least some experienced people in the room. If the number is limited, make sure these special people do not all end up in the same group. Spread the wealth!

The discussion exercises should all take similar forms: a discussion phase, a documentation phase, and a presentation phase. During the discussion phase, the groups might be discussing a specific situation provided by the instructor or they might first be asked to come up with a relevant situation from their own past. Obviously, if your group has limited experience, this latter choice will be harder to implement. For the documentation phase, try and think of different portions that can be written up by different people, otherwise you will have one person writing frantically while the others sit and watch. An option is to have this documentation going on during the discussion. The last phase is the most interesting, as each group presents its results to the entire class. It is usually quite enjoyable but I have seen situations where one group got a bit defensive when others challenged their process too aggressively so be prepared to intervene if needed.

Remember that these group discussions always have two objectives: to practice the specific skills that were just taught and to provide general practice for facilitation and elicitation. Watch the groups carefully and note interesting things that are happening, such as control or leadership. Note examples of things like recapping to ensure complete understanding or negotiation between two different positions, and make sure to bring those up in the after-exercise review.

## Planning for Training

How will the training effort begin and how will it proceed? Each training situation will possess its own unique circumstances, driven by the company and its policies and procedures, but there are a number of major steps that will always occur, in one form or another. The training will eventually be designed and conducted, of course, but first, the training requirement must be assessed, analyzed, and planned.

Start by conducting a careful review of each BA's individual capability and needs. Once this is complete, look for similarities and start thinking about individual training elements that could be used to deal with many needs at once. Think also about leveling the training field for the entire staff. Consider, for example, a set of basic BA courses, even if some in your group are past that level. Most people think about training as a mechanism for taking someone with no skills to a place where they have all the skills, but more commonly, it is to take someone with some skills to the finish line. A student with no experience in a subject will take away 50% of the subject material while someone who already has 50% will emerge with 100% and a big smile on their face. Training like this works very well, with the added benefit of stocking your class with those experienced people that make group exercises so excellent.

Once your analysis is over, document your results and create three separate plans: best case, middle case, and a plan for the bare-bones minimum training required to get the job done. Document these like a business case and be prepared to present and defend your recommendations. Remember that to the Governance Committee, your recommendations are about money, which no one wants to spend unless forced. By the way, contrary to your cynical viewpoint, it is not the bare-bones scenario that is most likely to be accepted; statistically it is the middle ground plan that they will pick. Push for the best-case scenario!

# Conclusion

- Training is a major function of a successful manager.
- There is a standard for Business Analyst knowledge, and the training should reflect and develop that standard
- Training is fun—make good use of it!

Training is management and, as a manager, a large part of your thoughts should be directed toward training. Training for BAs must be arranged so that it addresses the needs of the company and the students, and is conducted to deal with the learning style of adults in general and BAs in particular. The best method for BA training is face-to-face instruction with a world-class professional instructor. If the funding for such is not in the cards, consider virtual training or even online training. The only other option is no training at all!

The training subject matter should cover the *BABOK° Guide* Knowledge Areas, general communication skills, elicitation and facilitation, business knowledge, solution-side knowledge, and even Project Management and Quality Assurance, if possible. BAs live to talk so these subjects should be taught in a group environment and the exercises should be done as groups and presented to the whole class for further analysis. Treat your training plan as a project and remember that projects have to be approved and funded.

Training is vital but it is also fun. With a combination like that, we should do as much of it as possible!

# About the Author

Rick Clare, OCP, PMP, CBAP is the Business Analysis Practice Director and a Senior Instructor for PMCentersUSA, with over 20 years of experience as a Developer, Business Analyst, Trainer, and Project Manager. Rick is responsible for maintaining the company's BA courseware, providing expert consulting services to companies moving into the Business Analysis world for the first time, and constructing customized training material targeted at an individual company's methodologies. Rick's early career experience was as an Oracle Database Developer, performing analysis, design, development, and documentation on numerous database systems using Oracle and its complete set of development tools. He managed an Oracle training school for 2 years.

In addition to performing general management, Rick has worked on many projects as a Business Analyst, and his Project Management experience includes projects in Retail, Healthcare, and Banking. He has presented papers, seminars, and workshops at numerous conferences such as the IIBA's own BBC, Oracle's IOUG, the Oracle Developer Tools User Group (ODTUG) conference, and the Project Summit/Business Analysis World conference series. Rick is heavily involved with IIBA®. As a volunteer, he served on the Chapter Council, joined the Senior Leadership Team as VP, Chapters from 2010–2011, and was the managing editor for this book. Rick is originally from Canada but now lives and works in Pittsburgh, PA.

# BUSINESS ANALYSIS SOFTWARE AND TOOLS

By Marcelo Menezes Neves

Business Analysis is a team sport. During business analysis activities, including elicitation of requirements, documentation, analysis, tracking, prioritization, and management, it is essential that the whole team be aware of what is going on and has a firm understanding of the needs of the organization. It is the manager's responsibility to keep the whole team working to meet the goals and objectives of the project/initiative. Software can make this job much easier, if the manager understands what is available and how to get the best use out of it.

There are many tools available on the marketplace. Each tool has distinct characteristics and applications, attending to a wide range of needs for business analysis teams. Some of these tools are made available as a service (Software as a Service or SaaS) through the Internet, while others require installation onto each user's machine.

In this chapter, I will look at several of the most popular types of tools used on a day-to-day basis to manage the work of a team of Business Analysts. I will describe the type of software, rather than providing the actual brand or program names, since programs come and go. These tools facilitate the management, communication, and collaboration of many of the business requirements processes. I will provide insight into the following types of software tools:

- Email
- Project Management Software
- Presentation Tools
- Collaboration and Communication Tools
- Account and Invoicing Tools
- Spreadsheets
- Word Processors
- Incident Management Tools
- Drawing Tools
- Requirements Management Tools

## Email

Communication is the most important factor in the success of any project. Sending messages, responding to messages, and attaching files are everyday tasks that help maintain day-to-day communication with the team. Electronic mail is a vital means of communication within almost all businesses. Email can be used to invite members of the team to meetings, to notify them about project changes, to sent reports, and so forth. The manager should establish usage guidelines, such as a 24-hour response time for all email.

Written communication may sound extremely unfriendly if it is done improperly. Communication is composed of four elements, and three of them (intonation, non-verbal, and context) cannot be utilized in an email. Only the written word remains for email and it must be carefully used.

The number and frequency of one-on-one emails received from a manager will influence the team member, both in his sense of importance within the team as well as the level of perceived respect from the team leader. Remember however that face-to-face communication is always the most effective form, and that too much email at the expense of other types of communication can be detrimental. It is important that the manager and the team members use common sense when deciding that to stop sending emails and move on to telephone calls or face-to-face meetings. A rule of thumb is to try to make at least one call for every ten emails and one face-to-face meeting for every ten telephone calls.

Utilities commonly available in email tools:

- Send and respond to messages
- Attach files
- Save messages
- Organize messages by category
- Print messages

## Project Management Software

Project management tools allow the manager to apply control over the duties that each of the team members is to carry out. This becomes critical when the project has a wide variety of activities, especially when the team is virtual or multi-national.

This kind of software assists managers with many tasks related to the directing of projects and initiatives within the organization. They assist in time management, task management, and budget control. Usually the BA manager will use these tools in cooperation with the project manager to monitor the team's effectiveness in completing its tasks.

There is a growing tendency towards project management tools based on the Wiki concept. These tools work well on the web and allow the team to add documents, share content, and collaborate electronically: tasks, pages, discussions, and results can be easily linked to the status of the project. Some of these tools allow for the possibility of each team member having their own blog, introducing informal communication between the manager and his or her team. Project management tools help managers to clearly define success criteria for their team. That way, analysts can visualize the project's scope and tasks in a properly prioritized fashion.

Project failure usually comes from a lack of clarity in defining the requirements. Some of the project management tools available on the market allow you to record requirements and even provide space for discussing them. During the course of the project, the team may share ideas and solution options by publishing them on their blogs. The manager can then compile this information and call for meetings to discuss the critical points. Project management tools allow managers to continually monitor the team's progress.

Commonly found features and utilities for project management software:

- Project creation and planning
- Cost management
- Task management
- Project resource control
- Project status reports
- Resource status reports
- Potential risk alerts
- A multi-user environment
- Centralized, shared database
- Security and access control

## Presentation Tools

When managers need to present new ideas and gain a group's buy-in, they use presentation tools. These tools help you illustrate project concepts, plans, or business cases on products that need to be developed. Presentations facilitate the productivity of meetings by allowing the participants to see and hear the information.

New tools are popping up on the marketplace that allow managers and teams to create corporate presentations at all levels. Many of these tools allow multiple authors to concurrently create presentations, and some allow managers to conduct presentations remotely via the Internet. This allows an easy and interactive channel of communication with the team, saving unnecessary travel costs on projects. During online presentations, certain tools allow the team to interact with the presenter by jotting notes, asking questions, and receiving or sending files. Many of these tools also allow presentations to be recorded and made available afterwards on the Internet.

Common features found in presentation software:

- User-friendly editors
- Enhanced slides with special effects and sound
- Public or private presentations
- Presentation via Web
- Save presentations as recordings
- Chat during presentations

# Collaboration and Communication Tools

Collaboration tools help managers and teams involved in common tasks to reach their goals. These are also referred to as groupware or workgroup support systems—the term groupware was first used at the end of the 1980s in the writings of Richman and Slovak:

*"Like an electronic sinew that binds teams together, the new groupware aims to place the computer squarely in the middle of communications among managers, technicians, and anyone else who interacts in groups, revolutionizing the way they work."[1]*

These tools facilitate the manager's work by automating tasks and centralizing crucial day-to-day information. Some collaboration tools include electronic calendars, workflow systems, and project management systems.

As already mentioned, there are a number of tools on the market that allow the manager to conduct online meetings. Many of these allow for the scheduling of the meetings and inform the team of the meeting via email. This email often contains both the agenda and a link on which the professional may click to participate in an online session.

Here are some applications that assist with collaboration:

- Electronic Calendar—Allows the team to manage their own appointments while letting the manager view the appointments of each team member. Many electronic calendar tools are available on the Internet or included with various development environments.
- Workflow Systems—Workflow systems allow the manager to define a series of tasks that the team must execute in order to attain a final result. When a task is completed, the tool makes sure that the user responsible for the next task is notified.
- Social Media Software—Social media software allows the team to share data and allows the manager to establish and maintain connections between the members of the team.
- Wikis—Wikis are websites that facilitate the creation of interconnected web pages. Wikis assist managers in promoting collaboration among the team. Requirements themselves, plus all the supporting documents, can be stored on Wiki pages. The Wiki might include workflow management, blogs, image and file galleries, chat, and calendaring.
- Video Conferencing—Video conferences let two or more people interact via video and audio simultaneously. Managers can use video conferencing when communicating with the team. Video conferences are preferable to email since more elements of communication are involved. Many of these tools make use of VOIP technology.

---

1    Richman, Louis S. And Julianne Slovak, "Software Catches the Team Spirit". *Fortune Magazine* (June 8, 1987): http://money.cnn.com/magazines/fortune/fortune_ archive/1987/06/08/69109/index.htm

- Surveys and Questionnaires—This kind of tool allows the manager to conduct questionnaires regarding the team's needs, evaluation of the team's work, and so on. Surveys are also a valuable elicitation technique and the many free tools available make this once difficult task quite easy.
- Knowledge Management Software—Provides a means by which the manager and his team can innovate, build group knowledge, and thus improve the team's experience. This kind of knowledge base can help the team develop self-awareness and increase their productivity. If a company has a comprehensive knowledge management system, all documented information becomes available for your project, and for subsequent projects after your project finishes.

# Billing, Accounting, and Invoicing Tools

Billing tools are for managers who have to keep track of services in order to bill for them. Billing tools can handle multiple billing situations, including different billing rates with different combinations of flat and hourly rates and more.

Common features for tools like this:

- Billing rates per client, project, user, activity, and hour
- Flat rates per entry and per project
- Flexible billing rates and billing combinations
- Override rates per entry
- Overtime billing rates
- Separate reporting for billed and unbilled activity
- Record payments received
- Make balance adjustments
- Multi-currency support
- Track expense taxes
- Accept electronic payments directly from the source
- Create invoice batches to speed up the invoice creation process
- Choose from several invoice layouts and designs
- Create a "Pre-Bill" for preview
- Customize amount of invoice details
- Apply discounts to invoices
- Submit invoices electronically

## Incident Management Tools

Management involves remaining in control when problems occur, therefore managers need to be concerned with the concept of Incident Management— the process whereby the leader must restore normal operation after an incident. The following activities are involved in dealing with incidents:

1. Being able to detect and report the incident
2. Being able to compare the incident with existing problems
3. Being able to resolve problems promptly
4. Being able to prioritize problems with respect to their impact and urgency

There are many tools available on the market to assist managers with incident management. These are some the benefits of using software to manage incidents:

- It allows management to gather real time and historical data information as to what transpired.
- It allows identification of bottlenecks regarding team performance.
- It speeds up the restoration of operation, as the causes of incidents can be clearly identified.
- It minimizes the recurrence of incidents by informing users of the impact that the incident has had on the system.

## Spreadsheets

One of the most prevalent of software tools, spreadsheets are used for many purposes at all levels in the project process. Spreadsheets can be used to make lists, display data, design the critical path, perform calculations, keep track of costs, etc.

The ability of spreadsheets to do financial projections and complex calculations is unsurpassed. Their ease of use, intuitive interface, speed, and flexibility remain unmatched by more cumbersome database-driven applications. It is the software tool of choice for millions of managers in every conceivable business sector and profession.

Spreadsheet features such as data and pivot tables can help managers deal with the uncertainty in the decision making process and perform what-if analyses. With the ease and flexibility that is built into spreadsheets, data can be manipulated, transformed, and dissected to provide views from different angles. Graphs of the resulting tables are easily generated. Through spreadsheets, some of the more 'mathematical' models are easily comprehended and used by the manager. Managers may use spreadsheets to plan and report expenses. Small projects can be planned using Gantt chart spreadsheets rather than larger Project Management tools.

# Drawing Tools

In the same way that presentation and communication tools assist the manager in sharing information and ideas with the team, drawing tools make expressing ideas and concepts even easier by allowing them to become visual.

General drawing tools can be used to produce useful BA diagrams. Here are some examples of useful charts and diagrams that can be created:

- Flow charts are created by a wide range of users. They help managers define and analyze processes, and identify areas for improvement.
- Data flow diagrams are used to describe the flow of data inside a system. They are very useful in facilitating communication between programmers and systems or Business Analysts.
- Entity Relationship Diagrams are used to show how the information managed by the project's software will be structured.
- A Process Map or Activity Diagram uses swimlanes to document the various steps that a process follows and can include the analysis of problems with a process.
- Control charts offer a way to analyze output data collected by an information management system. A control graph shows a center line or an average of all samples collected of output. It also shows the upper and lower boundaries, or controls, on both ends of an acceptable range, and the data over time. When managers analyze control charts, they look for variations and for the causes of points out of the control range.

# Word Processors and Wikis

Gone are the days in which only secretaries and administrative assistants used word processing computers and programs. Now it is just as necessary for members of the management team to have top-notch computer and typing skills. It is *critical* for a manager to know how to operate a word processor.

In recent years, word processing tools have changed radically. Managers can find a multitude of word processors on the market, some of them even set up for SaaS. These services allow managers to work with documents anywhere with an Internet connection, without having to install a program on a desktop computer. Most word processors support the inclusion of material from other tools such as drawing programs or spreadsheets, directly into the document.

An interesting fact that has been observed lately in organizations is the growing replacement of word processors with Wiki tools. Maintaining long documents can be a problem for managers. They are hard to produce and the reader will read it carefully only once (if that). Minor errors can damage credibility and distract the reader from the critical message. Replacing the formal document with a Wiki offers a number of benefits:

- Documentation becomes more useful since each person reads only the sections relevant to him or her. Business managers can read the business section, the engineering staff can read the product requirements sections, etc.

- The publishing cycle is streamlined. In the word processing world, everyone waits while you write. They provide their comments, you incorporate feedback, and eventually publish another version of the document.
- You are now free to build your document from rough notes. With a Wiki, the whole ritual of document creation is changed. The document is always published, even in rough form. Everyone understands that the document is never "finished"; it is always a work in progress.
- The document can be created in pieces. You can put out a section for feedback while you work on the next section.
- The document becomes a group conversation. Reviewers can comment on each page and can react to one another's comments (unlike change-tracking in word processors).
- It's much less daunting for a reviewer to re-read just the sections they care about.
- The document is always up-to-date. You can incorporate someone's comments immediately, even while meeting with them. Everyone always gets the most up-to-date thinking available. They don't have to wait for the next publishing cycle.
- Wikis are hyperlinked. This means less repetition and it lets the material be scaled to the needs and interests of the reader.
- Wikis can be created collaboratively.
- Wikis are globally searchable.
- No more wasteful printing of huge documents.
- Managers can document everything that needs to be documented. You don't have to arbitrarily leave out important information just because it makes the document too cumbersome.

Using a Wiki in this manner is like employing an Agile method for document processing: you put out something small but quickly useful, and keep adding to and refining it.

## Requirements Management Tools

One of the biggest impacts on the Business Analysis community in recent years has been the advent of numerous software tools designed to make the recording and tracking of Requirements easier.

These tools provide many useful features:

- Record requirements one at a time, rather than as part of a document
- Register rRequirements at different levels (Business requirement AND Business Rule!)
- Automatically provide traceability between Requirements, horizontally and vertically
- Produce documents from the central repository, allowing them to be re-created easily when things change
- Built-in change control
- Diagrams built-in to support the requirements

Sometimes these tools even connect to development environments where code can be generated based on the requirements information. In practice, of course, this code will need to be modified prior to production but it can often provide a leg-up in the development process.

These tools are wonderful and they provide a great many advantages to a project team. Ironically, however, they almost never solve a company's requirements problems but can serve a group well that is already firmly in control of its requirements process. This is an important fact about require-ments management tools that has been borne out time after time in the real world: Never install a tool like this until you can function well enough without it. If your requirements process is not well understood or followed, a tool like this will only make things worse, as the team struggles to get a grip on its projects **and** somehow fit a whole new process into the picture. Wait until you are firmly in control of your projects before considering the implementation of such a tool.

## Business Rule Engines

Business Rule Engine (BRE) is the term used to describe software used to track, manage, and revise enterprise business rules. Software of this type tracks and, in some cases, executes business validation that might be derived from legal regulations or in-house corporate policies. BREs can be used alone or in conjunction with other technologies.

BREs help managers better manage and automate business decision criteria without expensive custom programming. Using BREs, organiza-tions are able to respond quickly to rapidly changing business requirements. Organizations of all sizes and across all industries can benefit from business rules software if their applications require frequent changes to decision-making criteria due to changing regulations, prices, or policies.

Many BREs work by providing a mechanism for documenting and executing simple business rules. The objective is to guarantee that the company's policies are followed and the clients are treated in a consistent and proper manner. Many BREs only allow the rules to represent simple tests, in other words, the possible responses can be 'true' or 'false'. This is a common complaint about the more simple rules engines because specialists in busi-ness don't often say just 'yes' or 'no'. For example: a typical business rule might be 'bill after ten days'. The majority of BREs can implement the rule in this manner: 'if the day after conclusion > 10, then send a bill' but if a client wants to push back his or her billing, the BRE may interfere. Some BREs can be programmed to access client records so they can analyze factors which could justify a postponement of billing. Some of the more complex BREs allow this kind of flexibility but that complexity comes at a price: much greater installa-tion and implementation costs.

With BREs, business decision criteria can be managed as an enterprise asset and used consistently across multiple business processes, applications, and platforms.

Common features of a BRE:

- Business users can modify rules frequently without a need for IT resources
- Business regulation criteria are entered using a graphical, wizard-like interface
- Rule definitions are reusable
- Changes to business rules immediately take effect on running processes
- Provides a rules-based evaluation of activities and process tasks
- Enables users to define exceptions to Key Performance Indicators (KPIs)

## Conclusion

Tools are a vital part of a project's success story. With the wealth of software available for Business Analysis Managers, it would be counter-productive to ignore the options. However we must be careful not to get to a state where the tool is dictating the process rather than the other way around.

## About the Author

Marcelo Menezes Neves is President of Anelox and has over 15 years of practical experience in software systems development, project management, client relationship management, and business analysis. Marcelo started his career in the information technology area as a programmer with progressive experience in other roles such as Systems Analyst, Business Analyst, and Project Manager. He has detailed knowledge and years of experience in methodologies (waterfall, client-server, object-oriented, Information Engineering, JAD, RUP, BPM, PMBOK®).

Marcelo's areas of expertise include business analysis, project management, software and business methodologies, facilitation, applications development, business process reengineering, and continuous improvement. His experience covers many industries. He conducts formal and informal training sessions, consistently receiving excellent student evaluations. Actively involved in the Rio de Janeiro IIBA® Chapter, he is a member of the founding Board of Directors for the Chapter, and has served as President since 2009.

# DEVELOPMENT AND ANALYSIS METHODOLOGIES

By Federico Palacios

*"I not only use the brains I have, but all I can borrow"*
*—Woodrow Wilson, US President*

Wilson's phrase above is as applicable to software development projects as it is to me in writing this chapter. As we get ready to immerse ourselves in the world of development and analysis methodologies, Wilson's quote helps me set the proper expectations from the start. As in many projects (whether software development or not), leveraging the expertise of others increases your chances of success; in writing a book, the research, in particular, on the work completed by many experts, increases your chances of providing the reader with valuable and accurate information.

I am not, by any stretch of the imagination, the foremost expert on project management, project life cycles, or development methodologies, rather an enthusiastic Project Manager and Requirements Manager who wants to provide you with a view of the various Project life cycle models and software development methodologies and the Project Manager's role in the context of software projects. To do this, I am blending information from my research (many other great brains) with that which I have developed based on learning from experience, and from studying projects and project management. The information I am about to present is not new. I didn't invent it. It is a consolidation of the many points of views from some of the 'real' experts out in the IT world with my added 'grain of salt'. I will try to provide you with a generic overview of the most popular life cycle models and some of the most widely used methodologies within them, along with presenting some of the pros and cons from the perspective of a Project Manager (PM). I hope that you can use this as a resource when needing a quick reference on the development and analysis of methodologies, and when facing the challenge to deliver a successful project.

## Methodologies

I embarked on this quest to get a simple, clear view on the best project life cycle models and methodologies that are available to Project Managers and Business Analysts. At some point during my research, believe me, I wished I hadn't.

I knew the options were many, as it all depends on your project conditions, but it wasn't until I searched online for a few phrases like project life cycle models, software development methodologies, SDLC, iterative, waterfall, etc., that I realized the task at hand was not going to be a light one! When your search returns over seven million results, you know getting the simple, clear view is going to take a while. Project life cycle models and the methodologies within them, in particular their adaptations to the diverse environments, come in all colours and flavours. The word to best describe the number of options: plethora.

Is there an excess or overabundance of project life cycle models and methodologies? Perhaps, but the issue is not the abundance, rather the ability to know which one to pick. Let's put this in perspective. Coming up with a straight list of the best project life cycle models and methodologies, and the reasons why one particular methodology is better than the other is not as easy as trying to figure out in Google Maps™ mapping service how to get from point A to point B. In Google Maps™, you have a point of origin and a destination, appropriately and respectively called 'A' and 'B'. I'll call getting from point A to point B the 'scope' of the trip. Your options on how to deliver the scope (to reach the destination) are limited and very clear: check if you want to avoid highways and tolls; indicate how you want to measure the distance (km versus miles); and last but not least, indicate whether you are going by car, public transit, or walking— since this will impact the directions you'll need. Having defined these, you get very clear step by step directions on how to get there, where and when to turn, what the distance is before the next turn, and an approximate (and very close to reality) time of arrival along with a few alternate routes, ensuring you keep within scope. In essence, you can, with a high degree of accuracy, estimate the time, cost, and even quality of your trip, while being assured that, thanks to the directions, you will stay on track (you will not get lost or need to get out of route unless something extreme happens). Aren't these treats the one elusive treasure in software development?

IT projects, like trip directions in Google Maps™, also have a starting point. A project may be an enhancement to an existing system, the replacement of a legacy system—so old that my youngest son, Pablo, would say "WOW! From the late 1900s, THAT's old! I'm from 2003!" Or, a project may be born from an organizational directive to look into new technologies and IT approaches that will enable the organization become more 'agile' (not specifically referring to the methodology) when it comes to reacting to market and industry changes, among many others. There is also a destination. But in software development projects, the destination varies greatly, however, it should always focus on delivering benefits and value to an organization. As Andrew Holmes points out in his book, *Failsafe is Project Delivery*, "Benefits realization should be the only reason why projects are initiated".[1] Unfortunately, based on statistics, a large percentage of projects still fail to get to their destination. While successfully getting from 'A' to 'B' is a straight forward activity in Google Maps™, the same quest eludes most Project Managers in the software development environment. That may be because the definition of project success is also viewed from different perspectives (finishing on time and on budget regardless of

---

1    Holmes, Andrew, *Failsafe is Project Delivery*, (Burlington: Gower Publishing Company, 2001), 96.

business value; providing value but with time delays or cost overruns, etc.) or due to the fact that options to reach the destination are many, vary in size and complexity, and are dependent on many conditions related to the project, team, organization, etc. In contrast to a road trip, your IT project cannot be easily predicted. Providing an accurate estimate on cost, time, and quality as well as staying within the original scope is particularly challenging. Even though there is a great variety of methodologies out there and a wealth of information at your fingertips, none of them on their own will allow you, as the Project Manager, to deliver the goods.

In the following sections I will attempt to provide you with a concentrated dose of the differences in the methodologies and management styles to help you make better choices when having to decide between a traditional or linear-sequential methodology and an iterative one.

## Methodologies:
## What Are They and Why Do I Need Them?

Do you say "t*uh*-mey-toh or t*uh*-mah-toh?" I've heard people ask the same question many times. The question, however, is not in the nature of the item or the spelling, but on its pronunciation. I, on a different note, have been wondering about project life cycle model or project methodology? Although phonetically not even close, the question that lingers in IT project conversations is related to the very essence of the concept. Is there really a difference between project life cycle model and project methodology?

I have seen people and websites use the terms interchangeably. I have also seen a few diligently trying to draw the line between them and explain how one complements the other. I have also felt lost and confused. And you? Do you know the difference?

To demystify them, I am presenting the concepts below and will explain the main differences I see between project life cycle models and project methodologies. let's start with the definitions.

*A project life cycle Model:* "A collection of generally sequential project phases whose name and number are determined by the control needs of the organization or organizations involved in the project. A life cycle can be documented with a *methodology.*"[2]

*A project methodology*: A system of practices, techniques, procedures, and rules used by those who work in a discipline.[3]

The way I see it, a project life cycle model provides the structure of the different phases needed to complete the main objective of the project, and the logical order in which those need to happen, while the project methodology tells you what you have to do to manage your projects from start to finish. It provides the process, practices or activities, and guidelines the teams will

---

2    Project Management Institute, *PMBOK® Guide*—3rd Edition, (PMI 2004), 380.
3    Ibid., 376.

need to follow within a project life cycle model to achieve the individual deliverables that will ultimately enable you to reach the project's objective. Table 1 shows an example in which the differences between the project life cycle model and the project methodology are highlighted.

### TABLE 1. PROJECT LIFE CYCLE MODEL VERSUS PROJECT METHODOLOGY

| | Project Life Cycle Model Phases | | Generic Project Methodology Steps per Phase | |
|---|---|---|---|---|
| No. | Phase | Description | Phase | Description |
| 1 | Analysis (Requirements) | The initial phase. You need to elicit requirements before you start. Need to know what to build (how deep will depend on the methodologies as we will see later). | Analysis (Requirements) | 1. **Determining the scope:** Understand what to build by going from visioning to scope and boundaries of the system. Identify stakeholders, key system functionality, etc.<br>2. **Deliverables:** Vision Document, Business Requirements Document (BRD), Systems Requirements Specifications (SRS), Business Process Diagrams, System Process Diagrams, etc.<br>3. **Team members involved:** Business Analyst, Data Architect, etc.<br>4. **Activities:** Hold brainstorming sessions, identify use cases, actors, glossary, perform some internal reviews, get business sign-off, etc. |
| 2 | Design | Based on the business and system requirements, the alternatives to build the solution are developed. These include tools and technologies to use, structure of the components, scalability of the system, etc. | Design | 1. **Determining the design:** Start designing how the solution will function (the how you will build it). May need to look at technologies, design database models, interfaces, screens, etc.<br>2. **Deliverables:** Logical Data Model, Design documents, Architecture Design Document, etc.<br>3. **Team members involved:** Business Analyst, Project Manager, Solution Architect, Data Architect, Systems Analyst, Developer, etc.<br>4. **Activities:** Finalize selection of technologies (if it hasn't happened), complete design of use cases (use case realization), create a preliminary logical database model, design interfaces, etc. |
| 3 | Development (Construction) | Point in the project where the solution starts to be built—coding is done based on the design. | Development (Construction) | 1. **Development:** Start writing the code and building the solution, solidify the architecture, finalize the design of the database, etc.<br>2. **Deliverables:** Code lines, builds, Disaster Recovery document, Logical/Physical Data Model, etc.<br>3. **Team members involved:** Project Manager, Solution Architect, Business Analyst, Systems Analyst, Developer, DBA, etc.<br>4. **Activities:** Enforce the architecture, do integration and system testing, implement and unit-test code, requirements traceability, etc. |

TABLE 1. PROJECT LIFE CYCLE MODEL VERSUS PROJECT METHODOLOGY

| Project Life Cycle Model Phases | | | Generic Project Methodology Steps per Phase | |
|---|---|---|---|---|
| No. | Phase | Description | Phase | Description |
| 4 | Testing | Once the code is available, testing takes place to ensure the solution meets the system requirements and that there are no errors/defects. | Testing | 1. **Test, test, test:** Need to make sure the solution is thoroughly tested against requirements and for errors/defects, bug fixing, identify areas for performance or usability enhancements, training material begins to be ready, etc. <br> 2. **Deliverables:** Test cases, defect tickets/reports, update to design documents, start Data Migration Requirements document, etc. <br> 3. **Team members involved:** Project Manager, Business Analyst, Systems Analyst, Testers, Developer, DBA, etc. <br> 4. **Activities:** Perform unit testing, regression testing, User Acceptance testing, defect metrics analysis (reports), etc. |
| 5 | Implementation | Once all tested and verified, the solution is moved from development to production (Go-Live) | Implementation | 1. **Implement:** This is where the solution is rolled out (Go Live), activities are carefully planned to ensure the business users are ready to take on the new application, users and maintainers are fully trained, etc. <br> 2. **Deliverables:** Training material, Implementation Plan, etc. <br> 3. **Team members involved:** Project Manager, Business Analyst, Trainers, Developer, DBA, etc. <br> 4. **Activities:** Train users and maintainers, prepare deployment site, convert operational databases, perform data migration (initial load), etc. |

## Why Use Them?

Regardless of how it's structured, every project goes through a series of stages during its life (project life cycle model). As we can see, the exact details on how the team delivering the solution interacts and completes those stages or phases, the processes, deliverables, who the individual participants at different points in time are, the expected inputs and outputs of each phase, and the way the phases take place—sequentially, overlapping, or iterative, to get to the end point, are outlined by the project methodology selected.

A project methodology helps by giving you a clear process for managing projects. It tells your team what has to be completed to deliver your project, how it should be done, in which order, and by when.

Without grouping the project activities into phases and without clearly understanding what those process activities need to be, the Project Manager and the core team will not be able to efficiently plan and organize resources for each activity, get things done, and objectively measure achievement of goals.

The Project Manager and the Executive Sponsor will not be able to justify their decisions to move ahead, make adjustments, or terminate the project.

Some of these decisions, like avoiding early termination of a project, may prove costly to an organization if not made in a timely manner. Sometimes the cost even means the organization goes out of business. 'Pulling the plug', although sometimes the best option, is normally the toughest decision to make. It's one that seldom happens until it is too late. Andrew Holmes' advice on this area is, as he would say, "spot on". Under the section 'Advice for the Chief Executive and the Board' in *Failsafe is Project Delivery*, one of his points reads:

*"Be prepared to pull the plug on a project that is spiraling out of control. It doesn't matter if it is an internally or externally run project, the outcome will still be the same: failure. It is far better to terminate it early, when you still have some money left to finance other projects."*[4]

It is clear, however, that a methodology is not a silver bullet. It won't fix projects by itself or guarantee success. An efficient, effective Project Manager is still required to deliver projects. No methodology will be a 100% applicable to every type of project. In addition to a good Project Manager, you will need to customize it to ensure it perfectly fits your project management environment. Ideally, you can gain efficiency on your approach, give your team a clear understanding of what you expect from them, and increase your chances of success if you can, through experience, find a way to manage every project you undertake in a similar way.

## Why Some Succeed. Why Some Fail.

On his website, Marios Alexandrou explains the value of knowing project management methodologies: "The reality is that the project management methodologies available to a project manager are often decided on long before a project starts. In many cases, the decision is based on nothing more than 'this is what we've always done'. At other times, the decision is based on an enterprise-wide initiative to adopt a particular process like the Rational Unified Process. Regardless, it is important to know the various project management methodologies if for no other reason than to be aware of where their strengths lie and where they fall short."[5]

Getting to know some of the basics of the different project life cycle models and methodologies will help you to better react or adapt them to your environment, increasing your chances of success. After all, "...Many of the problems [faced by software projects] have to do with choosing the wrong methodology, applying the methodology incorrectly, or following a methodology too rigidly"[6]

---

4    Holmes, Andrew, *Failsafe is Project Delivery*, (Burlington: Gower Publishing Company, 2001), 193.

5    Alexandrou, Marios, *Project Management Methodologies*, http://www.mariosalexandrou.com/methodologies.asp.

6    Alexandrou, Marios, *Project Management Methodologies*, http://www.mariosalexandrou.com/definition/project-lifecycle.asp.

Projects are very unique undertakings. Therefore, the methodology followed should be customized and scaled based on the many aspects of the project:

*Size:*
- Smaller projects may not need a formal methodology. They may, however, use some portions of it to add value.
- Larger projects require most of the steps and activities specified in a methodology and, since more structure and discipline is required, a formal methodology may provide the most value

*System to Deliver and Technological Content:*
- A different project life cycle model and a different degree of formality or flexibility will be required in the methodologies applied based on the type of system you are building and the technology being used
- Enhancements to a well known system
- Replacement of a legacy system
- Brand new system using experimental (super hi-tech) technologies
- Using a Commercial Off The Shelf (COTS) solution

*Culture of the Organization:*
- Is it a risk embracing organization or a very conservative one?
- Is there full or partial management support?

*Team:*
- The size and location of the team
- Their knowledge and experience regarding the problem domain
- Their experience using the different methodologies
- The availability of the team members
- The willingness to work with a particular methodology

*Project Criticality*
*Time Constraints*
*Industry Changes/Issues*
*Other*

Based on the above, it is clear that a one-size-fits-all process cannot exist. Consequently, you always have to adapt a process to fit your particular environment. As a Project Manager, use judgment and discretion to determine which methodology seems to be a good fit, and to determine the right process and activities to execute, within that methodology, to successfully deliver value to the organization.

Of course, project life cycle models and methodologies are not interchangeable. As stated before, to deliver a quality system, it's critical to know the many aspects and risks surrounding your project and to use the model that best addresses those.

Figure 1. Manager's Approach to Methodologies

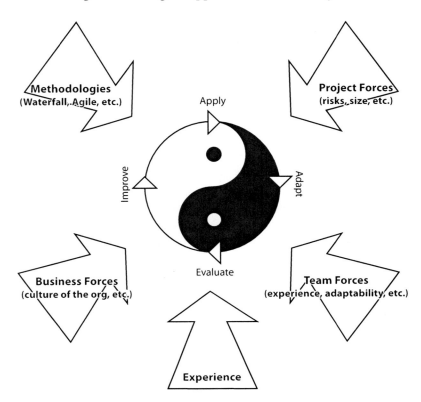

# The Adaptive Manager
## (*The PM/BA Factor in a Methodology*)

As a modern Project Manager, you now need to display not only the correct leadership style to deliver a successful IT project but also to understand the many options available to you for delivery of that project.

As a Requirements Manager, your functional role has also evolved to include strategic implications. As the Lead BA, you now need to develop a wider skill set of competencies than the more traditional BA of previous years, such as leadership, communication, project knowledge, strategies, technical areas, as well as your business acumen, to be able to lead a successful project or to support the Project Manager in the successful delivery of one.

Depending on the nature of the project, the effort required to manage the process and produce the solution successfully will require varying degrees of both intellectualism (brain power, new ideas, flexibility, and imagination) and craftsmanship (known work that essentially requires repetitive effort). From the perspective of management, it is the extent and balance between these components that provide the distinguishing features.

However, it is the production work in the execution stages of the project that results in the actual final product. And, with the exception for the Project

Manager, the project team members are going to be executing various parts of the project life cycle and methodology. So the application of people management skills during the project will also play a part in relation to the Project Life Cycle and methodology being used. If you do not understand the Project Life Cycle and methodology required for your project, you are going to have problems managing the project team, assigning them the right work, and dealing with their concerns.

In addition, nothing irritates the Executive Sponsor more than a project that has no clear idea of how much it will cost to build a solution and how long it will take to build it. Some of the project life cycle models try to provide an approach to address this issue while others state that the predictability desired is simply not possible. Martin Fowler calls these approaches the 'predictive and adaptive planning' respectively. According to Fowler, predictive planning focuses a large effort in the early stages of the project life cycle in determining what needs to be done to achieve some of that predictability required by the organization (this is known as requirements analysis, a BA functional role). By knowing up front what you need to build, you can predict what will happen later. Normally, the downfall of the predictive planning is changes in requirements in the later stages of the project due to industry changes, changing business priorities, or, misinterpreted requirements that deliver the wrong solution. This is called Requirements churn (again, here, the BA functional role is key in terms of proper requirements and expectation management).

Adaptive planning sees change as unavoidable. Therefore, the planning approach must treat change as a constant. Controlling the change to deliver the best software possible is the main objective of adaptive planning. You can only predict certain aspects of the project. In adaptive planning, you can predict the cost and time for delivery but not what functionality will be delivered. The downfall of adaptive planning, as seductive as the approach may be by offering productivity and/or error improvements in the development of the right solution, is that it often takes several iterations to get it right. The teams must understand the methodology and be aligned with it in order to be successful. Fowler provides two important pieces of advice on this:

1. "Don't make a predictive plan until you have precise and accurate requirements and are confident that they won't significantly change
2. If you can't get precise, accurate, and stable requirements, use an adaptive planning style

   Predictability and adaptability feed into the choice of life cycle. An adaptive plan absolutely requires an iterative process. Predictive planning can be done either way, although it's easier to see how it works with waterfall or a staged delivery approach."[7]

Accordingly, some of the methodologies, like waterfall, are heavy on process and structure, where certain steps must be completed in one of the

---

7    Fowler, Martin. *UML Distilled Third Edition—A Brief Guide to the Standard Object Modeling Language*, (Addison-Wesley 2004), 24

pre-defined phases before going into the next, whereas other methodologies, like agile, are very light and flexible, where less documentation and iterative work is common. Either may be your best option depending on the many project factors.

So, how do you know which one to pick? And when you have solved that mystery, how do you then define to what extent do you need to apply it? What does your team need to look like? What will your own style need to be?

In essence, we can categorize most project life cycles models into two main groups:

- Linear, sequential model (e.g. waterfall)
- Iterative model (e.g. agile)

Let's take a brief look at the most widely used project life cycle models:

- Pure waterfall
- Spiral
- Agile
- V-Life Cycle
- Evolutionary Prototyping

## Waterfall

This is the classic system development model. In a waterfall model, each phase must be completed in its entirety before the next phase can begin. At the end of each phase, a review takes place to determine if the project is on the right path and whether or not to continue or discard the project. Phases do not overlap. Methodologies include pure waterfall, modified waterfall, and the Sashimi model.

It is important to note, however, that the first formal concept of the waterfall process (by Winston W. Royce) described waterfall as an iterative process. Although Royce never used the term waterfall, he believed the process, when used in large software projects, would be "fundamentally sound". "Hopefully", he stated, "the iterative interaction between the various phases is confined to successive steps."[8]

## Spiral

This model of development combines the features of the prototyping model and the waterfall model. It is intended for large, expensive, and complicated projects. The spiral is a risk-reduction oriented model that breaks a software project up into mini-projects, each addressing one or more major risks. After major risks have been addressed, the spiral model terminates as a waterfall model. Spiral iterations involve six steps:

---

8    For a more in depth examination of Royce's views, visit http://www.cs.umd.edu/class/ spring2003/cmsc838p/Process/waterfall.pdf.

- Determine objectives, alternatives, and constraints
- Identify and resolve risks
- Evaluate alternatives
- Develop the deliverables for that iteration and verify that they are correct
- Plan the next iteration
- Commit to an approach for the next iteration

## Agile

Agile is an umbrella term that covers many processes that share a common set of values and principles as defined by the Manifesto of Agile Software Development (http://agileManifesto.org).[9] Agile software development refers to a group of software development methodologies based on iterative development, where requirements and solutions evolve through collaboration between self-organizing cross-functional teams.[1]

Most agile methods attempt to minimize risk by developing software in short time boxes, called iterations, which typically last one to four weeks. Each iteration is like a miniature software project of its own going through all the process life cycle phases to release the mini-increment of new functionality: planning, Requirements analysis, design, coding, and testing. These new methods attempt a useful compromise between no process and too much process, providing just enough process to gain a reasonable payoff. They emphasize real-time communication, preferably face-to-face over written documents. In many ways they are rather code-oriented. Methodologies include Extreme Programming (XP), Scrum, Feature Driven Development (FDD), Crystal, and Dynamic Systems Development Method (DSDM).

## V-Life Cycle

Just like waterfall, it is a sequential path of executing processes. Instead of moving down in a linear way, the process steps are bent upwards after the coding phase, to form the typical V-shape. The V-Life Cycle model demonstrates the relationships between each phase of the development life cycle and its associated phase of testing. Testing is emphasized in this model more so than the waterfall model. The testing procedures are developed early in the lifecycle before any coding is done, during each of the phases preceding implementation. This lifecycle is, in part, the result of Royce's work. In his description of the waterfall life cycle, he also stated the need to develop a preliminary program design and involve testing early in the process.[10]

## Evolutionary Prototyping

Also known as breadboard prototyping, this model uses multiple iterations of requirements elicitation and analysis, design, and prototype development. The main objective is to build a very robust prototype in a structured manner

---

9    *Agile Software Development*, http://en.wikipedia.org/wiki/Agile_software_development.
10   Royce, Winston W, *Managing the Development of Large Software Systems* 331–338, http://www.cs.umd.edu/class/spring2003/cmsc838p/Process/waterfall.pdf.

and constantly refine it. After each iteration, the result is analyzed by the customer. Their response creates the next level of requirements and defines the next iteration. Other models include throwaway prototyping, incremental prototyping and extreme prototyping.

Let's now take a look at some of the most widely used methodologies within the two main model types.

# Pure Waterfall Methodology

As stated above, this is the most common and classic of methodologies. It is very simple to understand and use. In a waterfall model, each phase must be completed in its entirety before the next phase can begin. Figure 2 shows the different phases in waterfall.

Pure waterfall performs well for products with clearly understood requirements or when working with well understood technical tools, architectures, and infrastructures.

*Figure 2. Waterfall Methodology*

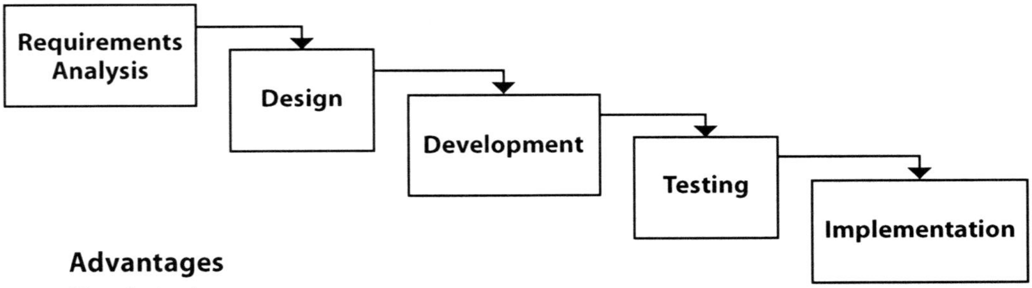

### Advantages
- Simple and easy to use
- Easy to manage due to the rigidity of the model—each phase has specific deliverables and a review process
- Phases are processed and completed one at a time
- Works well for smaller projects where requirements are very well understood
- Minimizes planning overhead since it can be done up front
- Works well for technically weak or inexperienced staff

## Disadvantages
- Adjusting scope during the life cycle can kill a project
- High amounts of risk and uncertainty as no working software is produced until late during the life cycle
- Poor model for long and ongoing projects
- Inflexible—poor model where requirements are at a moderate to high risk of changing
- Only the final phase produces a non-documentation deliverable
- Backing up to address mistakes is difficult

# Extreme Programming (XP) Methodology

The roots of XP lie in the Smalltalk community and, in particular, the close collaboration of Kent Beck and Ward Cunningham in the late 1980s. They refined their practices on numerous projects during the early 90s, extending their ideas of a software development approach that was both adaptive and people-oriented.[11]

XP begins with five values (communication, feedback, simplicity, courage, and respect). It then elaborates these into fourteen Principles and again into twenty-four pvractices. The idea is that practices are concrete things that a team can do day-to-day, while values are the fundamental knowledge and understanding that underpins the approach. The project usually begins with planning, the main component of which is the user "story", which parallels the use case in other development methods. With XP, the developer works with the business owners directly. Instead of formal project meetings, XP teams typically do "stand up" meetings at the beginning of the day. Developers use the stories to define the iterations of the project, or the pieces that define a block of work to be done. Iterations are no longer than three weeks in duration, the logic being that people like to see progress often. XP puts testing at the foundation of development, with every programmer writing tests as they write their production code. The tests are integrated into a continuous integration and build process which yields a highly stable platform for future development. Figure 3 shows how XP works.

*Figure 3. Extreme Programming (XP) Methodology*

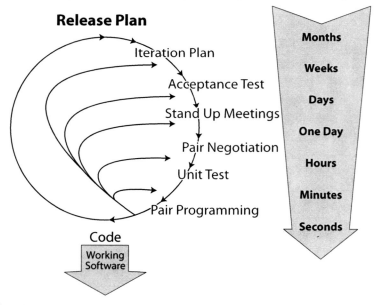

## Advantages

- Emphasis on customer involvement (rapid feedback)
- Emphasis on teamwork and communication

---

11    Fowler, Martin, *The New Methodology*.Source: http://www.martinfowler.com/articles/newMethodology.html

- Iterative, incremental development
- Frequent, extensive testing and continuous reviews

### Disadvantages

- No requirements traceability may impact the trust between customers and developers
- Lack of design documentation limits XP to small programs and makes it difficult to take advantage of reuse opportunities
- Lack of transition support: Transitioning any new process or method into general use is a large and challenging task
- Development team turnover: very difficult for new Developers to replace the previous Developers when they leave the project/organization due to lack of documentation

# Rational Unified Process Methodology

Named for the company where it was first developed, the Rational Unified Process (RUP), is another well-known process to have come out of the object-oriented community. Since RUP appeared about the same time as the agile methods, there is a lot of discussion about whether the two are compatible. RUP is a very large collection of practices and is really a process framework rather than a process. Rather than give a single process for software development, it seeks to provide a common set of practices for teams to choose from for an individual project. The key common aspects of RUP include being Use Case Driven (development is driven through user-visible features), iterative, and architecture centric (there's a priority to building an architecture early on that will last the project through).

It clearly defines who is responsible for what, how things are done, and when to do them. It also clearly articulates the essential milestones and decision points.

The RUP is organized along two dimensions: The dynamic aspect (horizontal) expresses cycles, phases, iterations, and milestones; the static aspect (vertical) expresses activities, disciplines, artifacts, and roles.

The Phases are: Inception, Elaboration, Construction, and Transition.

The Disciplines include: Business Modeling, Requirements, Analysis and Design [BA functions], Implementation, Test, Deployment, Configuration and Change Management, Project Management, and Environment.

### Advantages

- Iterative, incremental development
- Manageable, traceable
- Process is tunable
- Use Case driven and architecture centric

### Disadvantages

- Heavyweight on process side
- Not as much customer involvement as some of the agile methodologies
- Lots of artifacts (team members get overwhelmed)
- Process allows for too many variances from rigid waterfall to perfect agile

# Learning from Ancient Methodologies (Martial Arts)

As I stated at the beginning, the amount of information on methodologies and techniques can be overwhelming. In the end, it comes down to understanding the ones that are available in light of your understanding of the project and then adapting your personal style to them. Ultimately, you need to become one with the methodology by mastering the different artifacts, techniques and steps to deliver the goods! As with the many martial arts, the key lies not in memorizing the techniques but in 'knowing' them to the point that they become a natural movement—almost subconsciously knowing how and when to apply them. It takes time! As great as the techniques are, some are ineffective under certain circumstances. The PM or the BA Manager, very much like the martial artist, needs to develop the knowledge of the methodology to the point that it becomes instinctive. The Manager can then decide what process to apply and what to omit, and learn how to be flexible enough when the circumstances require working through unconventional steps, to deliver a successful project.

**"Early in the project the PM realizes it wasn't as simple as just setting the course" —FP**

Is agile for everyone or all projects? I certainly don't think so. But if you are willing to try it, make sure you do your homework. Find a suitable project to try agile on. Get a team that knows how to work with the methodology or that is willing to try it out. Engage the customer (without their collaboration you will not be successful), and if you can, get a Project Manager or a consultant who has done it before.

Similarly to when you are in a situation where you need to defend yourself (compared to a project you need to run), if you have practiced many styles and techniques (methodologies), you need to pick one you can adapt to your situation. Select one from your short list. Then, consider what adaptations of those techniques (processes) you need to make to fit them to your current scenario. Then it's just a matter of applying and improving as you go.

Just as Aikido and Karate are two opposite martial arts that work well depending on the circumstances—the first one trying to blend in with the opponent and using his own strength and power against him while the second one forcing the conflict between the two opponents and fighting back force with force—both iterative (e.g. agile) and sequential (e.g. waterfall) methodologies can be powerful approaches. It all depends on the context of the engagement. You must learn to pick the right methodology for the right project, the right client, and, in particular, the right team. Project teams cannot be successful unless they understand the project life cycle that is applicable to their project. Remember that building and managing according to a life cycle model is partly an art that requires flexibility and creativity. A good methodology provides the framework, processes, guidelines, and techniques to structure the work. It increases the odds of being successful, and therefore provides value to the organization, your project, and your project team.

*"To me, the extraordinary aspect of martial arts lies in its simplicity. The easy way is also the right way, and martial arts is nothing at all special; the closer to the true way of martial arts, the less wastage of expression there is."—Bruce Lee*

# About the Author

Federico Palacios, President of Pharos Edge Consulting Inc., has over 11 years of experience as an independent Senior Consultant who specializes in project management, business analysis, software development, Business Process Management (BPM), and business analysis training and mentoring of staff, among other things. He has consulted for various government organizations, as well as global companies in the private sector, such as Deloitte Consulting, Royal Bank of Canada, CryptoLogic Inc, etc. on multi-million dollar programs, projects, and business transformations. He specializes in Business Analysis Management and best practices assisting organizations make the transition from an unstructured analysis and development approach to achieving Business and Product Success through successfully Identifying, Managing, and Specifying Business Requirements and applying the process that is just right for their specific project context. He is currently working on his first book on the structure of the staffing and consultancy industry and the challenges and gaps that exist in the model in use today.

# INTERNATIONAL AND CULTURAL IMPACTS

By Bina Mehta, CBAP, PMP

## Influence of Globalization

*"Globalization has changed us into a company that searches the world, not just to sell or to source, but to find intellectual capital—the world's best talents and greatest ideas."*
—*Jack Welch, ex-CEO of GE*

## Business is Global

### Global Business Needs Global Thinking and Understanding

Globalization has become pervasive. We have corporations with employees spread across the globe. All employees need to understand the culture of the 'headquarters'. In a situation where the company is based in the United States (US), Business Analysts (BAs) working in another country need to be aware of American culture and traditions. If a team of Business Analysts is based in India and their stakeholders are in the US, managers need to ensure that BAs on the team are aware of the business practices, etiquette, and culture prevalent in US. In this instance, the BAs should understand GAAP (Generally Acceptable Accounting Principles), SOX (Sarbanes Oxley), and other US regulations that may apply to their projects. In order to be effective however it is equally important for BAs to understand American culture. Generally, Americans prefer to be addressed by first name and they are also very particular about punctuality, are process-oriented, and have strong belief in freedom and equality. Business Analysts can earn credibility by being aware of American holidays, traditions, and trivia. The same applies when dealing with any other country.

If a manager and BAs are from different places with different cultures, there will be additional challenges. Be it task assignment, monitoring, team-building, performance review or conflict resolution, having different locations, cultures, histories, and backgrounds will create different opinions and perspectives. If a manager can handle these dynamics effectively, the team will be strong and enriched. Otherwise, there will be dissatisfaction and reduction in performance.

### Strategic Advantage of Regional BAs

As businesses enter markets in different countries around the globe, their success depends on how well they understand the local market and mindset. Cellphones are a great example to demonstrate this phenomenon. Until recently, cellphones in the United States were used predominantly to make phone calls. In comparison, people in Europe and Asia became the leaders in using SMS or text messages with cellphones. In India, there is also the concept of what is referred to as "giving missed call'. Parents tell the kids to give a missed call when they need to reach out. A *missed call* is where you call a person and hang up after a ring. Parents use this as a signal that the child has reached the destination or the child needs to talk. This was extremely effective if parents had a cellphone plan with lots of minutes and the children did not. Another notable point is the proliferation of cellphones. India has been adding around 20 million new subscribers each month for a while now and by the end of October last there were some 705 million subscribers: over 50% year on year growth.[1] Consider a project where such a product or application was being developed. If the Business Analysts were local (in India, for example), they would understand the context within which the customers were to operate the cellphone. Requirements of usability, features, connection strength, and sturdiness of the phone will be different from a phone being manufactured for a developed country. If a manager or project manager were to assign Business Analysts from US or Canada for this project, they would start with a huge handicap of not *getting* the environment and the context. In this scenario, requirements analysis would be much more efficient by leveraging local BAs. A company doing business in different countries benefits by having local BAs or international BAs with a strong understanding of the local business practices and regulations as well as local culture.

For Business Analysts, performing an environment analysis is a good practice for effective requirements gathering. It provides a clearer perspective for their requirements planning effort especially for international project.

# Teams are Global and Virtual

## Foster Collaboration

As per Wikipedia, collaboration is a recursive process where two or more people or organizations work together in an intersection of common goals, such as an intellectual endeavor that is creative in nature—by sharing knowledge, learning, and building consensus.[2]

Collaboration is crucial to team success. Most aspects of business analysis need collaboration within large teams; be it Enterprise Analysis, Requirements Elicitation, or Solution Assessment—business leaders, stakeholders, Project Managers, Business Analysts and technical teams get together to understand a problem and build a common vision for the solution. This requires meeting of minds, mapping of ideas, and managing expectations. Collaboration can

---

1    Source: Julian Stretch OBE, Chairman of India Briefing Centre, in an article on India Inc: http://www.indiaincorporated.com/component/k2/item/84.html

2    Source: http://en.wikipedia.org/wiki/Collaboration

be complex even within a homogeneous group of people gathered in the same room. When teams are global and virtual, complexity grows exponentially. If management can build synergy within these teams, it can reap the benefits of multitude of ideas, knowledge, and skills.

## Capitalize on "Centers of Excellence"

A Business Analysis Centre of Excellence within an organization can provide a unified front for the BAs as well as to the Business and other teams interacting with BAs. The members become practitioners of the art of business analysis. They take pride in the role, follow a consistent methodology, and become better team players. Team building is one of the most significant tasks for any management. BA management is no exception. It is management responsibility to select team members representing various geographic and diverse business perspectives and experiences, all based on the common assumption that teams comprised of multi-ethnic, multicultural members that are more effective than homogenous teams. Global teams can be more effective than local teams, if managed properly. Management's commitment to respect cultural differences and encourage participation and team building is crucial to the Centre of Excellence for BAs. Business Analysts may need cultural training to understand their own cultural profile and the cultural profile of their team. This training should facilitate understanding of potential areas of conflict, as well as convergence. Teams cannot ignore the fact that working as a multicultural unit will require negotiating key areas of differences that could impede their effectiveness.

## Establish Consistent Processes and Terminology

I'd like to share an anecdote about processes. In the mid-nineties, a German company had took over a 51% stake in an Indian company where I worked. The Indian Company had homegrown financial applications and the parent German company had a popular ERP (Enterprise Resource Planning) system. It was decided that the Indian subsidiary had to adopt and transition over to the ERP system. The German project team came to Baroda, India for a preliminary assessment of the Indian systems. Business process diagrams and presentation were prepared for the visiting team. Although language was one of the barriers, the team survived, with some accent issues on both sides. There was, however, one acronym used in the Indian subsidiary that caused confusion. While explaining the Purchasing process and system, the Indian subsidiary had listed as part of their documentation a "Goods Inward Note" (GIN) document. Two days after the discussions, the German team was still confused about this "GIN". They kept asking about it. Both teams had to go through hoops before coming to a common understanding. The Industry-standard and more prevalent terminology for "Goods Inward Note (GIN)" is Goods Received Note (GRN), a document that is created to record receipt of goods against a purchase order. Because the Indian subsidiary was used to the acronym "GIN", they could not get away from it. The German team did not confirm nor was clarification sought to ensure both teams were referring to the same thing. Instead, the team kept going in circles potentially impacting project timelines.

This incident highlights the importance of having common terms and definitions. BA management teams should identify and document common terms regarding business analysis itself–like BC (Business Case), BRD (Business Requirements Document), RFP (Request for proposal), SOW (Statement of work), etc. It is not sufficient to know the acronyms and their meanings, there must bee a common understanding of terminologies across teams. BAs should have a common understanding of the templates, sections, and format of each of the documents. In addition to business analysis and project management terms, BAs should also understand common terms within the company and within the industry. These could be business terms like *PCI Compliance* for credit card encryption, *VSOE* for revenue recognition, or technology terms like *SaaS* (Software as a Service), and *Cloud computing,* etc.

In addition to facilitating common terms, BA management teams are also responsible for establishing a consistent process of planning, conducting, and documenting as well as managing changes to requirements analysis. This process should fit within the overall project management and systems development methodologies. Also, BA management teams should be very cautious in introducing any process. If it is overly convoluted with lengthy workflow, teams can get stuck and spend unproductive time in chasing the paper through the process rather than keeping the focus on the end game—effective requirements analysis and a solution which best meets the requirements. Process for the sake of process benefits no one—customers, BAs, or companies, except if it creates value and meets the needs of the business.

# Effective Communication is Crucial

*"The difference between the right word and the almost right word is the difference between lightning and a lightning bug."*
—*Mark Twain*

## Challenges in Communication

### Language Barriers
One of the definitions of communication is 'the imparting or interchange of thoughts, opinions, or information by speech, writing, or signs'.[3] Be it vocal, written, or sign language, communication varies between nations,

---

3    Source: dictionary.com (http://dictionary.reference.com/browse/communication).

communities, and cultures. In some cases, language itself is different—Japanese, Hindi, Spanish, or English. Even when it is the same language, such as English, its usage and interpretations may be different. I grew up in India and have settled in the US for the past decade. Indian English takes after Queen's English. People in India and Britain use the phrase 'phoning someone'. In USA, people use the phrase 'calling a person' and to *phone someone* seems to be wrong usage. When there can be such differences between British and American English, think about the permutations when we bring in Canadian, Australian, Irish, and other nationalities using the same language in their own way. When translation from one language to another comes in the play, things get even trickier. There is the infamous incident when Pepsi's "Come alive with the Pepsi Generation" slogan translated into "Pepsi brings your ancestors back from the grave" in Chinese.[4]

These were just few words or phrases that caused confusion. The job of a Business Analyst involves extensive communication—reading documents, writing requirements, conducting meetings, workshops, interviews, and surveys, etc. In global environment, they have to deal with language barriers every step of the way. They need to be very sensitive while listening, reading, or interpreting communication from the others on the team. In order to keep their own communication effective, Business Analysts must ensure feedback and confirmation from the recipient. Interpretation of accents is also very difficult especially on the phone and during conference calls. If a BA is in the same room with their audience, then lip-movement and gestures can provide a basis for better interpretation through observation of non-verbal communication signs. However, when voice is the only medium, there is a greater probability of miscommunication. Message tone and non-verbal communication also play a big role in effective communication and a Business Analyst has to pay close attention to both.

## Culture Barriers

Just as language can be a barrier, culture can also become a barrier to communication. Managers, Project Managers, and team leads must ensure that Business Analysts on their team are aware of the cultural background of the stakeholders. Wordless messages or kinesics are the way we communicate by sending and receiving signals using body language, gestures, postures, proximity, and facial expressions. Some signals are consistent across cultures. To a certain degree this is good news; if you do not speak the foreign language, you can still communicate with people of another country by using body language and facial expressions. Even if you do speak the local language and are able to communicate with the local people, you may still be puzzled by the use of body language and facial expressions at your destination country. Why? Because non-verbal communication has also cultural meanings and is interpreted according to the cultural context in which it occurs. Cultural

---

4     Source : http://www.chinesetranslationpro.com/brand-translation.php

norms regarding kinesics vary considerably between countries; if you are not familiar with local body language, you may be misunderstood or misinterpret the local non-verbal signals. The table below shows some gestures and cultural behaviors in different countries.

### TABLE 1. EXAMPLES OF CULTURAL CUSTOMS AND GESTURES

| Country | Customs |
|---------|---------|
| China | During conversations, be especially careful about interrupting—listening is a sign of politeness and of contemplation. |
| France | The "okay" sign, made with index finger and thumb, means "zero." The French use the "thumbs up" sign to say "okay." |
| India | Indians value personal space. Don't stand too close; allow an arm's length space. |
| Japan | The Japanese find it hard to say 'no'. The best solution is to phrase questions so that they can answer yes. For example, "do you disagree with this?" |
| Mexico | Time is a very flexible thing in Mexico. Don't be offended or surprised if your contacts in Mexico don't show up on time. |
| Britain | There is some protocol to follow when introducing people in a business: Introduce a younger person to an older person. Introduce a person of lower status to a person of higher status. When two people are of similar age and rank, introduce the one you know better to the other person. |
| USA | Arrive on time for meetings since time and punctuality are important to Americans. Stand while being introduced. Only the elderly, the ill and physically unable persons remain seated while greeting or being introduced. |

## Distance and Time Zone Barriers

We examined language and cultural barriers so now let's look at the situations that can arise due to distance. Globalization has made businesses function 24 hours, 7 days a week, 365 days a year but each individual employee works as per his or her time zone. If a manager has Business Analysts located in different time zones, just the logistics of meeting times can be difficult. Consider a scenario where a company is spread over three countries—US, Ireland, and Singapore. There is an eight-hour time difference between the US and Ireland, and eight hours between Ireland and Singapore. It is very challenging to find a common time for meetings among stakeholders, Business Analysts, Project Managers, and other team members. If you have to invite people from American, European, and Asian countries to a conference call, it is almost impossible. Managers should be very careful in assigning BAs on projects. If one BA is assigned to multiple projects with people in three time zones, it creates a no-win situation. BAs can be overworked and dissatisfied, causing the productivity on each of the projects to suffer. Both managers and PMs should be sensitive to time zone barriers. It has become inevitable that most people will work beyond their time zones in order to facilitate communication but the managers must ensure the BAs do not burn out in the process.

Figure 2 shows how effective communication incorporates feedback and considers potential barriers that can reduce communication effectiveness.

### Timely Follow-Up and Closure
Communication is successful if the receiver gets the point or idea that the sender wanted to send. The sender should always check the feedback and confirm it with the receiver. Feedback loop, open items or action items, regular follow-ups, and drive to closure are extremely important in communication.

*Figure 2. Communication Model*

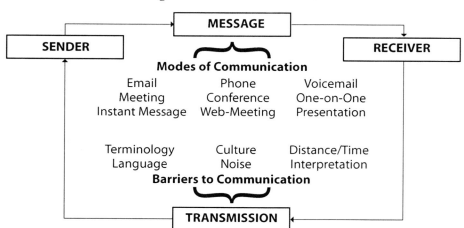

## Constant Feedback and Verification

### Leveraging Tools and Technology for Communication
Globalization has become possible thanks to technological advancements in networking, Internet and the plethora of applications leveraging these technologies. Technology has also given us many tools to overcome the barriers in communication.

### Virtual Team Meetings
Audio conferencing, web conferencing, video conferencing, document sharing, and content management systems are some of the technologies that have enabled the world to come closer. These tools and techniques are used across the organization for disseminating information, collecting information, brainstorming, training, meetings, or collaborative sessions. BAs use these for conducting requirements workshops, verifying or validating requirements, or even for brainstorming or problem-solving sessions. Whether a person is

sitting in the next cubicle, working from home, traveling, or attending from across the seas, it does not matter. Management needs to invest in these technologies in order to improve the efficiency and effectiveness of the BAs. Many options are very affordable and even video conferencing should follow suit in a few years. Managers should plan to train their BAs so that they can maximize the available resources.

## Synchronous and Asynchronous Communication

Communication can be both synchronous and asynchronous. Email and documents sent via email are examples of asynchronous communication. It is a very effective method when the receiver needs to spend some time reviewing the details or needs to have some discussion with few members and then reply or provide feedback. Social networking media like Twitter or Facebook also tend to be asynchronous but they have the potential of very quick turnaround and spreading the message virally in a very short amount of time. Many companies have started cautiously adopting these media.

Synchronous communication happens in conference calls, in-person meetings, and instant messages. Text messages can act as synchronous or asynchronous depending on the availability of both parties. Synchronous communication is more effective whenever a decision needs to be made or an issue needs to be addressed. Both forms of communication are extremely important.

## Document Repositories

Business Analysts are to be trained to follow a common methodology, understand and adjust to communication barriers, and be aware of social and cultural differences among members of global teams. Will this make them effective in their role? Not unless their work is accessible and maintained in a common repository with proper change management system. Efficient document management and version control is important in any situation; it becomes critical for disbursed teams. Many tools are available for content management and collaboration. Structured organization of documents within these systems along with proper naming conventions and consistent version control can enable the teams to work seamlessly. Even if a BA is in the US and the development team in India (with a 12 hour time difference), they can still work as a cohesive team if a common approach is followed for communication and information sharing. If there is a gap in understanding, it can be a costly waste of time, in this case, an entire day.

# Setting Expectations

## Clear Definition of Roles and Responsibilities

By establishing a BA Centre of Excellence, methodology, process, and templates, an organization can create a well-defined role for a Business Analyst. But when there are many BAs spread over various regions working on cross-functional initiatives, there can be overlaps in the roles and responsibilities of BAs in the context of a particular project. A BA could be a lead or accountable for one project, responsible for another, and just informed for the third project. This can be achieved by appropriate use of Roles and Responsibilities Matrix (RACI). The purpose of the RACI matrix is to assign departments or individuals to activity categories, define role responsibilities, and define relationships between groups. If the manager fails to clarify roles and responsibilities, it can lead to a situation where everybody thinks that others are assigned to the task.

### Ground Rules for Communication

Be it a sports team or BA team, ground rules are an essential element of collaboration. For global teams, the location, time zones, holidays in respective regions, and preferred modes of communication should all be laid out at the beginning of a project or assignment. The worldW is not perfect and not all situations can be pre-defined. In case of any conflict or lack of productivity, the manager or Project Manager should step in and understand the root cause. Sometimes, it is miscommunication or inaccurate expectations among team members.

# Cultural Impacts

*"What managers do is the same around the world. How they do it is determined by tradition and culture"*
—*Peter Drucker, management guru*

## Organizational Culture

### Leadership Style

Managers and leaders need to tweak their style for global, multicultural teams. Here are some of the points to consider in managing Business Analysts:

- Selection of BAs with right skills, abilities, and motivation
- Provide training on technology use, virtual communication, and cultural sensitivity
- Align reward systems with nature of distributed work
- Disseminate information among BAs and other team members
- Allow time for information sharing in video and teleconferences
- Make communication norms explicit and encourage openness
- Develop team building exercises
- Ensure remote BAs do not feel isolated
- Communicate frequently with all BAs.
- Encourage knowledge-sharing among BAs
- Assign primary and secondary BAs for projects

### Values of Organization

Managers should understand the values of the organization and share the same with all BAs. The values generally include how company wants to be perceived by the customers and the core values expected of every employee in order to meet customer satisfaction. It is also important that the Business Analysts understand corporate goals and objectives. Enterprise Analysis stems from these objectives. Correct interpretation of values, goals and objectives is important and it is the role of managers to ensure that Business Analysts from different cultural and national backgrounds grasp the organization's true values, its meaning, and spirit.

## Regional Subcultures

### Social Behaviors and Customs

We have looked at some of the customs of different countries. Business Analysts and management should also be aware of subcultures within a country. Big cities in most countries have a diverse population and a greater acceptance of diversity but smaller towns and inner cities will generally be more rigid. In a country like India, there are many different languages and cultures. Age also plays a great factor—the younger generation from most parts of the world is technology-savvy and embraces Western culture while older people tend to be slower to adapt to change and more apt to try to stick to old ways. Managers should take these dynamics into consideration before assigning resources on tasks. They should also train the BAs on group dynamics among stakeholders.

# Conclusion

## Synergy of International and Cultural Diversity

In this chapter, we learned that:

- Globalization is pervasive and it affects the role and management of Business Analysts.
- Managers have to ensure that BAs understand the context of the business, business practices, and the rules and regulations within different countries.
- Regional BAs can provide a company strategic advantage in business analysis.
- Key to the success of BAs is effective collaboration, Centers of Excellence, and consistent processes.
- There are language, culture and time zone barriers to communication. These barriers can be overcome by provide cultural sensitivity training and using appropriate tools for communication.
- It is important to set expectations and define ground rules.
- Managers should choose a leadership style that takes the challenges and opportunities of a global environment into account and manage to create synergy.

All in all, it is an exciting time for business in general, and Business Analysts in particular, to take advantage of globalization. They can get to know business practices and BAs from other countries and ethnicities, and enrich their knowledge and exposure. Global business does not support a 'my way or highway' philosophy; it thrives on multiple viewpoints and insights.

*"The Whole is Greater than Sum of its Parts"*

The great philosopher Aristotle's quote from 4th century BC is very appropriate in the 21st century for our global, multi-cultural, interconnected, and inter-dependent village.

# About the Author

Bina Mehta is an accomplished IT professional with over 15 years of experience in the areas of business analysis, software development, project management, and people management. She holds CBAP® and PMP® certifications. Her strengths include large-scale ERP implementations, integrations for mergers & acquisitions, SOX & PCI compliance, engagement with offshore & onshore outsourcing vendors, and global cross-functional projects. Bina excels at building relationships among cross-functional teams and  solving complex problems. Currently, she is working as IT Business Architect on the strategic demand management team for a software company. In this role, Bina is working on enterprise analysis and strategic planning initiatives. She is also serving as VP- Marketing & Communications for IIBA®, Silicon Valley Chapter. She also provides training for the CBAP® preparation course.

In the past, Bina has worked as consultant for large technology and construction clients. She has also served as program manager, communications for PMI®, Silicon Valley chapter, and as club president for the Toastmasters organization. She holds the Competent Communicator™ (CC) and Advanced Leader Bronze™ (ALB) credentials from the Toastmasters program. Bina won the area level public speaking contest in 2010.

# OFFSHORING, NEARSHORING AND BUSINESS ANALYSIS

By Charles Bozonier, CBAP

## Offshoring, Nearshoring, and Business Analysis

### Terminology Clarification

The terms offshoring and nearshoring, when used in this text, specifically refer to the contracting of resources on a technology solution. Offshoring indicates that the provider is based outside of the country of the client, such that a significant difference in time of day or significant travel time of more than one day exists. Nearshoring indicates the provider is outside of the country or regional area of the client such that little or no time of day difference exists. Both offshoring and nearshoring are distinctly different from the term outsourcing. Within this text, outsourcing is defined as the external resourcing of an entire process, not just a portion, to an outside company regardless of that company's physical location, whether in or out of the country.

*Figure 1. Servicing the Four Relationships—Overview*

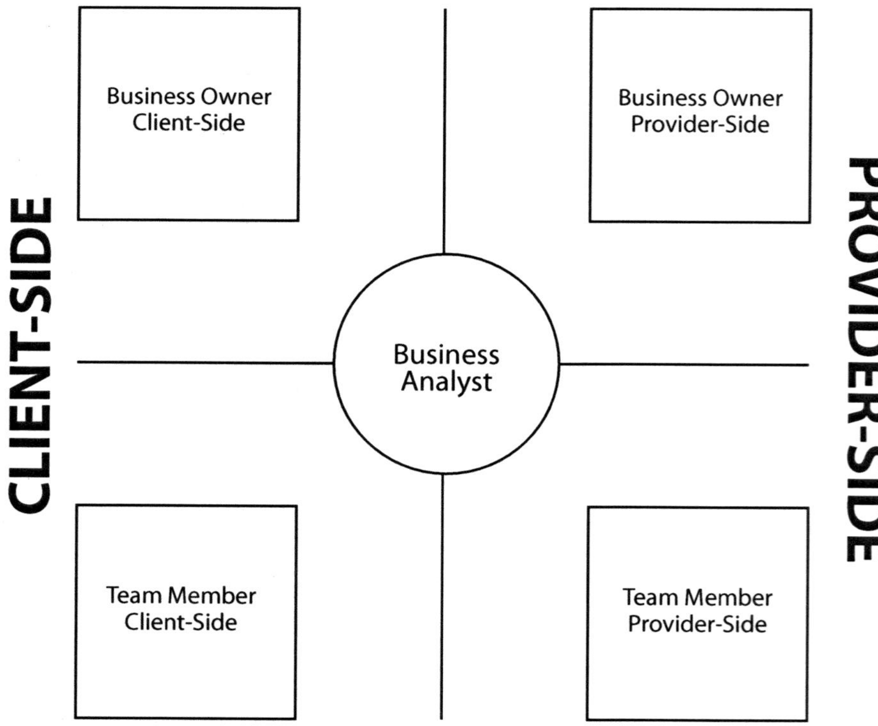

# The Perspectives and Agendas

The offshoring and nearshoring of technology services is unique in vendor-client relationships. While the relationship most often presents itself outwardly as a simple business decision to meet demands for technology capacity while controlling costs, the relationship has at least four distinct perspectives and agendas. Each primary role in the relationship has a perspective and an agenda which, though often hidden, profoundly impact the work that will be done and the manner in which it is accomplished. The role of the BA is to support the needs of the business by facilitating the progress of the solution development by acting as a liaison between each of these divergent perspectives and agendas.

## The Client-Side Business Owner Perspective—Responding to Pressure

The technology manager or director on the client-side is often presented with a difficult decision prior to openly considering offshoring or nearshoring. This controversy has not diminished after a decade and a half of widespread use of offshore and nearshore technology outsourcing. The client-side business owner is typically faced with the need "to do more with less" and is looking for a long-term relationship that services the needs without complicating the overall situation. A few of the fundamental questions that the business owner may encounter from the client-side team members when they learn the company is considering offshoring and nearshoring solutions are:

1. Where is the organization headed with near and off shore development?
2. What does it mean to the existing technology staff?
3. Do roles change?

How these questions represent opportunities for business analysis is at the heart of this chapter.

For the client-side business owner, an internal company directive or statement about offshoring or nearshoring engagements can answer questions and help put to rest rumors or misunderstandings. Leadership-hosted conversations and dialogue can do even more. The formulation of a company policy about offshoring or nearshoring is a backstop that should be discussed, developed, distributed appropriately, and understood before the serious negotiations and on-site visits of offshore or nearshore solution providers begin. When the scope, impacts, and benefits of the relationship are defined, a large degree of the anxiety is abated. As in all other business decisions, the pros and cons on the new relationship should be made readily available to the individuals with a need to know or those who could benefit by knowing.

Even if the client-side business owner is not responding to pressure to do more with less but is "multi-sourcing" or "right-shoring" (complex tasks completed near the client, simple tasks offshore), the perspective held by the business owner is that the problems they faced when attempting to have the work completed in-house will be reduced and that the new relationship with the outside provider is strengthening and bringing relief to his or her organization.

A key difference between the points of view of the client-side business owner and the supplier-side business owner may manifest over time. As the relationship matures, the client-side business owner often places more value on the relationship with the vendor's onshore representatives and less value on the terms of the contract which fade in significance. The supplier-side business owner has the precisely opposite perspective—the terms of the contract are of paramount importance to the offshore or nearshore provider in order to ensure survival of his organization as the relationship matures and re-work and development corrections work into the project. This difference in values is worthy of consideration and should be considered a risk that should be addressed early and throughout the relationship.

## Opportunities for the BA—
## Supporting the Client-Side Business Owner

*Figure 2. Business Analysis Support*

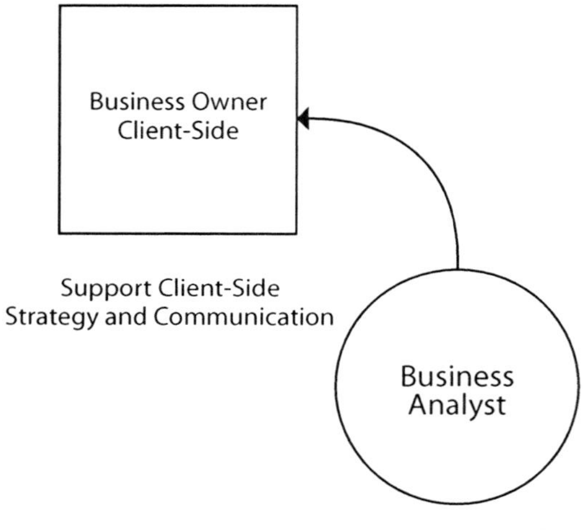

The opportunities to support the transition to an offshore or nearshore development model will vary from organization to organization—but the opportunities are there nonetheless. The BA can assist the business owner in getting ahead of concerns that can impact productivity, morale, and team confusion by helping to establish and communicate the objectives that the business owner has been tasked to meet and the means available to achieve them.

Here are two examples of how the BA can provide value to the business owner:

1. *Cost Benefit Analysis:* To improve the understanding of the strategy and to answer questions as to why offshoring or nearshoring is a good approach for the organization, the BA may provide the business owner with an analysis of all work to be done on a project versus the cost benefit of the specific aspects of the project which are being considered for offshoring or nearshoring.

Keeping the ratio of cost to benefit as a positive number is a simple way to demonstrate the rationale of the business owner to a broad audience.

2. *Work Value Analysis:* A shift in thinking on the best way to utilize internal resources is a common driver in decisions made by business owners. The BA can support the communication of the business owner's strategy by providing analysis as to how work is done today, the way things should be done in the future, and a practical way forward to reach the business objective of having high cost employees working on high value efforts.

## The Provider-Side Business Owner Perspective—An Opportunity to Grow

These pressures have placed added importance on the details of the contract between the provider and the client. In contrast to the client's perspective of the importance of the client as a mere formality, the seasoned provider views the contract with extreme importance. The provider's perspective is driven by the fact that tighter margins have driven the need for terse contract language to protect the offshoring or nearshoring vendor from excessive cost. The overhead of initiating a contract is high—travel expense, initial estimation, contract negotiation, and high caliber talent needed to convince the client that productivity and quality will meet expectations. In order to maximize the return on the investment, the provider is naturally looking to expand their opportunity and persist as a provider as long as possible.

## Opportunities for the BA—Defining the Benefits Driving the Relationship

*Figure 3. Defining Relationship Drivers*

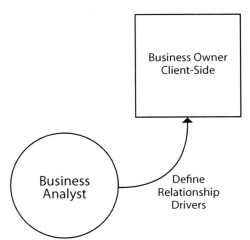

The documentation that was developed to communicate the purpose and boundaries of the offshore or nearshore relationship to the client-side team members can be foundational in establishing the boundaries with the provider-side business owner. The client-side business owner must define the scope and scale of the relationship. The BA can assist in providing the context of the work to be performed and the areas of cost benefit that are driving the relationship.

## The Provider-Side Employee Perspective— Measuring up and Making an Impression

Often the most motivating opportunity for the offshore or nearshore provider-side employee is access to travel to the client country or locale and the opportunity to establish contacts, gain experience, and grow as a professional. The tremendous competition to be selected as a candidate to travel to the client drives the provider-side employee to make as much of an impression as possible. It is often the case that these travel-worthy individuals from the offshore or nearshore provider are in fact the best resources that the provider company has and they are utilized to form the initial team that engages the client. Over time, the agenda for the offshoring or nearshoring company is to reassign the best performing staff to new or even prospective accounts. This inevitable transition of high-caliber provider-side talent off of their assignment from one client and on to new clientele is important to address early so as to control the negative impact on the projects productivity. The provider's team members will inevitably change over time. This cannot be changed, however, the experience level or core competency of the talent on that team is something that can be defined and agreed upon.

## Opportunities for the BA— Comparative Analysis of Productivity—Provider-Side

*Figure 4. Comparative Analysis of Productivity*

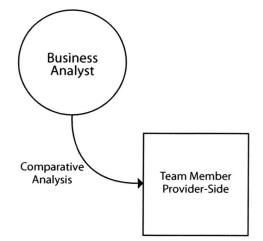

As the composition of an offshore or nearshore team changes over time, it is important for everyone in the relationship to be aware of the impact on productivity. Clear and accurate recording of hours to task by the individuals involved is important and the BA can provide comparative analysis of feature value to hours worked over time to demonstrate any change in performance. If, over time, the value of work produced slips when key offshore or nearshore resources are rotated off projects, the business owner needs to have quantitative information at their disposal to support their position during negotiation.

## The Client-Side Employee Perspective— Flourishing in Change and Providing Leadership

*Figure 5. Providing Leadership*

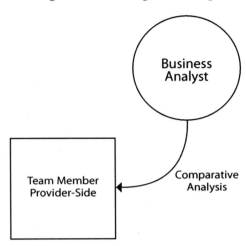

Things change. Companies change. Employees who change along with the organization in the adoption of new methods and who show leadership in finding ways to prosper are of the highest value. The BA that can support his fellow team members in new ways that add value will help everyone on the team. BAs that thrive as the "middle" in the relationship relieve a great deal of the pressure due to change. The BA can provide leadership, ease tensions, and model forward thinking behavior as he or she integrates with the changes that result from offshoring or nearshoring of resources. These change-leveraging behaviours help everyone on the team.

## Opportunities for the BA— Comparative Analysis of Productivity—Client-Side

The BA can provide a tremendous service to his client-side team members by sharing with them the results of their hard work in a changing workplace. Teams which have adapted well to change should be recognized and the comparative analysis between teams can be healthy ways to demonstrate what works and what does not work in nearshoring and offshoring situations.

BAs bridge the gap between the perspectives and agendas of offshoring and nearshoring roles through innovative and supportive techniques which ease transition, maximize productivity, and deliver valuable analysis to support strategic thinking.

### Opportunities for the BA—Bringing it All Together

The BA has an opportunity to play a unique and important role in the offshore or nearshore business relationship. Engage your BA team to consider the important ways that they can contribute to the success of the relationship by seeing themselves as the facilitators of progress and healthy agendas on both sides of the relationship.

*Figure 6. Business Analysis Opportunities*

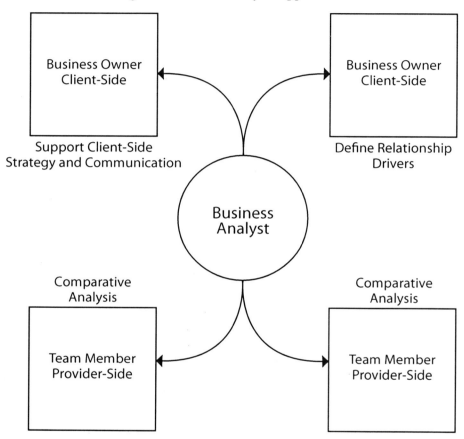

## Realizing the Opportunity of Nearshoring and Offshoring

Offshore or nearshore business relationships may have origins in cost savings but these savings have diminished over time. Cost savings represent only a small part of the total opportunity in most situations. Following is a list of factors that all BAs should consider as a reminder of the services that client-side companies value when determining the benefits of offshoring or nearshoring:

### A.    Convenience

A good service provider makes it convenient for a customer to do business with them. This convenience equates to ease of engagement. Terms and conditions are simple, methods of payment are clear and standardized. Complications are kept to a minimum. Hiring full-time equivalents can result in costs and delays that nearshore or offshore development resources just don't incur.

## B. Capacity on Demand

The ability to add and reduce development resources with just the right expertise as needed would give organizations the capacity to quickly meet the short term needs without the risk of needlessly overstaffing once the demand subsides. This is a clear win for the business but it is generally only possible with a sustained relationship with the right vendor. It is likely this is most effective for services such as on-call support, initial product launches, or peak seasonal demands that can be planned for in advance of the need.

## C. Multiple Solution Paths

The ability to assess more than one solution design can be a remarkably effective method of development and leads to the next reason why companies persist with offshore or nearshore solutions. Engage your BA team to determine the benefits of multiple solution paths.

## D. Healthy Competition

Every professional organization knows the value of competition. We get better with it and grow complacent without it. Engage your BA team to determine the benefits of competition through comparative analysis of burn down rates on similar projects and compare the solution quality by monitoring the number of post-implementation bugs.

## E. Expertise

There is often cause to utilize expertise that is not present in the client-side organization. The expertise could be in older technologies for which available resources is in short supply or in newer technologies that have not yet been fully adopted by the client-side customer.

## F. Elimination of Single Points of Dependency

Organizations often have key individuals who are the sole holders of a large amount of knowledge in one particular area of the company. In technology departments this can be especially common. Single points of dependency can make it very difficult to change as an organization. An offshore or nearshore provider can provide resources to complete the daily tasks while the client-side resources who are the sole members of their area of expertise can participate on new projects and new technology solutions.

## G. True Customer and Provider Relationship

Many IT departments consider their business partners their customers and go out of their way to establish a customer service model that supports the businesses needs with as much customer-centric communication as possible. However, there is no substitute for a customer-provider relationship that can result in one party (usually the customer) taking their business elsewhere. The customer is king in a true customer and provider relationship and is not subject to the political undercurrents so common in so many companies.

## The BA Role in Embracing Change

Perhaps the largest factor that will determine the success or failure of an offshoring or nearshoring solution is the ability for the client-side organization to embrace the change that these relationships represent. The BA can play a vital role in this area by enabling the engagements early success through high quality requirements, documentation, and defined terms and business rules.

The effective BA can provide support in all of the following areas that set the tone early on in the business relationship:

- *Setting up for Success* - Preparing the way for eased engagement through organized delivery of critical information and company tribal knowledge is a remarkably effective means of breaking the ice and setting the stage for an effective partnership. Engage your BA team to provide an overview of appropriate documentation.
- *Refining the Deliverables* - Prior to assigning work deliverables, it might be highly advantageous to reduce the complexity or the volume of deliverables that perhaps have become dated, redundant, or of lower value over time. Ask your BA team to set up a review of the deliverables in detail with the external solution team. This goes a long way in ramping up productivity and minimizes lost time in the transition.
- *Identifying the Initial Effort* - Getting a scope and success criteria of an initial effort that is meaningful, achievable, and valuable sets the tone and builds the reputation for a new relationship. Challenge your BAs to assist in gaining a high degree of mutual understanding of the first set of Requirements and acceptability criteria.

## Sustaining and Refining

In order to establish a cycle of development that is suitable for both sides of the relationship, an effective method for handling change is a smart place to start. Engage your BAs to take the opportunity to include process flows for changing requirements, changing acceptance criteria, and changing test plans. These are "gotcha" areas of any solution development process and especially so when engaging external sources.

Establish a pattern of periodic reviews as opportunities for gathering and sharing feedback and lessons learned. Quarterly reviews for refining processes and measuring progress and performance is critical to a successful partnership.

## Exiting the Relationship

While the BA likely won't play a role in terms of an agreement, it is safe to say that steps can be taken to limit the exposure through good BA habits.

Documentation and the maintenance of a knowledge base and functional specifications can be hugely important hedges against strained relationships.

## Concluding Thoughts

Managing BAs within an offshore or nearshore business landscape is a great opportunity to extend the meaningful work your team performs in ways that most IT workers in the company are less equipped or less inclined to provide. The natural "middle" people that often make good BAs make the transition or the optimization of an offshore or nearshore relationship easier. Like any other venture the company may enter into, the objective is always to be successful—help your team make offshoring or nearshoring a huge success for your company by encouraging them to take the first steps in inclusive and adaptive tasks that build the strongest foundation for effective communication and engagement.

Encourage early BA involvement amongst the company leadership team by communicating the benefit of a well-prepared team that provides details to information dependent staff augmentation teams.

Finally, ensure that your BA team considers the entire enterprise as they provide information to the external work resources. The critical areas of the company that remain largely unseen to external resources will remain a mystery to them without the help of an informed internal resource that is forthcoming with the high value information that will make a difference. The BA's ability to traverse the enterprise and provide access to business rules, company knowledge, and policies puts the offshore and nearshore resources much further down the road to understanding how to be successful in their role with your company.

# About the Author

Charles Bozonier works as a Principal Business Analyst for REI and is a University of Washington Professional and Continuing Education instructor for the Business Analysis Certificate program. He is a frequent speaker at BA World Conferences in Seattle and Vancouver. He specializes in group facilitation to build consensus, complex cost benefit analysis, data modeling, and decision modeling. His business expertise includes analysis delivery in Investment Advisory, Capital Markets, Accounting, Finance, Retail, Ecommerce, Product Life Cycle Management, and Education sectors. Charles is a Certified Business Analysis Professional® having earned that designation in 2008. He holds a BS in Computer Information Systems.

# DEVELOPING A BUSINESS ANALYSIS CAREER MODEL

Angela M. Wick, PMP, CBAP

## Introduction

Imagine for a moment that you are a Business Analyst (BA) with a job description that does not match what you do or the direction you are getting from your leadership team. In addition, as a Business Analyst, you are wondering what the future holds for your career as there is not a clear career path defined for you as a Business Analysis professional. Perhaps the expectation is that Business Analysts grow into Project Managers. As a BA, you are curious by nature and passionate about helping implement solutions that drive business value; you are passionate about not just executing the project but ensuring that what is being delivered provides business value; you see the big picture and the details. You may feel that project management, other than the perceived career growth, does not align to your desires or skill set. What would make you more excited about your career? What opportunities would spur excitement and engagement to grow and contribute more?

The work of business analysis has been happening for many years although has not always been called business analysis. Today, there is a lot of business analysis happening within the roles of many professionals other than those titled Business Analyst. In some organizations, this work has happened under the structure of many roles; each performing a different part of the present day definition of business analysis. Some organizations adapted the title of Business Analyst many years ago with job descriptions partially covering what we see as today's Business Analyst. Many organizations have sizeable gaps between their current Business Analyst job descriptions and what Business Analysts actually do, and yet another gap in what leaders would like Business Analysts to be doing. International Institute of Business Analysis™ (IIBA) has defined the globally-accepted standard of what a Business Analyst is. IIBA® *A Guide to the Business Analysis Body of Knowledge® (BABOK® Guide)* has defined what a Business Analyst does, and the IIBA® Competency Model has defined job profiles, levels of BAs, and what success in a BA looks like along with the defined competencies and indicators.

Although still quite varied, we are seeing more commonly used definitions of the Business Analyst role from organizations around the globe. Organizations are further exploring what the Business Analyst career path looks like and those that have already developed a career model need to continually evolve them as this critical role takes shape. Career models for Business Analysts in organizations are evolving from a single individual contributor role into paths that can take a business analysis professional into the C-suite. Even well-established career models for Business Analysts formed in the '90s and early 2000s need refinement and redefinition to leverage the value that a BA can bring to the agility needed by organizations in the twenty-first century. The business analysis role is vital to enabling organizations to operate efficiently and compete in today's market.

Many organizations use career models to create a common language for defining roles. Benefits of a well-defined career model aligned to organizational talent strategies and goals:

- Foster employee engagement; increasing productivity
- Create accountabilities and role expectations
- Use as a tool to recognize, reward, and retain employees
- Motivate employees seeking growth opportunities
- Increase employee versatility and adaptability
- Promote professional growth and competency development

This chapter is dedicated to understanding the business analysis career and how, as a manager of business analysis professionals, you can foster a positive career model that will benefit your team and drive organizational value through better business analysis.

## How Does One Become a Business Analyst?

Before looking at business analysis career models, we must first look at where business analysis professionals start. Every career model has an entry point, and understanding the possible paths to get to that entry point is an important piece of making the career model work. If you are managing a team of Business Analysts, you are likely wondering where to find more great Business Analysts and how to develop the great business analysis resources you already have. There is growing appreciation of what a BA is and how to develop a high-performing BA. Experienced business analysis professionals are difficult to find so developing and growing them internally is an increasingly popular talent management strategy for many organizations. Organizations need to find creative and alternative ways to find and develop Business Analysts.

Business Analysts come from a large variety of backgrounds and levels of experience. Each of these paths to becoming a BA needs knowledge, training, and mentoring, plus exposure to and practice in business analysis skills. Each also has a unique perspective from which to learn these new skills.

- *University:* Upon completion of a university program with little to no professional experience and from a variety of academic backgrounds, anyone from computer science to music major may become a Business Analyst. Developing these professionals into great Business Analysts takes a solid training program, mentoring opportunities, and work experiences that match and grow their competency levels. An established career model will help guide these professionals, helping monitor how each grows and develops through the experience managers are able to expose them to during the first few years of their careers.

- *Business Units:* From business unit operations, corporate audit departments, product managers, trainers, and many other business backgrounds with or without knowledge of the business or systems with which they are working. Business Analysts coming from business unit experience have operational knowledge, business relationships, and cultural knowledge. They need training and mentoring to develop understanding of technical aspects of the role including analytical techniques, the software development process, business rule/process/data constructs, and some basic understanding of technical architectures. These skills will help develop the business knowledge into capability identification skills critical to business analysis success.

- *IT Departments:* From technical backgrounds; former developers and software engineers, tester and quality assurance backgrounds, and help desk backgrounds, among others. These professionals often make a natural transition into the business analysis role as they already have deep technical knowledge, software development knowledge, and some business knowledge. These professionals typically need training in skills related to abstracting technical details into higher-level business terminology and concepts. Besides knowledge of the Business Analyst role, these professionals need to look at their underlying competencies, technique usage, and the level of abstraction used in techniques. Typically, these professional are experienced in many business analysis techniques, however, they may need to refocus the usage of the technique to a more conceptual and higher-level for some audiences and phases of the project.

- *Leadership Roles:* Recently I have increasingly seen Business Analysts coming from leadership roles such as project managers, IT managers, and business managers; all with the passion to do great business analysis and ensure solutions are providing value back to the organization. These professionals usually have well-developed underlying competencies and need to focus on learning the techniques and knowledge of the Business Analyst role.

- *Consultancies:* These professionals have a background in a variety of industries working on teams and usually under a structured process of solving for problems and opportunities. These professionals may come with a vast variety of knowledge and experience with different aspects of the Business Analyst role. Their knowledge, technique usage, and competencies will vary greatly. They will likely have deep experience and knowledge but identifying which aspects of the Business Analyst role they are experienced in will be important and will vary based on their unique consulting background.

- *Independent Contractors:* Those with contracting backgrounds tend to have specific skill sets in business analysis or related competencies and have applied them in a variety situations and organizations. Like professionals from consultancies, they will each have a deep and unique skill set. Understanding their true competency set will be important to growing and developing them through a career path.

- *Software Development Companies:* Those in pre-sales, product management, functional expertise, and support roles often have many competencies in business analysis. Similar to consulting and contract backgrounds, these professionals will each have a deep and unique skill set. Understanding their true competency set will be important to growing and developing them through a career path.
- Other career backgrounds may also provide a solid foundation for a business analysis career. Backgrounds with a strong balance of analytical and human interaction skills are often worth a further look to determine if competencies fit the organization's business analysis needs.

There are competency overlaps with all of these backgrounds, however, so organizational support for training and mentoring as well as individual knowledge, experience, skills, behaviours, attitudes, and motivations need to be in place to craft each of these potential Business Analysts into a high performer.

# A Business Analysis Career Model

With Business Analysts being critical to an organizations success, providing them a career model becomes a key talent management strategy. In developing a basic business analysis career model, the key components that come into consideration are:

- Job family
- Job levels & job descriptions and expected competencies for each
- Career progression and potential paths
- Process for the BA to review and discuss options, and provide input into their own path
- Process for the organization to evaluate business analysts and to provide feedback and direction on development
- Development options, opportunities, and support that align with required competencies needed in job descriptions

Each of these areas is an important piece to creating a career path in your organization that will have the potential to give your organization and employees the benefits of highly engaged and motivated employees who want to build a career in the organization.

## Job Family

Job families are groupings of jobs that are of similar nature. Business analysis can be a job family itself in an organization. Some related job families that may also be a fit for business analysis: business improvement, business capability enablement, strategic initiatives delivery, and so on. Some organizations have the BA role in a job family with other roles such as project management or application development. Many organizations are discovering that aligning the business analysis role with project management or application development is not meeting the needs of the organization nor the business analysis professionals. Business analysis has a distinct set of knowledge, training, experience, and competencies that are different from project management and application development roles. There may be overlap in the roles and heavy collaboration needed however the focus of each role is completely different. The essence of the BA role and the talents that make one successful are unique.

## Job Levels and Descriptions

As the BA role evolves, the job levels and descriptions do as well. Many organizations are managing Business Analysts with outdated job descriptions and levels. Organizations are finding that what they need their BAs to be doing is not what the job descriptions have specified. This is making the entire talent management process difficult for managers, as it is challenging to recruit, manage professional development, and manage and motivate the needed performance and behaviours while following outdated job descriptions. Both Managers and Business Analysts are in need of more tools to manage BA careers.

Many business analysis job descriptions are narrowly focused on either a specific technology application or business processes; and some focus on tasks versus business value and results. Effective BA job descriptions are centered more on behavioural competencies that drive results and business value versus tasks to be completed.

Business analysis is a knowledge worker role. Similar to lawyers, doctors, and other knowledge professionals, a Business Analyst needs to rely on applying a set of knowledge to complete a variety of tasks that require using, acquiring, and sharing knowledge to successfully perform. Tasks BAs perform have varying inputs and unpredictable circumstances that make the role reliant on the application of knowledge and techniques critical to completing the tasks effectively. Selecting the right knowledge, technique, and behaviour for each situation becomes more important than simply completing a task or deliverable. Successful BAs alter their approach to each work effort to maximize the best results instead of simply completing the task.

There are vast differences in the quality of business analysis work for completed tasks. BAs draw on their knowledge of business analysis techniques, experience, and underlying competencies to perform effectively in their role. Merely completing a requirements specification does not equate solid performance or a high quality requirements document. The BA role is more about the process and techniques used to get the information needed for a requirements package, and packaging that information in a way that makes sense to the audience. A job description that focuses on the responsibility to gather requirements and document them falls short in realizing the true essence of the Business Analyst role. Facilitating and eliciting the discovery of business needs and decomposing those needs into details that enable a solutions implementation may be a better description of what is expected. These are very different ways of looking at one of the most common elements seen in a business analysis job description.

Organizations also struggle to define and implement job levels and descriptions that reward employees for competencies that the organization truly values. Some job levels, descriptions, and reward systems motivate the BA to acquire detailed knowledge of an application's inner workings or to follow a specific and defined task list. This may be effective for some job descriptions in the business analysis job family, however, it does not motivate BAs to facilitate change, identify the root cause, and identify and implement solutions true to the business need.

To begin discovering how to evaluate, create, or update job levels and descriptions, you will need to research and collaborate with others in your organization. Consider getting an advisory group or committee together to discuss and develop answers to the following questions. There is no set standard for this as the roles and needs in each organization are different.

Things to consider when updating or creating job families, descriptions, and levels for Business Analysts:

1. *Job Families, Levels, & Descriptions:*
   - What job family should business analysis professionals belong to?
   - Is a business analysis job family a possibility?
   - How many levels are appropriate for the organization in this job family?
   - At which levels is it appropriate to have multiple roles and job descriptions?
   - At which points in the career path is there an easy transition to another job family (in and out)?

2. *Behaviours and Results:*
   - What behaviours and results create ideal performance in the role and each level?
   - What does success look like in the role at each level?
   - What behaviors do you want to resonate through all talent management processes related to the role?

3. *Knowledge:*
   - Does the description motivate knowledge sharing and flexibility in how knowledge is used?
   - What types of knowledge does the role need and what level of experience using this knowledge? (Knowledge of: standards of the profession, common techniques of the profession, organizational knowledge, industry knowledge, detailed business process or system knowledge).

4. *Autonomy:*
   - How much direction, instruction, and supervision is needed in the role at various levels?
   - Is the BA expected to work independently or under the direction of a more experienced resource?

- What kind of review and direction from others is necessary to complete tasks and get the results needed?
- Is this role and level in a lead role to other Business Analysts?

5. *Scope and Complexity of Work:*
- How large and/or complex of a work effort should this role or level be able to perform effectively?
- How does scope of work and autonomy come together for the role?
- How much ambiguity is this role and level expected to be able to work with?

6. *Experience:*
- How much experience is needed in various tasks with what type of results, autonomy, and complexity to enter into the role and level?
- What types of results, experiences, autonomy, and complexity need to be achieved to look at roles and levels that are next in career?

7. *Rewards:*
- What is the industry range of pay and rewards scale for similar levels of experience, knowledge, autonomy, and complexity of work?
- Does your organization value different types of knowledge or experience? Internal and external knowledge and experience?
- Are the rewards aligned to what knowledge, skills, experience, and behaviours the organization needs to grow, develop, and sustain talent?

8. *Cohesiveness:*
- Does each job level have progressive competency expectations?
- Does each job level have more complex expectations that align to the leadership competencies the organization values as one progresses through the career model?
- Does the career model allow for the organization to value and balance longevity and competency?

9. *Expected Competencies and Behaviours at Level:*
- What competencies and in what context are professionals at this level expected to display?
- What behaviours and in what context are professionals at this level expected to display?
- To what level of detail is your organization comfortable managing behavioural and competency expectations for each job level and description?

The IIBA® BA Competency Model outlines job levels and context information for each level of BA. It also outlines the behavioural-based competencies and results for BA activities in the Knowledge Areas of *BABOK® Guide*. Using these behaviours in combination with the work context outlined in the competency model for each level spells out under what autonomy, supervision, complexity, etc. a BA should be able to successfully achieve.

## Career Progression and Paths

Figure 1 represents a conceptual model of what a business analysis career path may look like. Also depicted are conceptual linkages to related job families like project management, quality assurance, application development, and leadership roles. This visual gives an example of how a business analysis career model can incorporate movement in and out of the business analysis job family, movement up towards leadership levels, and movement laterally within the business analysis job family.

Movement between job levels and job families is depicted with arrows. Many arrows are bidirectional indicating that professionals from each job family may move in and out of the job family with relative ease. An effective career model needs to provide opportunities to enter, leave, make lateral moves, and advance; and the business analysis profession is no different.

Many BAs are frustrated with the career options for advancement. Many organizations have project management as the default option for BA advancement. BAs recognize that the project management competencies and role is very different from that of a BA. They are frustrated that there is not have a path to continue to contribute and grow within the business analysis domain using true business analysis competencies. They are frustrated that a role with so much influence on strategic initiatives can have a non-existent career path for those with advanced level of contributions and skills.

# Entering a Business Analyst Career Path

A business analysis professional may enter the business analysis career path as an Entry Level Business Analyst or at any other level or place in the career path based on competencies developed from within other job families or experience external to the organization.

# Moving Up or Within the Career Model

Business Analysts have different motivations for being in the business analysis career. An effective career path needs to give BAs the options to move up, specialize, or remain a positive contributor while staying at the same place in the career path. Often BAs are great candidates for management positions, they're great individual contributors but they lack options in the career path and end up leave the organization. Many BAs want to remain Business Analysts, doing great work and being rewarded for their experience and contributions.

*Figure 1. BA Career Progression and Paths*

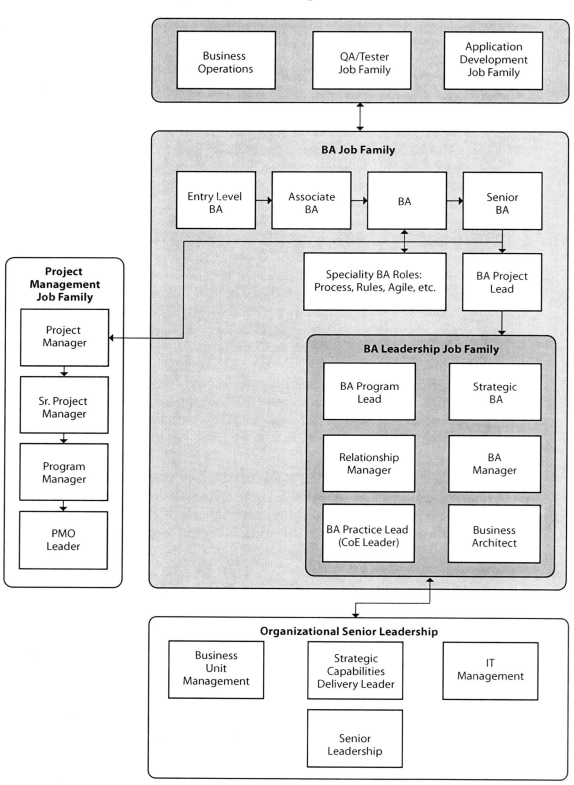

A common challenge that BAs, managers, and organizations face is creating options in career development for BAs after they achieve the Sr. BA level. With the field of business analysis growing in recognition as well as importance, more options for business analysis professionals are evolving. The IIBA° Competency Model v3 identifies a handful of roles for business analysis professionals ready to move beyond a Sr. BA position and take on more challenges in the business analysis domain. The roles are: Business Architect, BA Project Lead, BA Program Lead, BA Practice Leader, Business Relationship Manager, and Strategic Business Analyst. Each of these roles provides an opportunity for a business analysis professional to remain in the business analysis domain while further contributing to the organization. Each role also has a different focus where professionals and organizations can align organizational needs and an employee's strengths and competencies.

There are also career-advancing paths for BAs outside of the business analysis domain. Some common paths may be: Project Management, Product Management, IT Management, Program Management, Business Management, Strategic Initiatives Management, Enterprise Architecture, Business Architecture, and many others. If an employee's desire and talents match to these other job families, how will the organization foster this transition and retain the employee with a high level of engagement?

## Moving Out of the Job Family

An effective career model gives managers and Business Analysts the tools to recognize when the business analysis career path is no longer a best-fit career choice. This is achieved by focusing on behavioural competencies versus tasks. Focusing on behavioural competencies will allow the BA and manager to develop awareness and discuss what competencies, behaviours, strengths, and the development options that are available and align to past, current, and desired future experiences. They will be able to identify, recognize, and reward positive results and behaviours while discussing constructive feedback on desired and undesired results and behaviours. Behavioral models will help BAs and managers identify and leverage the natural strengths and identify if the business analysis career path is the right fit, or if another job role may better leverage the professional's strengths.

A career model is a tool for management and Business Analysts alike; it facilitates many pieces of making Business Analysts and managers successful. One of the many benefits of having a career path is allowing business analysis professionals to have significant input into their own path. This motivating activity for any professional helps keep employee engagement high and gives managers a tool and forum to have critical manager/BA discussions.

## Entry Points to the Business Analyst Career Path— Fitting Existing and New Business Analysts on the Team into a Career Model

Once a career model is established in your organization, those involved in executing on the model need to be comfortable with two scenarios:

1. Determining the fit of the existing team of BAs into the model
2. Determining a process to fit new BAs into the model: job postings, recruitment, interviews, and selection process to align to the model.

The most important question to remain focused on in both scenarios is addressed in the next section.

## Where do Their Competencies Fit into the Model?

It is typical for salary expectations of new hires and the salaries of existing BAs to pose a challenge when aligning competencies, salary expectations, years of experience, and cultural norms into a new competency-based career model. When the model is set up correctly, there should be few discrepancies. Where there are discrepancies, it is important to not deviate from the model but address the competency gaps in development plan processes and also look at specialist and lateral moves outside the career model if a true competency fit is not a possibility.

If the rewards system and career model focus on organizational asset knowledge versus competencies, new resources will be challenged to effectively perform and long-term resources are not motivated to grow new skills. Motivations will align to grow and maintain knowledge versus share and facilitate knowledge. A level playing field of skill development and knowledge sharing versus tenure and knowledge attainment is needed.

When transitioning existing business analysis professionals into a new business analysis career model, the organization and manager need to consider:

- What competencies does the Business Analyst have?
- How do the current competencies align to the new model?
- How can we educate existing business analysis professionals on what a competency- and behavioural-based model is?
- Where in the new model do they expect to be?
- What fears will existing BAs have about the new model?
- How will the organization transition the team into the new model?
- How will the organization handle discrepancies and morale of the team members that are not in agreement with their place in the model in terms of compensation and skill development?
- Is a gradual progression or transition to the new model needed to mitigate the impact of a large change in cases where the current state of competencies and new model are largely divergent?

When bringing new BAs to the team, there are a number of things to think about to ensure you align your team with well-rounded competencies and maintain the career model. The questions a hiring manager needs to consider are:

- What competencies does the potential BA already have?
- In what context have these competencies previously been applied? How will the business analysis context be different for this person on my team?
- What basic training in the role do they need to get started?
- Given their competencies entering the role, what level is the best fit?
- Once a level is determined, what type of work complexity and autonomy is appropriate to ensure positive results and a learning environment?
- How can I, as a manager, track the experiences and competencies the BA is developing so I can manage and build their skills?
- What competencies do they bring to the team that my team currently does not have or is weak in?

Think of entrance criteria for the role this in terms of competencies, scope of work experience, and autonomy. Too often, I see years of experience as criteria and this has many drawbacks. Some Business Analysts with only two years experience have more business analysis knowledge and competencies than those with 30 years experience working on the same application. Both have business analysis competencies, however, one has deep knowledge and may greatly struggle to perform business analysis outside of the context with which they are intimately familiar. The other lacks application specific knowledge but has the business analysis competencies to effectively elicit the knowledge they do not have. How and when Business Analysts learn the business analysis competencies has less to do with years of experience and more to do with what they have done in those years to build competencies and knowledge.

If you are a manager in an organization that rewards and recognizes knowledge in their business analysis career model; and it could be knowledge of the organization, industry, a specific business area, or technology. Some things to consider if your organization rewards based on years of experience and knowledge:

*Questions to consider:*
- Is acquiring knowledge and years of experience alone enough to move in the career model?
- How will the organization ensure that knowledge is shared and not kept only in employee's heads and organizational silos?
- What skills and competencies will this person be missing compared to others at the same level?
- What consistency do stakeholders of the role need from professionals with the same job title and level?

- Are there are career model options that recognize knowledge is important to the organization?
- What knowledge is important to the organization?
- What knowledge will be critical to the organization in the future?
- Is the need for knowledge a human capital need or is there another way to share that knowledge as an organization and motivate other skill-building in the individual?
- Are you willing to reward knowledge over skills and results?

## Supporting Processes for Career Models

An effective career model needs support and alignment from all stakeholders to be a valuable tool that benefits all. The three main components of this support structure are:

*Figure 2. Career Model Support Structure[1]*

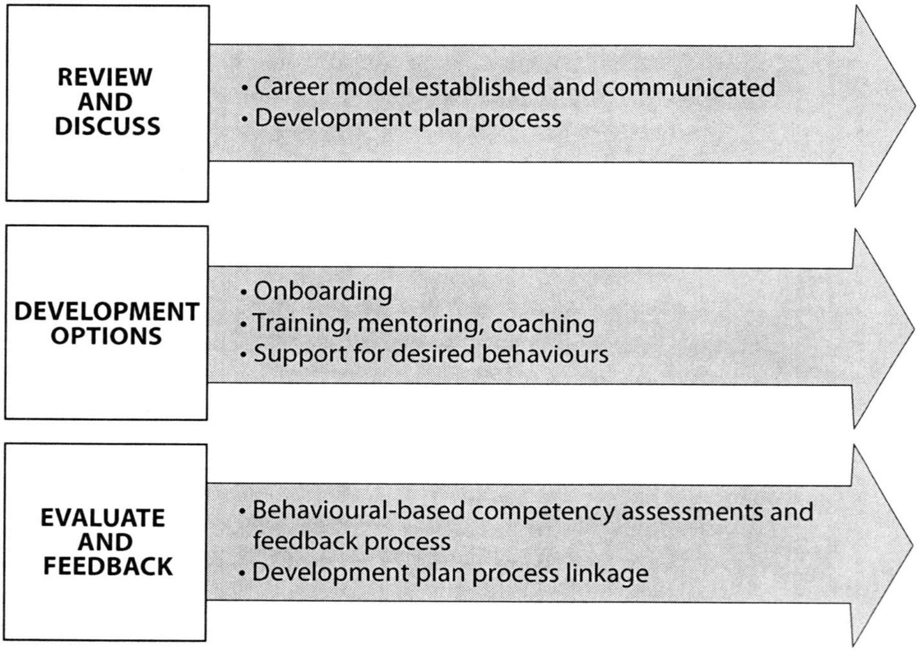

**REVIEW AND DISCUSS**
- Career model established and communicated
- Development plan process

**DEVELOPMENT OPTIONS**
- Onboarding
- Training, mentoring, coaching
- Support for desired behaviours

**EVALUATE AND FEEDBACK**
- Behavioural-based competency assessments and feedback process
- Development plan process linkage

---

1    Wikipedia defines as: Onboarding, also known as *organizational socialization*, refers to the mechanism through which new employees acquire the necessary knowledge, skills, and behaviours to become effective organizational members and insiders (Bauer & Erdogan, 2011). Tactics used in this process include formal meetings, lectures, videos, printed materials, or computer-based orientations to introduce newcomers to their new jobs and organizations. Research has demonstrated that these socialization techniques lead to positive outcomes for new employees such as higher job satisfaction, better job performance, greater organizational commitment, reduction in stress, and intent to quit (Ashford & Black, 1996; Kammeyer-Mueller & Wanberg, 2003; Fisher, 1985).

*Review and Discuss:* Process for the BA to review options, discuss options, and provide input into their own path. To make this support element relevant, the career model must be established and communicated. There must also be a development plan process in place aligned to the career model providing Business Analysts and managers with a tool and framework to use for discussion.

*Development Options:* Development options, opportunities, and support that align with required competencies needed in job descriptions and levels. An onboarding program and process for the business analysis role will help set up a new BA for success. Training programs aligned to build new skills and further develop existing competencies should be aligned to the career model. Include mentoring and coaching programs to allow more senior business analysis professionals a leadership opportunity to mentor others and to provide newer BAs critical relationships, mentoring, and coaching to build competencies.

Assigning BAs to appropriate work efforts also becomes a critical part of supporting development options as part of a career model. Assigning a new BA, with little experience, to the largest and most complex project the organization has done this year and expecting them to perform independently with great results is unrealistic. Assigning an experienced BA to a large and complex project whose competencies rely on detailed system knowledge versus business analysis practice and technique knowledge and expecting high performance levels with great results is another unrealistic expectation. Job and project assignments need to be understood in context to assign the correct resource, skills, competency, and development opportunity for the resource and assignment. Detailed knowledge of a business process or application is not enough competency alignment for a BA to be successful on a large complex effort.

*Evaluation and Feedback:* Process for the BA to self-evaluate and get manager and/or peer feedback on business analysis competencies. Part of this process is the opportunity to discuss competencies with a manager, examples of scenarios to apply competencies, and opportunities to gain and share experience in competencies. Note that this is a separate process from a performance evaluation and salary determination process.

## Creating Momentum for Changes to the BA Job Family

If your organization is looking to update your business analysis career model, you likely need to rely on other peers, leaders, and their acceptance of a change to the model.

*Compelling Reasons for Change:*
- BAs are a pivotal role in the organization that bring strategic priorities into implementation reality
- BAs have a foundational skill set and with experience they can evolve into great leaders for the organization
- The business analysis role is continually changing and evolving as a career and you want your BA to be up-to-date on skills and experience

- Retention of great resources to your organization
- Create high engagement levels

*Signs Change is Needed:*
- Currently a business analysis career model does not exist
- Current business analysis career model rewards knowledge versus competency; not promoting the right skills to help the organization move forward
- Current business analysis career model is aligned to another discipline
- Current business analysis career model job profiles do not match reality of what BAs are actually doing
- Current business analysis career job profiles are task-focused versus results-, behaviours-, and competency-focused
- Current business analysis career model does not allow BAs options to choose to stay in individual contributor role or to grow in leadership and specialize

*Implementing a Career Path or Changes to One*
When looking at developing or changing the business analysis career model for your organization, consider the following in your planning:

- Defining the "What's in it for me?" for all parties impacted
- Develop a change and communication strategy and plan
- Changes to the career model are fear-provoking for both BAs and leaders
- Get buy-in for the new paths from others
- Develop an advisory team with all levels represented
- Competency versus seniority
- Competency assessment process
- Development opportunities for BAs to build competencies

## What's In It for Each Impacted Group?

Like any organizational change, new or rewritten job descriptions and career paths are huge changes for the organization impacting numerous resources. For lasting change and momentum, gain buy-in and support from peers and leaders.

Without a compelling story about what each stakeholder will gain from this change, others will not see the value of using their time and energy to support you. Some ideas to get you started on what's in it for each stakeholder group to help you gain support:

*Other BA Managers:*
- Reduced turnover and retention
- Longevity, performance, continuing development
- Employee engagement levels
- Retention of valued employees who are motivated to advance their careers
- Attracting high quality employees with the opportunity to advance in their desired job family

*Other IT Managers & Leaders:*
- Consistent skills levels and expectations for BAs
- Attract and retain business analysis talent
- Align expectations of roles with other IT roles
- Competency alignment to bring technology closer to the business
- Competency alignment to build better relationships with the business

*Business Leaders:*
- Consistent expectations for the business analysis role
- Competency development for better project delivery
- Development of upcoming leaders for the business, IT, and project delivery

*Human Resources:*
- Support leaders in making informed decisions on compensation, staffing, promotions, and succession planning
- Support for skill development aligned to talent management strategies

*Business Analysts:*
- Career growth opportunities aligned to skills that align to leadership development
- Career growth opportunities aligned to industry standards and competencies for their profession
- Alignment of roles to better support the work they do as BAs
- Rewards and recognition for the competencies that define career, business analysis skills, and experience
- A structure to help determine what development, experience, and competencies are required further develop the BA's career

*Some overarching benefit statements that may resonate with large and diverse stakeholder groups:*
- Higher retention rate of key resources in the organization that understand the organization's business and technology capabilities
- Stronger engagement from a team of employees who can directly influence strategic initiatives
- Motivated BAs with an established path to grow
- Options for BAs to move inside the organization and to share skills and knowledge across the enterprise
- Consistency in the BA role throughout the organization
- Alignment of job profiles to the strategy of the organization
- Development of self-awareness of career fit
- Alignment of rewards to motivate consistent and desired behaviours
- Alignment of recruitment and selection processes
- Succession planning for organizational leadership positions; position BAs to be part of succession planning; alignment to leadership development planning.
- Alignment to individual development plans, goals, and training

## Monitoring the Effectiveness of a Career Path

Once you have developed or made changes to the business analysis career model, it is important to monitor the effectiveness. Know and accept that you will make changes and continue to evolve the model as the organization responds. Also, expect to move some employees around that were potentially misplaced in the implementation of the new career path.

To monitor the new career model, like the planning process, rely on an advisory group to help determine how to measure and improve.

Some questions that may help guide how you and the advisory team when monitoring the effectiveness of the career path:

- What were some of the unexpected benefits from various stakeholder perspectives on the career model?
- What expected benefits have materialized, formally and anecdotally?
- What unexpected challenges have arisen? What can we do to prepare better for those challenges moving forward?
- How is change management progressing for the employees impacted by the new model? What are their concerns and areas of excitement?
- What benefits have we experienced from a behavioural competency-based model?

# Summary

More and more organizations are realizing the benefits the Business Analyst role brings to the organization. Organizations that wish to fully leverage the BA role need to develop a career model that empowers business analysis professionals to grow in their careers. Organizations need to provide them with a career model, career path, and development options to support growth in the business analysis domain. A career model becomes a vital tool for BAs and mangers alike.

Organizations that provide a comprehensive career model for business analysis professionals will benefit from higher employee engagement, resulting in increased productivity and higher retention rates. Organizations can also benefit by positioning the business analysis career model in their overall talent management strategy and align the role to leadership succession planning.

Business analysis is a knowledge worker role that depends largely on a set of knowledge and critical skills in facilitating the usage, application, and sharing of that knowledge. Organizations that are able to shape the business analysis role to facilitate the sharing and empowerment of knowledge will see greater benefits from the role.

Business analysis work assignments need to be aligned to a professional's competency level and development plans if at all possible. This allows the BA to effectively practice and gain experience in the needed skills, fosters knowledge worker mentality, and motivates both the manager and BA to align experiences and development discussions towards the career path and competency development.

Developing a behavioural competency-based career model is significant to moving towards a knowledge-sharing culture. Behavioural competency-based job descriptions and levels allow the organization to motivate and empower the behaviours critical to the organization's success and role alignment. Management of a behavioural competency-based career model allows for a mechanism to expect and deliver feedback on critical behaviours for success as well as enable positive development discussions.

# About the Author

Angela Wick, CBAP, PMP, is a Business Analysis Consultant and Trainer with deep experience developing business analysis best practices, business analysis communities and centers of practice, practice and competency assessments, business analysis improvement initiatives, and business analysis curriculum. Through these experiences, she has gained considerable exposure to and experience in assisting organizations with the development and updating of career models for business analysis professionals. Angela is passionate about improving the value Business Analysts bring to organizations and is in tune to balancing risk, organizational readiness, and human change management.

Angela serves as a volunteer for IIBA® as the IIBA® Competency Model Product Manager and Committee Chair. In this role, Angela leads a global committee in the development of the IIBA® Competency Model.

Angela resides in Minneapolis, Minnesota where she enjoys playing tennis, running, and cooking for family and friends.

# BUILDING A BUSINESS CASE FOR BUSINESS ANALYSIS

By Courtlan Telford, CBAP

## Step 0: Know the Basics

### What is a Business Case?

Isn't it an old saying that you have to spend money to make money? If companies make more money than they spend, that's the bottom line of success. The secret to that success is spending money on the things that in turn make the company money, right? Most companies have a long list of things that they can choose to spend money on. A business case outlines a particular investment and its return on the company's bottom line, thus giving decision makers the information they need to determine if the investment is worth it. The investment may aim to generate revenue. For example, a coffee shop may decide to invest in building a drive-thru. The additional planned revenue from new customers may justify the upfront cost of construction. A business case may also outline an investment that plans to save the company money. For example, an apartment complex may decide to replace aging water heaters with new energy efficient models. The long-term savings in energy bills may justify the initial cost of the upgrades.

A business case may be a formal document or informal presentation but, in the end, it must persuade the audience to say 'yes' to the investment. The author of the business case is usually the requester of funds or leader of an organization. The audience is usually a management team or financial decision maker. For example, a Director of Product Development at a shipping company may present a business case for building a mobile application to give customers tracking capabilities from their wireless phone. The executive team of the shipping company would most likely evaluate this investment along with other new product ideas and determine which should move forward.

### Why Do I Need a Business Case for Business Analysis?

New technologies have a lot of impact in the marketplace but there are many costs to developing them. One of those costs is the manpower to manage IT projects and translate information from the user community to the technical community. The Business Analyst role assumes the responsibility of this information translation and is becoming an essential component to the success of IT projects. This role costs money and is often confused with other project roles. Leaders of organizations without resources that focus on business analysis may find themselves in a position of creating a business case to present the need for this role on IT projects. A business case is usually the best way to present the information to the designated decision maker, offering bottom line persuasion and demonstrating how spending money can in turn make or save money.

# How Do I Create a Business Case for Business Analysis?

A business case for business analysis should outline the purpose and plan for including the role of the Business Analyst. The format should be simple and should include the following components:

- *Foundation:* Overall Vision, Goals & Objectives
- *Problem Analysis:* Current State, Facts & Figures
- *Solution Proposal:* Organization, Plan for Action, Alternatives
- *Enterprise Advantage:* Bottom Line Factors, Benefits, Risk

Each component of the business case is necessary to tell the complete story to decision makers. Don't skip a key section. It important to be organized, to include real facts, and to record only organizational specific information. Don't waste time on information that isn't necessary to make a decision. Most decision makers have limited availability and will review information quickly. Offer a concise and clear business case for business analysis so the leadership can make an efficient and informed decision.

Writing a business case for business analysis may seem challenging at the start but following this simple five step process will break the tasks down into more manageable pieces. These steps will help to sort through the myriad of details and focus on the most important points for the designated decision makers.

# Step 1: Build a Foundation for Business Analysis

## Articulate Overall Vision

As with any persuasive story or selling process, it is important to articulate the overall vision. Incorporating a business analysis function in an enterprise must support the company's mission and offer a strategy for improving the company's performance and position. How will IT projects benefit from a business analysis organization? How will better IT projects impact the company's bottom line and time to market? For example, "The time has arrived to increase our IT project success by maturing our business analysis practices, introducing cost savings, higher user satisfaction, and competitiveness in the marketplace. Is this measureable?"

## Identify Goals & Objectives

It is important to hit the highlights of the initiative early on. What are the goals and objectives for realizing the overall vision? This may be a narrative or a bulleted list of what needs to be tackled. This is where the decision makers see the first glimpse into the real requests so take caution when creating this list. For example, a list of goals and objectives for the initiative might be:

- *People:* Build a Centre of Excellence for Business Analysis
- *Process:* Supporting a Business Analyst role on all large IT projects
- *Tools:* Incorporate software package for requirements management and business process modeling

## Find Sponsor

It is essential to have a Sponsor support the business case for business analysis. This person does not necessarily have to be the author of the business case but rather the planned support system and champion for the business analysis discipline and/or organization. This is most likely a member of a management or executive team. The business case should be reviewed with the Sponsor as it is developed. It may be beneficial to have this person present the final business case to the designated decision makers.

# Step 2: Understand the Problem

## Assess Current State

The first step to offering a particular solution is to understand the problem that it will solve. The problem is usually found in the current state of the IT organization, IT project pipeline, the Software Development Lifecycle, and/or feedback from the user community. Assess each one of these factors and choose the most appropriate or significant limitation to support the need for business analysis. Remember that the decision makers will be most concerned with the bottom line so focus on how each of these factors affects the company level financials.

## IT Organization

Examine how the organization is structured in reference to business analysis activities. Do application teams have dedicated staff for gathering requirements and talking to stakeholders? Are they trying to do both jobs? Are there specific teams that are charged with doing business analysis but they are not trained or fully functional? It's possible that several teams are doing business analysis but they are not consistent with their methods or software tools. What is the leadership situation? Is there a dedicated manager or leader advocating the business analysis discipline and investing in the right resources?

Identify which disciplines in the organization *are* at an effective competency level and illustrate why business analysis needs attention. For example, an IT organization may have a dedicated team of Project Managers who are drifting from excellence in project management because they get interrupted doing sideline business analysis work.

## IT Project Pipeline

Assess the current state of the IT project pipeline. This is always a good indicator of organized chaos in the business analysis discipline. How many projects are waiting to get started? How are the scope boundaries of the project requests? If there is a jam of projects waiting in line to be looked at by technical resources, this may indicate a need for the project initiation and enterprise analysis activities which are most typically owned by a business analysis team. If projects are not scoped well initially, it is difficult to prioritize multiple projects and properly estimate timelines. Are multiple projects impacting the same applications or processes? This may be an indicator that business analysis activities at the enterprise level could help segment projects more effectively by understanding dependencies and cross-functional impacts. If most projects in the pipeline are an unreasonable size, it could indicate a need for enterprise analysis activities to form projects with more achievable sizes.

## Software Development Lifecycle (SDLC)

Regardless of the type of SDLC supported (e.g. waterfall, iterative), communication lines may fail between the users and the developers. Understand the relationships between roles in the current SDLC and where the lines of communication are failing. If the SDLC is documented, identify gaps that could be filled with business analysis. If the SDLC is undocumented or poorly documented, research which activities *are* occurring and the role that each person is responsible for. It will become apparent that business analysis is missing or lacking in focus. Research the deliverables produced by the developers. Do they understand the consumer's point of view? If the deliverables, roles, or processes for communicating with the developers are not consistent, this will present a need to mature the business analysis discipline.

## User Community

The true test of IT project success is the report card from the user community. Gather feedback from business project sponsors and users. What are they saying about the process to get work done in IT? Is it difficult to communicate? Are they saying the same thing to multiple people for the same project? Determine if the users are happy with the implemented solutions. If they indicate that IT doesn't understand what they need, it may be an indicator for business analysis.

## Capture Metrics

As with all research, information must be presented with facts or numbers to know that it is reliable and meaningful. After assessing the current state, assemble the most significant metrics to prove the need for business analysis. Use numbers and facts. Don't use vague statements. For example, instead of "users are not happy with IT projects," utilize survey results such as "55% of the user community that interacted with IT last year felt their needs were misunderstood." There is more credibility with a statistic and it shows that there was some diligence used rather than just opinion gathered. Another example would be "After reviewing twenty-five IT projects, it was found that requirements deliverables were delivered to the same application team in ten different formats." Numbers like this give some context to how big the problem is but still reflects an ability to solve the problem.

# Step 3: Propose Solution for Business Analysis

## Outline the Immediate Actions

Once the problem is identified, it's time to outline the solution and explain how business analysis will reduce or eliminate the problems identified in the previous section. The first step is to determine the immediate requirements to put business analysis into action. This may include plans for leadership, resources, training, organization restructuring, and pilot projects. Be specific about what is needed and describe how the change will solve the problem. It is important to have a firm and decisive plan. The plan should demonstrate confidence that the proposed solution will actually change the current state in a positive direction, influencing the bottom line of the company.

## Leadership

The most important immediate action is to select the right leader for the business analysis function. This may be an existing member of management that has passion and knowledge of business analysis or it may be a position that needs to be filled by an external resource. If the leader is an existing member of management, they will most likely be involved in the creation of the business case. If the position needs to be filled, it will be important to present a sense of urgency in order to be effective in a rollout of business analysis.

## Resources

Dedicated staff is needed to perform business analysis functions. It is important that the resource needs for the immediate future are identified. This may include hiring new staff or utilizing existing staff. The business case should be specific about the number of resources that are needed. Based on the current IT project pipeline, what is the minimum amount of manpower needed to be successful? The initial plan may need to include time to survey the existing staff for business analysis competencies and to select the appropriate resources based on those findings.

## Training

It is imperative that an ample amount of ramp-up time be allocated to train the selected resources. Adequate analysis must be performed to determine if this training will be facilitated in-house or if an external vendor will be needed. Perform early research on the training courses, costs, and availability. Include specifics about the planned training.

## Software Tools

Based on the assessment of the current state, it may be determined that software tools are necessary to jump-start or mature the business analysis discipline. This may or may not be a part of the immediate actions necessary. Weigh the cost of incorporating software tools and when it would be appropriate to do so. It may be more important to purchase training on how to elicit quality requirements versus implementing a requirements management tool. If software tools are a must, then they should be included as part of the immediate actions.

## Organization/Restructuring

It is important to make initial decisions on how the business analysis resources will be organized. If organization changes are needed, include this in the proposed solution. Don't recommend organization change without first being sure to understand how the change will help solve the problem. Time is money in business; therefore, time used to reorganize will obviously affect the overall goals and objectives.

## Pilot Projects

The proposed solution may also include a target list of pilot projects to utilize the newly identified business analysis resources or tools. If possible, select a pilot project that is similar in size and complexity to a struggling current project. This will help the decision makers identify with the pain of the current project. Describe how changes to the pilot project will assist in dissolving this pain.

## Knowing When Success has Been Met

Be sure to include how the company will know when the problem has been solved. Use metrics from the current state as the measures for improvement. The proposed plan may include a repeated survey of the same current state measures after some time has passed. It is important for the decision makers to know that the success of the solution can be measured in a concrete way.

# Step 4: Prove the Enterprise Advantage of Business Analysis

## Determine Cost

Decision makers are concerned with one thing at this point: how much is this going to cost? The heart of the business case is proving that the financial investment of a business analysis function will in turn reduce long-term IT project costs and improve the company's bottom line. It may be helpful to have two perspectives on the cost of business analysis. The first is focused on a per project cost. What percentage of the IT project cost will business analysis consume? The second leans more on resource cost as a whole. Considering the total planned resources, determine what the overall cost will be on an annual basis. This number may seem small in comparison to the total annual budget for IT projects. Putting those numbers side by side can help illustrate an enterprise perspective. It is also important to include any upfront costs, such as costs for training or software tools, as well as any ongoing maintenance and support costs.

## Determine ROI

After outlining the costs, it's time to prove that those costs are worth it. Determine the Return on Investment (ROI) for establishing business analysis in the enterprise. Perform research to determine where the bottlenecks of costs are on IT projects. Recruit someone from the finance area to support the validity of the numbers. For example, calculate the cost of problem tickets or production support activities resulting from post implementation of new projects. The dollars spent upfront in analysis may be much less than the sum of a backlog of problem tickets. Another avenue is to research how many projects never finished or were canceled. Find out why those projects failed. If it was due to lack of understanding or poor scope definition, calculate the wasted time and compare it to the cost of performing proper analysis. The bottleneck of costs may be a factor even before the project even starts. How many projects are waiting to get started due to lack of enterprise analysis and prioritization? If any of these projects are adding new products or customer-facing capabilities, compute the cost of the time to market delay. The ROI should be gleaned from company specific measures. It's good to reference industry-wide metrics for the success of IT projects but the best reference for decision makers will be from within the company's measures.

## Non-Financial Benefits

Determine the non-financial benefits of establishing business analysis in the enterprise. These might be things such as career opportunities and employee retention, higher satisfaction among the user community, and better relationships between non-technical and technical staff. There are many wins to having more successful IT projects. Listen to the company culture and understand what is causing pain. If the proposed solution addresses the pain point, include it as a non-financial benefit.

## Identify Risks of Changing

There are always risks to implementing something new or changing the way people work together. Identify any organizational risks that may surface in a changed environment. Identify any risks with project work. Adding a new role to a SDLC or changing a deliverable format always causes some stirring and initial confusion. Call out awareness to those factors.

## Identify Risks of Staying the Same

There may be more risk to the company if the decision is to remain the same. Communication will continue to decline and projects will follow the same failing path. It is important to understand what risks are present now and how they may multiply if no action is taken. Make the decision makers aware of how the trends will continue if business analysis is not established as a core discipline.

# Step 5: Communicate Business Case

## Determine Audience

It is crucial to know who the audience is for the business case. The audience will determine what type of format is used and how it is presented or published. The audience should be the management team or financial decision makers.

## Document Steps 1–4 in Appropriate Format

Once all the information is gathered, document the business case in an appropriate format. If the audience is an executive team, it probably makes sense to create summary slides with quick reference visuals and bullet lists. These slides should be geared for an in-person presentation or discussion. If the audience is a group of people or a remote organization, it might be better to distribute a document with a more narrative format. If the audience is unknown at this point, the format might not be as important as documenting the information for later use.

## Present/Publish Business Case

The final step is to present or publish the business case. Ensure the credibility of the presentation or publication by making the author accessible. Don't just send the documentation and disappear. Expect questions and be available to answer them.

Be sure to include the sponsor and selected leader in any presentations (they may be the presenter). It is likely that a decision cannot be made immediately following a presentation or distribution so plan to follow-up with the audience in an appropriate manner.

## Final Thoughts

Don't let the task of building a business case for business analysis scare you. Be forward-thinking and focus on the company's bottom line in all areas. Stay attuned to the company's mission and goals throughout the process. Be bold and communicate with confidence. Business analysis is a beneficial discipline to IT projects but it does require spending money and we all know that you have to spend money to make money, right?

## About the Author

Courtlan Telford is a Principal Consultant and CBAP' with PrimoPoint Consulting, Inc. in Overland Park, KS. She has extensive experience in enterprise analysis, process modeling, user interface design, and Requirements gathering. Courtlan excels in customizing business analysis deliverables for each project, making them simple and usable for the right audience. She has had a lot of experience with implementing software tools for business analysis teams,  as well as training and mentoring junior Business Analysts. In her personal time, Courtlan enjoys the creative arts, participating in a variety of music and theatre events.

# ESTABLISHING BUSINESS ANALYSIS IN AN ENTERPRISE

By Nan Schaefer, CBAP

Companies invest in what brings them value. Many companies today are investing in business analysis practices. They are recognizing the value that business analysis resources can bring to their software development and process improvement initiatives by bridging the gap between the business and technical departments. This support includes identifying business problems, defining business processes, and communicating comprehensive requirement specifications *before* designing solutions.

Establishing a business analysis practice can take many different forms. It can be a dedicated team whose role is to focus on analysis or an existing employee within the business or development organization who takes on the role in addition to other responsibilities. One emerging trend is to establish a Business Analysis Centre of Excellence (BACoE) to establish BA processes, conduct training, and oversee results. What is a Centre of Excellence (CoE)? It sounds a bit intimidating but basically it's a *team of people that promote collaboration using best practices around a specific focus area to drive business results.* The BACoE is a team dedicated to promoting business analysis to drive business results. In the past, enterprises have successfully established Project Management centres (usually called Project Management Offices) to promote higher standards for managing projects. Having seen positive results in project management, companies are now applying that same focus to business analysis.

Why are companies so interested in increasing their competency in business analysis? With the enormous cost associated with development and transformation projects, companies are looking to work smarter, not harder. They understand that business as usual will continue to get them results as usual. How bad is it?

- Software projects have a 32% success rate compared to 35% from the previous study in 2006 and 16% in 1994. (The Standish Group International, Inc.)
- 50% of projects are rolled back out of production. (Gartner)
- Research has shown that business analysis practices can directly impact these dismal numbers through a consistent and pro-active approach to analysis and requirements. This research represents input from companies worldwide and across multiple industries.
- An estimated 60–80% of project failures can be attributed directly to poor requirements gathering, analysis, and management. (Meta Group)
- Poorly defined applications have led to a persistent miscommunication between business and IT that largely contributes to a 66% project failure rate

for these applications, costing U.S. businesses at least $30 billion every year. (Forrester Research)[1]

Reducing the number of failed or late projects can mean tens of thousands to millions of dollars to a company. Think about these statistics within your own enterprise. Companies are desperate to reap more benefits from complex projects and leverage their development budgets.

# Getting Started

If you've done the due diligence on establishing a business analysis practice and received "thumbs up" for the business case, then you're ready for the next step. But before jumping in, put that business analysis hat on and treat this initiative like you would any other project.

This section outlines some important considerations when starting your business analysis practice. Our intent is to share insight and lessons learned to aid you on your journey.

## Focus

First things first—just as in any successful project, identifying your goals and objectives and putting deadlines to them will enable you to know at the end of the day if your efforts have been successful. Start with understanding the business challenge. If you have multiple areas for improvement, prioritize them to tackle the one with the biggest payback first. Once you zero in on the area you need to tackle, you can create the objectives that will drive this effort. Being able to articulate both the business problem and your response to it will help you build the right solution for your situation.

The following table gives some examples of common business problems and proposed BA solutions:

### FIGURE 1. COMMON BUSINESS CONCERNS

| If Business Problem is | Practice Might Focus |
| --- | --- |
| Projects are over time/budget primarily because of misunderstood or poorly defined requirements? | Requirements development and management |
| Projects starting, then getting cancelled due to competing priorities? | Feasibility studies and assisting in preparing business cases |
| A merger/acquisition requiring entities to select and adopt common systems and processes? | Documenting the business architecture |

---

1    Hass, Kathleen B. *Business Analysis Centre of Excellence: The Cornerstone of Business Transformation.* Management Concepts (2007): http://stlouis.theiiba.org/download/BACoE.pdf

Being able to clearly articulate your objectives in a charter can be used as a rallying call for the enterprise; use it to get other teams behind your efforts. Remember, a business analysis practice cannot create change by itself, it requires the support of all impacted stakeholder organizations to be successful.

It takes time for change to be adopted and to become part of a corporate culture. Make sure your deadlines are realistic and doable. Setting up the practice may happen relatively quickly but it takes time to see results. The establishment of business analysis best practices needs to become a part of the culture and practiced by all organizations. Change is adopted starting within the practice and continues to spread outwards to groups with which the practice interacts. Success happens when all teams accept the processes of the practice.

## Executive Support

When making organizational changes, it pays to have friends in high places—the higher, the better. It's critical to the success of this endeavor to have senior executive support and to have it on both sides—business and IT. These champions will help build the momentum while the organization is getting set up and then keep the organization alive during its fledgling years.

It's important to keep your champion informed of progress, sharing success stories along the way. The group's livelihood may depend on it. Encourage your executive champion to communicate frequently about the progress of the initiative, reiterating the corporate as well as their personal commitment.

All teams will be very interested in the progress of the new practice since it will impact their world. There will be people in the company who are on board from the beginning but be prepared for the majority of people to be skeptical. They'll question why the change is needed and if it can achieve any real improvement. Companies have become somewhat 'shell shocked' by what they consider to be constant change. Your job is to break through that apathy and create a sustainable change that will become part of the corporate culture and produce real results. Unfortunately, you'll have the weight of all those failed attempts on your shoulders as you try to achieve this.

As important as executive support is to the new practice, just remember it only gets you started. It's not a substitute for results. When setting up a business analysis practice, you must deliver results to ensure adoption and acceptance by the entire organization.

## Measuring Progress

When building the business case for the practice you might have defined some metrics. Make sure what you measure is meaningful. After all we become what we measure, therefore be sure to measure the right thing. If we measure the wrong things, we encourage the wrong behavior. For example, if we are solely focused on reducing cycle times in a project, that's exactly what will happen. We will focus on doing it quickly and not necessarily with quality.

Here are some additional points to consider when developing metrics:

- Build the collection of metrics into the Business Analyst processes. Trying to measure them after they occur is very difficult and no one ever has the time to go back. Try to build your processes so they capture the data needed to generate metrics as you execute the process.
- Make the metrics bulletproof. Don't be caught with slip-shod numbers that can easily be disputed or distrusted. Questionable numbers will not help the credibility of a new practice.
- Communicate loudly and broadly every time there is an improvement in one of the measurements. Success for the new practice is success for the entire company.
- Measure your baseline (the current state) before you implement any improvements. After all, if no one knows how bad it was in the beginning, they won't appreciate the improvement.

## Communicating Results

As with any change that affects the culture of a company, it doesn't happen overnight. Since changes in how we do analysis are only measurable after we're done, it's going to take awhile before the numbers come in—especially if you start with large, strategic initiatives. Be patient. The important thing is to take victories along the way if possible. Don't go dark on communications; companies need to know things are moving in the right direction, even if the final results will not be in for some time. Metrics that substantiate improvements will be a weapon to use in the massive PR campaign that you have to wage while setting up new processes and organizations.

# Setting up the Practice

The following are thoughts on setting up the practice and getting it operational. There is no prescribed order or priority but each is intended to help you to make decisions.

What is the scope and approach for the new practice? As discussed earlier, knowing what problem the new practice is trying to solve will aid in defining the scope. It's generally easier for a new practice to start with a limited scope and add other functions as the practice matures. Phasing in functions gives the new practice a chance to gain experience while leveraging early successes to increase their charter over time. After all, Rome wasn't built in a day.

Once the scope of the practice has been decided, then it becomes a question of "how" the new practice will organize to achieve the objectives. There are many factors to consider. For example, when considering a dedicated Business Analyst role, think about the skill sets of the available resources—*will existing teams be able to take on the additional responsibilities of the Business Analyst or are the roles too diverse*? On the other hand, if you are thinking about creating a centralized practice with a dedicated Business Analyst role, you need to consider the amount of change that your organization can tolerate—*will other teams view the new practice as diminishing their responsibilities? Is it just another change on top of all the others?*

There are many approaches to setting up a new business analysis practice:

- Establish a business analysis governance organization, responsible for defining BA role, standards, and governance for projects
- Establish a centralized team whose role is to perform requirements development and management functions
- Establish a federated model with the BA role performing requirements development and management functions within existing groups

Don't forget to do your homework. Ask other roles and organizations for their input when deciding this. Their support will be crucial and their input invaluable. When building a practice, start small, quickly achieve successes, and build based upon need.

Once you have established the approach for the new practice, where is it best placed in the enterprise, in the business or IT organization? And once that's decided, should it be a dedicated, centralized team or one that is federated out within existing organizations. There are no easy answers to these questions, it's dependent on each company's specific situation.

You may want to consider the following when trying to decide what's right for you:

- Will the new practice be assigned to projects or providing governance over projects?
- Is there already an Enterprise Project Management Office in place? If so, would it make sense to co-locate the practice there, possibly changing group's name to show the enlarged scope (e.g. Business Change Office)
- Which organization is providing executive support?
- Is the IT organization more progressive in adopting new processes? If so, it might be the place to start.

If the new practice is a dedicated team, always place the new organization as high in the company as possible. This helps give it some political clout to challenge the status quo and implement needed changes.

## Building the Team

There are many important aspects when setting up a business analysis practice. Among the first steps is ensuring you have the right people in the right positions.

Putting leadership in place is foundational. Their job will be to take the conceptual (business case) and make it operational. No small feat. Remember, they'll be on the frontline of change, which can be a challenging place to be. Select someone adept at negotiating but tenacious in getting the job done.

Once leadership decisions have been made, one of their first tasks is to resource the practice. So, what is the right skill set for Business Analysts? The charter will outline the functions of the new organization and that in turn should determine the skill sets needed. Some thoughts to keep in mind:

- Actual BA work experience should always be further examined, since the role varies widely.
- Can the BA work in an ambiguous environment? Analysis is about figuring things out, which means there's generally a lot of ambiguity to deal with.
- Does the BA have strong facilitation and negotiation skills? The BA role is about collaborating while leading the stakeholders through analysis.
- Strong business acumen is a necessity. BAs need to understand how a business runs.

Look for people with a mixture of passion and knowledge but who know how to get the job done. One is not good without the other. When staffing the new organization, make it a small but powerful team. It's best to start with a few "A" players. Look for the willing and the able, with stress on the "able"—they need to be good to give the new organization a good showing right out of the gate. Early successes are important for new practices; many don't survive long enough to prove their value. Don't be just another failed attempt. Get in and get going!

## Defining the Processes

Your charter should already have decided this but consider starting with requirements, it usually is the area easiest to start with and where help is generally welcome. Once you know the objective of the practice then you can start building your process and procedures.

Whenever possible a practice should integrate rather than invent new processes. Examine processes already in place. What is the smallest change that the new organization can make that will have the largest payback? In starting, you want to be as non-invasive as possible. The burden of the new processes should rest primarily on the BA role and impact other roles as little as possible. Enthusiasm dampens when people hear about a new process that piles another thing on their plate. Realizing that Business Analyst practices are heavily dependent on stakeholder involvement, the art is to make it easy for them and still get what you need.

It's always a good idea to pilot new processes, seeking feedback from all stakeholders along the way. Piloting with a small team allows you to easily modify your processes as you go. Listen to the feedback and build upon what works and throw out what doesn't.

Leadership must measure to ensure that the new practice is delivering on its promises and that the processes in place are adding value. This is where those metrics that were defined earlier will be helpful. They point out any adjustments or fine-tuning that is needed. The business analysis leadership needs to solicit feedback from the Business Analysts and stakeholders to keep abreast of progress or the lack thereof.

### Choosing the Tools

Just remember and keep repeating—A tool is NOT a process, a tool is NOT a process. It's one of the most common mistakes made by start-up organizations. If you don't have your processes defined, no tool will do it for you. After all "a fool with a tool is still a fool". Start with a process and keep it simple. Graduate to a tool when you have the need, not just because you have the money.

Always start with the tools at hand. For instance, Microsoft® Office applications are more than sufficient to get you started. These can take you a long way; they allow you to work out the kinks in your processes. You can set-up templates within each tool to standardize how the practice uses the tools. You don't need the headache of implementing and learning a new tool while you're defining your processes and setting up the practice.

You'll know when it's time to move on to more sophisticated tools. A few indicators that you may need to invest in more robust tools are:

- Traceability of requirements. It's taking too long and it's too cumbersome. A tool can help with linking requirements and generating different views for reporting.
- Reusing and sharing of process diagrams. A tool with a repository and configuration management will make sharing easier.
- Quality checks on analysis deliverables. A repository and naming standards will aid in the quality review process.

Requirements development and management tools should be incremental thoughts, not foundational to start up activities. Give yourself time to figure out what you need before you jump in and buy. It can be an expensive mistake if you buy tools before understanding what you need.

## Ready, Set, Execute!

Okay, you've found your place in the organization, the team is getting staffed, the processes are defined, and you're plugged into the pipeline. Get started! Don't wait until everything is perfect, it never will be so you just have to start anyway. Get going and adjust as you go. The company needs the improvements that the business analysis practice will bring them, and they need it now. Look to get some early wins and build on that. Always work with a sense of urgency.

Communication should be occurring as you do each of the steps outlined above. It's as important as all the steps you go through to get going. Be sure you are communicating and training all organizations that are involved in the development life cycle. Almost every organization is impacted by development initiatives and they all need to understand what the Business Analyst's role is and how their roles interact. Communicate often and on a regular basis, once is not enough. It takes a lot of communication for change to become part of a company's culture. You'll want these organizations as your allies and they all have an active role in producing positive results.

Tailor your communications to your audience. Stakeholders who are directly involved in projects require a different level of communication than executive management. Recruit all members of the practice (as well as the executive sponsor) to deliver communications to the groups they interact with and develop a communications plan which shows:

- Audience (IT or business organizations, Operational groups , Executive Management, etc.)
- The frequency of communication (weekly, monthly, quarterly, etc.)
- The channels (all hands, team meetings, email, newsletter, etc.)

## What's Next?

For practical reasons, if your practice couldn't tackle all the functions wanted in its start-up, how do you know when it's time to expand the practice to take on some of those other responsibilities? Consider some of the following when making your decision:

- Build upon successes. If your team has achieved some positive results, that's a good indication that they're mastering what they're doing. It's good to build upon that foundation to expand into more functions.
- Receiving a mandate from the people. Project stakeholders and upper management have realized the value of business analysis and are now strong supporters of what the practice does. They want Business Analysts involvement in other areas.
- Is there an urgent business need? The company may be going through some kind of transformation (merger, new line of business, etc.) and there is an urgent need for Business Analysts to lead the effort. Timing is everything; recognize an opportunity and act!

It may feel at times that you are more of a salesperson than a Business Analyst but it is critical to the practice to constantly evangelize the purpose, the process, and success stories. The Business Analyst role can make a huge difference in an organization, but it cannot do it alone. Success happens when the Business Analyst and the stakeholders work together. One cannot succeed without the other.

## In Summary

- Get strong executive sponsorship
- Establish metrics which will best chart the practice's progress
- Find the best fit for the practice—be it within the Business or IT organization
- Select leadership with the qualities that can take on this type of a challenge
- Focus on creating a small but powerful team
- Define the optimum processes, integrating into the current SDLC
- Get started executing, act with a sense of urgency
- Communicate and train at every opportunity
- Evangelize!

A Business Analysis practice is a game changing play. It takes some of the unpredictability out of software development and process improvement projects. Any time you take on the task of changing a culture, you need to be prepared for a journey. It's not a short trip. It takes time and it's hard work, but it can reap huge benefits for an organization. Welcome aboard!

# About the Author

Nan Schaefer is a Principal Consultant and CBAP® with PrimoPoint Consulting in Overland Park, Kansas. She has an extensive background in defining business analysis activities within software development environments and projects. Prior to co-founding PrimoPoint in 2009, Nan worked for several Fortune 500 companies, holding a broad range of positions. Her responsibilities included managing large programs, leading complex analysis efforts, and developing start-up organizations. Nan specializes in integrating and right-sizing Business Analyst functions within a company's existing software development process.

# INCREASE PERFORMANCE THROUGH A COMMUNITY OF PRACTICE

By Julian Sammy

*A manager's guide to increasing performance by integrating a self-sustaining, continuously improving Busniness Analyst Community of Practice into your group and your organization.*

You manage a group of Business Analysts with a mandate to deliver business analysis services—and you have to deliver. You are measured against significant key performance indicators and are responsible for creating a culture and environment that encourages your staff. Certainly, there are many things outside your control, such as enterprise standards and human resources policies. It is your challenge to work within these limits and still meet your objectives. You care about delivering value but you're measured and rewarded for the performance of your team.

You believe that your BAs can create both value and performance—and they can—but you may not be sure how to use them to best effect. Why do they demand so much time and effort for requirements, when they can get the job done in whatever time they're given on a project schedule? What would they do with the extra time? How do you help them be more effective? How should you deploy them to best effect? Can you give them space where needed and boundaries that will reduce risk and increase consistency and quality?

A mature Community of Practice (CoP) is one tool to help you drive performance and to help your team help itself. In this chapter, we discuss communities of practice from a manager's perspective, using an evidence-based management approach. We consider the CoP as an agent for change, for both individual BAs and the organization.

In the first part of this chapter, *What is a Community of Practice*, we describe the kinds of impact a CoP can have on your organization and the stakeholders who will need to be engaged in these changes. The second section, *Performance and the Community of Practice* explores the complex relationship between a CoP, individual competency, organizational maturity, and performance. A CoP can increase performance but significant improvements require a mature active CoP. The last section, *Which CoP is right for me?* examines how to implement a CoP in your organization, considering the size, business sector, and other factors.

# What is a Community of Practice?

One definition of CoPs is "groups of people who share a concern or a passion for something they do and learn how to do it better as they interact regularly."[1] While this is true, it is incomplete from a manager's perspective; the benefits that BAs provide each other through a CoP are relevant and important but managers want a CoP to increase the performance of the group. Many of these performance benefits are found in the interactions between a CoP and the rest of the organization. To understand the benefits of a CoP, we will look at it three ways:

- The roles a CoP can play in the organization
- The operation of a CoP and how this relates to organizational change
- The stakeholders who are involved in these changes

This chapter refers to a community of practice within an organization, rather than the worldwide community of practice. In this section, we begin with a high-level look at the roles a CoP can play in an organization. Since implementing any of these capabilities involves considerable change management, the next section discusses the ways a CoP can prepare, provoke, and prevent change. In the last part of this section, we list the many stakeholders with an interest in a CoP.

## What Can a CoP Do in My Organization?

A mature CoP can take on many responsibilities beyond their role as advocates for business analysis in the organization. Broadly, these fall into two categories: *review* and *recommend*.

- *Review:* Assess changes that impact BA practices and practitioners
- *Recommend:* Propose changes to BA practices and practitioners

In many cases, *review and recommend* go hand-in-hand. The table below lists some of these, including direct support for peer BAs in a CoP and a variety of other relationships to the rest of the organization. These roles are based on real CoPs in several large Canadian financial institutions but are not comprehensive. Any particular CoP may have other roles or some portion of the roles listed here.

---

1    http://www.ewenger.com/theory/index.htm

FIGURE 1. EXAMPLE ROLES FOR A COMMUNITY OF PRACTICE

| Role | Description | Benefits |
|---|---|---|
| Peer Support and Mentoring | • BAs with experience and expertise in one area provide ad hoc assistance to other BAs in a CoP. This spreads BA knowledge across organization. Includes peer reviews. | • Encourages standardized practices<br>• Increases quality of BA outputs<br>• Uncovers common problems across the organization |
| Peer Performance Assessment | • Senior BAs in a CoP evaluate the work of other BAs against internal standards.<br>• BAs in a CoP work with the standards group (if any) to set performance standards and baselines. | • Improves workforce management<br>• Fairer performance assessment process |
| Peer Competency Assessment | • BAs in a CoP evaluate each other using a standard competency model.<br>• CoP maintains private records of BA competency across groups and over time. | • Foundation for many aspects of performance improvement (see Performance and a CoP in this chapter) |
| Curriculum Assessment | • BAs in a CoP provide feedback to the group responsible for BA training on the quality of courses taken and advice on which courses should be taken. | • Better use of training budget<br>• Evidence for contract negotiations with education providers |
| Standards and Improvements to Processes, Techniques, and Tools | • BAs in a CoP work with the standards group (if any) to establish and maintain standards for the practice. | • Track BA work against standards<br>• Improve standards based on CoP feedback |
| Advocacy, Outreach, and Communication | • BAs in a CoP interact with stakeholders in a consistent and positive way.<br>• Single point of contact for stakeholder groups with interest or influence on BAs.<br>• BAs in a CoP reach out to stakeholders to educate and inform them about business analysis and the BA role in the organization. | • Increases assertiveness of BAs in CoP<br>• Better coordination with project practitioners (PM, Design, Testing) and other stakeholder groups<br>• Improves change management when BAs are initiating change |
| BA Focus Group | • Representative sample of BA population available to advocate for BAs in any organization changes that will impact BAs.<br>• Single point of contact for BAs | • Better coordination with organizational stakeholders<br>• Improved change management when BAs are targets of change |

In the early days of a CoP, it will focus on supporting the BAs in the CoP directly. As a CoP matures, it becomes more tightly integrated into the organization. The group can turn its focus outward, to relationships with stakeholders in other parts of the organization.

The diverse interests of a CoP can be a challenge, particularly for a small group or when the group is forming. For example, what should be the purpose? How should they run their meetings? Options include:

- Promoting the learning activities of CoP members through workshops and mentoring sessions
- Gaining buy-in for business analysis from key stakeholders through lunch-and-learn sessions
- Creating practice standards in working groups

As the manager supporting a CoP, you may need to focus them on one or two opportunities for improvement and table the others as future efforts.

### Time Commitment

BAs in a CoP will need to spend at least one hour a week working for the CoP, including working sessions with other BAs and with you. In large organizations that can support a Centre of Competency (COC) and a Practitioner Champion Group (PCG), Champions will also need to spend time working with BAs in their local groups. (See *1.3.3 Practice Support* for more information on Champions, PCGs and COCs.) Most CoPs should also meet as a group for about one hour a month to discuss progress and challenges. This meeting helps you coordinate plans, develop organizational messages, and learn from each other's work.

These minimums are practical: less than this, and the group is unlikely to build any momentum. It is possible to spend considerably more time on a CoP—particularly in the early days of the group—so it is important to set organizational expectations for how much time BAs can dedicate to it. Participation should enhance their regular BA work, not interfere with it.

## The CoP and Change Management

A CoP delivers value when:

- Practitioners in the CoP alter, adapt, and improve their work practices
- Organization adjusts its processes to absorb new work practices
- CoP participates in enterprise process improvements

In other words, a CoP delivers value when it is engaged in change.

The change management roles described in this section can and are done by individual BAs, with or without a CoP. An organized CoP supports and directs these change management activities but individual BAs must still participate. The coordination a CoP can bring is a big advantage for individual BAs. As a team, a CoP can present business analysis to the organization in a unified, coherent way. An established CoP can become a trusted resource by the organization at large, helping BAs to be trusted by default, instead of starting from scratch with each new stakeholder.

The change management roles of a CoP can be summed with three words: provoke, prepare, and prevent.[2]

- *Provoke:* Advocate for good changes to individual practitioners and to the maturity of the organization. For example, if the roles described above do not exist in the organization, a CoP advocates for them.
- *Prepare:* Communicate the benefits of good change to stakeholders, and help ease the transition from current to future state. For example, a CoP can act as a communications hub, both when BAs are making a change (e.g. improving the system development lifecycle by updating the business analysis process), and when they are targets of change (e.g. updated job profile and career path from HR).
- *Prevent:* Control damaging changes, or reduce the negative impacts of these changes. For example, a CoP may participate as a stakeholder in organizational changes that impact BAs. This helps ensure coordination and reduces churn (e.g. a new process from the Testing team is created with input from a CoP). A CoP may also monitor the quality of BA peer reviews to ensure that they are consistent across the organization.

A CoP plays these roles in two contexts: changes to the practice of business analysis and changes that impact the business analyst practitioners themselves. (These are not the changes BAs help implement while working on projects in the normal course of their jobs.) Changes to BA practices affect standards, processes, techniques, and tools that define the scope of the BA role. Changes to BA practitioners affect everything related to the BA, including performance, competency, assignment, hiring, firing, education, certification, career ladders, promotion, and benchmarking.

We will discuss the stakeholders who are interested or impacted by these changes in the next section. Here, we describe the role of a CoP in managing these changes as the organization and the CoP mature. A BA CoP is particularly well-suited to this because BAs are constantly immersed in exploring and implementing organizational change.

---

2    IIBA® workshop, *Helping Business Do Business Better*, by Kathleen Barret (President and CEO).

## Preparing for Change

Change management is a complex discipline that often begins with preparing for change. A CoP can be a working group and focus group to:

- Look past the symptoms, to discover problems and opportunities to improve the BA practice or the BA practitioners
- Analyze the impacts of change to BAs, other stakeholders, and the organization as a whole
- Describe the stakeholders who will be impacted by changes to BA practitioners and BA practices
- Validate your plans to create, implement, and monitor the change

## Provoking Change

A CoP is also a key group in implementing change. If the BAs in the CoP believe in the improvements you discover while preparing for change, they can form a passionate, self-supporting team of advocates and evangelists. A CoP helps BAs deliver a more powerful, unified message to the organization, partly by reducing individual risk and fear of reprisal.

When BAs are not competent enough or follow poor practices, the people who depend on them will have trouble doing their jobs. In this case, a CoP can help you make useful changes to the practice of business analysis. Unfortunately, there are many cases where BA performance depends on the competency and practices of some other group. Individual BAs might complain about the situation or suggest local, one-time changes to address the problems but they have no power to demand changes to the other groups' practices. A CoP can call on these other stakeholder groups to discuss ways to improve the situation at an organizational level.

## Preventing Change

Many organizational changes are poorly managed, often because the impacted stakeholders are not engaged appropriately. BAs often feel negative impacts of poorly defined changes because the BA role is not well understood by the groups initiating the changes. For example, a poorly informed HR group could position BAs as junior PMs on a career ladder, without seeking input from BAs or PMs.

A CoP can help stop bad changes before they get too expensive or do too much damage. As a single touch point for other organizational groups to engage, a CoP can make it easier for these groups to get accurate information about the BA role. A CoP can also be proactive in advertising and promoting the BA role and teaching others the impacts they have on business analysis. A CoP can influence organizational leaders, develop and deliver strong messages to management, and engage powerful groups in productive discussions. This influence can be used to provoke change as well.

# Stakeholder Groups

The stakeholders in a CoP are:

- People needed to start change
- People needed to make change stick
- People who feel the impact of the change—positive or negative

With this definition in mind, it is easy to see that there are many stakeholders in a CoP, concerned with BA practices and practitioners. They can influence or direct changes to both the practice and the practitioners, which means a CoP needs the support of many groups to be successful.

Stakeholders in a CoP can be grouped into four categories:

- *Practitioners:* Individuals who perform business analysis
- *Project Participants*: Groups and individuals who produce information BAs need, or who need information BAs produce
- *Practice Support:* Groups and individuals who support and govern the execution of business analysis in the organization
- *Organizational:* Groups and individuals who have reporting relationships with BAs in a CoP

Practitioners and Project Participants are most interested in the services that BAs deliver and the way BA deliver these services. Organizational and Practice Support stakeholders are more focussed on everything BAs do when not delivering BA services. These categories are conceptual, used to describe the roles, responsibilities, and activities of each stakeholder, and their relationship to a CoP. In some organizations, one group may have several stakeholder relationships to a CoP. For example, a BA Office, analogous to a PMO (Project Management Office), could manage the performance of BAs (Organizational) and be responsible for BA processes (Practice Support). In another organization, Project Managers might assign BAs to projects (Organizational) and then work with those BAs on the project (Project Participant).

These stakeholder relationships are described from the perspective of a large organization but any organization has someone in these positions, formally or informally. In your organization, one person could have responsibilities in more than one category or one category could be split between several people.

## Practitioners

A CoP provides a forum for BA practitioners—the people who perform business analysis tasks—to help each other. An individual practitioner may be interested in a CoP for many reasons, such as:

- Providing a forum for discussion and self-improvement
- Defining standards for BA practices

- Creating a sense of identity
- Arranging networking opportunities

Over time, a CoP can become a significant conduit for practitioners to influence and direct the maturation of their profession within their organization. Ongoing participation of BAs at a local and organizational level is the core of a CoP, no matter what their current job titles. A CoP may have participants in hybrid roles, specializations, and at any level of the organization (see sidebar, *A Selection Of...*).

## Project Participants

Many people interact directly with BAs on projects, whether in person, through shared processes, process hand-offs, or documents. These are CoP stakeholders with a project focus and an interest in the services that BAs deliver. They care how projects are executed because it affects them.

Since a CoP plays a significant role in improving the way projects operate, these people care about the work a CoP does, and vice versa. These are distinct from the people BAs call *solution stakeholders*—the people who will use a solution that a project delivers. Solution stakeholders are interested in the BAs they work with, not with a CoP that supports those BAs.

One way to identify Project Participant stakeholders is to consider the processes in the Solution Development Life Cycle (SDLC), whether formal or informal. Each process has inputs and outputs that form hand-offs to the other processes in the SDLC. Any process that requires business analysis work as an input or output should point to stakeholders in a CoP.

## A Selection Of...

**BA Titles**
- Business Systems Analyst
- Business Consultant
- Enterprise Architect
- Enterprise Business Analyst

**Hybrid BA Roles**
- BA and Testing
- BA and Project Management
- BA and Design
- BA and Management

**BA Specializations**
- Methodology (Agile, RUP)
- Knowledge Area (Elicitation, Enterprise Analysis)
- Industry (Financial, Gaming)
- Sector (Public, Private)

**BA Roles, by Seniority**
- Project BA: Work primarily inside projects
- Transition BA: Work primarily at the boundary between projects and the organization
- Enterprise BA: Work primarily at a portfolio level, working with business cases

In most cases, there are a relatively small set of outputs of business analysis services but these are used by many people: plans, requirements, diagrams, matrices, change requests, and so on.

The inputs to business analysis services are quite a bit more complex; BAs need information or resources the BA from many groups, including steering committees, project managers, design/development teams, solution support teams, test teams, customer representatives (users), and clients. It may also include project governance groups such as information security, legal, audit, enterprise architecture—and don't forget vendors and other third parties.

## Practice Support

Practice support groups are responsible for development of BA Practices and for supporting a CoP. For them, a CoP is a focus group, advisory panel, and communication channel; it helps them make useful change.

Practice support activities have an organizational and a practitioner perspective: the Centre of Competency (COC) and Practitioner Champion Group (PCG). In this chapter, Centre of Competency and Centre of Excellence are treated as different names for the same thing.

### Centre of Competency

In a large organization, a COC usually has a mandate and responsibility for all aspects of the practice of the profession. This includes overall responsibility for the Community of Practice and management of many of the relationships between the CoP and stakeholders in the business environment. This group may have a mandate to implement many or all of the roles of a CoP. In this case, the CoP and COC are partners, with interdependent roles; the COC supports the work of the CoP, and the CoP supports the work of the COC.

A COC is not usually an 'office' with functional reporting responsibilities for individual BAs. These roles are described in the Organizational section.

### Practitioner Champion Group

A Practitioner Champion Group (PCG) is usually part of a large organization. It is made up of BA Champions who represent the interests of the rest of the BAs in the CoP. Champions are passionate advocates for the BA profession. They can discuss the value of business analysis to the organization and from a global perspective. They take leadership roles, discussing the value of business analysis with colleagues, supporting peers, and are assertive—with or without organizational support.

Champions are a small percentage of the BA population but when working together in a PCG, they do everything a CoP does while they lead and coordinate BAs across the organization.

A PCG can be a formal or informal group of Champions. In some organizations, Champions band together as a grassroots movement. In others they are a formal team with organizational objectives and are supported by management, leaders, and the COC. In this case, 'support' often means taking on many of the administrative and organizational tasks that are part of a traditional council or committee, such as meeting scheduling and minutes. This helps Champions focus on activities that are most valuable from an organizational perspective, such as:

- Reviews and recommendations
- Developing and implementing objectives for the CoP (with the COC)
- Playing an active leadership role in local groups by engaging BAs to contribute to the CoP

A PCG should be structured in a way that represents the culture of your organization. This may mean small teams working on specific objectives, such as an update to one aspect of the BA process in the SDLC. It could also mean each Champion takes on an objective to work on with the BAs in his or her organizational group. The 'right' structure for a PCG is the one that works best in your organization.

## Organizational

Organizational stakeholders have functional reporting relationships with BAs, such as performance management, assignment to projects, or allocation of training dollars. A CoP helps these stakeholders manage BAs more effectively by giving them a single, unified communication channel to all BAs. Organization stakeholders can engage representatives from the CoP in changes to organizational processes and expect to get a reliable and realistic view of the needs of BAs. Organizational stakeholders can also deliver information to all the BAs in the organization through a CoP.

In general, organizational stakeholders fall into three categories: managers, leaders, and human resources (HR).

- *Managers:* BAs report to managers with day-to-day tactical responsibility for practitioners and power over the BAs. Managers are 'make or break' stakeholders in a CoP. Without manager support, it is extremely difficult to sustain the group. A manager is responsible for efficient delivery of BA services through the BAs in his or her group.
- *Leaders:* Managers report to Leaders, who have power over practitioners and strategic responsibilities for the BA practice. Like managers, leaders are 'make or break' stakeholders.
- *Human Resources:* Groups who define hiring practices, job profiles, career ladders, and performance assessments have power over BAs—power supported by the organizational structure. A CoP can help HR develop standards and practices that support effective business analysis.

Organizational stakeholders provide critical support for the development and ongoing operations of a CoP. This section takes the perspective of a manager of BAs; here we take a few moments to talk about leaders. They:

- Embody the goals of your CoP: set direction and maintain focus
- Commit resources to the development and operation of a CoP
- Remove organizational barriers to participation in a CoP
- Define measures of success and the associated rewards

For a CoP to develop in the ways discussed in the next section, you will need a strong leader to sponsor it, not just with words, but with tangible commitment of resources: people, time, and money. Be careful of leaders looking for superficial change instead of substantial improvement; they say they support business analysis and see the value of it but don't back up their words with resources. A Centre of Competency (COC) and Practitioner Champion Group (PCG) depend on strong commitment. Leaders can also influence or command stakeholders to participate in a CoP.

Leaders can have more subtle impacts on a CoP as well. Look for organizational measures and targets that conflict with the objectives you have for a CoP, and ask your leaders to help reconcile them. For example, in a big IT shop a target billable/non-billable ratio of 80% may seem quite reasonable. Leaders define the activities that count as billable and whether this ratio is measured at a group or individual level.[3] Depending on the details, this target can leave practitioners as little as one or two hours per week for all non-billable work—including staff meetings, time reporting, training, and a CoP. Ensure your Sponsor is aware of this sort of disconnect so he or she can work with other Leaders to resolve it.

# Increase Organizational Performance

A CoP can drive higher performance but performance is a broad concept. It refers to an individual's capacity to deliver useful outcomes and to the organizational capacity to deliver results. One component of individual performance is individual competency; similarly, organizational maturity[4] is a key factor in organization performance.

We start with the role of a CoP in increasing individual competency, particularly through careful use of a competency model. We will also discuss the complex relationship between individual competency and performance, from an evidence-based management perspective. Next, we explore how a CoP can

---

3    Calculated with 1 non-billable resource per 10 billable and 12 days vacation / year per employee, on average.

4    'Maturity' is considered in the context of organizational maturity models, such as CMMi and ITIL. A more mature organization operates in a more predictable way, with less wasted effort and better results.

help increase organizational maturity, and the impacts this can have on BA performance. Finally, we discuss the impacts of leadership commitment on a CoP and ways a CoP can influence leaders.

# Individual Competency

*"A supportive environment delivers more value than competent individuals."*

It is tempting to create a CoP primarily focussed on developing individual practitioner competency, because:

- You have significant influence on your employees' competency
- Employees usually like to increase their expertise
- It easy to measure real progress in competency development

While this is a worthwhile endeavour, it should not be the main purpose of a CoP because organizational factors have a larger impact on performance than individual competency does. Competent individuals in an unsupportive environment are seldom able to deliver real business value.

In the book *Hard Facts: Dangerous Half-Truths & Total Nonsense – Profiting from Evidence Based Management*, Jeffrey Pfeffer and Robert I. Sutton from Stanford University provide considerable evidence that a good team and business environment have a greater impact on performance than "stars" do. In other words, individual competency plays an important but limited role in performance. This means you should spend at least as much effort engaging the organization to create an environment for high performance as you do developing individual competency in your BAs.

Improving BA competency is still important for many reasons. It can be an integral factor in driving organizational maturity and a powerful way to engage BAs in a CoP—which helps a CoP play an active role in improving individual competency. For example, a CoP can facilitate these performance-enhancing interactions:

- BAs can easily and informally find peers and mentors for assistance
- BAs expose each other to different techniques, successes, and failures
- BAs can share organizational knowledge and influence

Real progress on developing individual competency is also a motivator for BAs. People who see opportunities to improve their skills are more likely to be engaged in a CoP and support it as a useful team. As a manager, you can support a CoP in maturing from a discussion group into a team that uses measurable objectives to improve performance.

## Understanding Business Analysis Competency Models and Assessment Tools

One powerful tool for driving results is a behaviour-based competency assessment. This kind of assessment is based on a competency model that describes the behaviours that are expected for practitioners with various levels of skill, knowledge, and experience. A competency assessment is usually an online survey with an array of questions intended to reveal a BA's ability to deliver BA services. It standardizes the collection and analysis of data about competencies, and provides an objective standard for comparing the competency of practitioners to each other and to organizational expectations. Assessment starts with individual BAs in a CoP. These are aggregated to show the competencies of a CoP as a whole.

Your organization may have a competency model already—bought or built in-house—or you may need to find one. The usefulness of a competency model should be assessed based on several characteristics:

- *BABOK® Guide Alignment:* All aspects of the model are traced directly and explicitly to the latest version of *A Guide to the Business Analysis Body of Knowledge®* (*BABOK® Guide*). This allows BAs to assess themselves—and to be assessed—against the industry standard definition for the profession of business analysis. It also ensures that BAs can compare their competencies across groups and industries, and track their development over time. *BABOK® Guide* alignment also translates competencies into a standard framework for organizational maturity planning (see page 214).
- *Extensible:* The model can be altered and updated to integrate into your business processes without destroying the validity of the tool. Other tools and processes can be built based on the model or on the data the model is used to collect. For example, you should be legally allowed to copy the competency model into a spreadsheet and add elements as needed.
- *Evidence Based:* Measures of competency are described in terms of behavioural indicators and services delivered. Behavioural indicators are evidence, not assumptions—objective descriptions of actions people take. For example, "knows three or more techniques for elicitation" is an assumption because an outside observer cannot say what another person knows. The statement "has performed three or more techniques for elicitation" is evidence. This subtle change in focus helps ensure that assessments are as objective as possible and favour evidence over opinion. This may be the most difficult characteristic to find because creating a model and assessment tool with these characteristics is very expensive and time consuming. It requires:

  - Substantial research into the behaviours of BAs
  - Psychometric[5] evaluation to ensure that it accurately measures the behaviours it is supposed to measure

---

5    Psychometrics is the field of study concerned with the theory and technique of educational and psychological measurement, which includes the measurement of knowledge, abilities, attitudes, and traits.

Remember: competency and performance are not the same, and competency assessments are not the same as performance assessments. We will look at ways to bridge these is detail later in this chapter.

## Competency Assessments

The first step in improving individual competency is to evaluate the current competencies of BAs in the organization. A CoP can make this task much easier by:

- Communicating the purpose of the assessment
- Managing concerns over how the information will be used
- Using the results to help BAs in a CoP help each other

A CoP will need your support and guidance to take on the responsibility of measuring and improving the competency of BAs.

### The Purpose of Assessment

A competency assessment is a data-collection tool used to measure the competencies of individuals and groups. This data is the basis for discussion between a CoP and the organization. In turn, these discussions, along with more data collection and analysis, are the basis for taking joint action to improve BA competency in ways that make sense for the organization and for the BAs.

It can be difficult for BAs to hear, understand, and believe this purpose, and hard for you to stay focused on it. Organizational culture and individual attitudes can contribute to this. For example, if employees are worried that a poor assessment will be used to punish—by being used to figure out whom to lay-off, for example—they will be cautious of any competency assessment.

These risk factors mean your plan for the introduction of a competency assessment deserves great care and attention. Work with a few influential BAs in a CoP to acknowledge their concerns and assure the rest of a CoP that the results will be used in a positive way—or at least will not be used to punish anyone.

### Protecting the Results of Assessment

One way to reassure BAs that assessment results will not be used to punish them is to make a CoP responsible for collecting and analysing individual results. Ask a CoP to choose a few Champions to manage the assessment process, with timelines and targets. These Champions will collect the results and ensure the raw data is rendered anonymous before it is passed on to management.

Depending on the size of the organization and the number of BAs in various organizational units, a CoP may be responsible for aggregating the individual data—again, to protect anonymity. Control of this information also helps build engagement in a CoP and reduces resistance to change.

### Using the Individual Results in a CoP

Individual BAs will use their personal results in at least three ways: personal development, mentoring, and building baselines.

- *Personal Development:* The data from individual self-assessments should describe what the BAs believe about their own competencies, compared to the industry standard (*BABOK® Guide*). This data can help BAs make professional development decisions about the competencies they want to improve.
- *Mentoring:* If each BA in a CoP shares their strongest results—the Knowledge Area (KA) and Tasks where they self-assessed as most competent—everyone in the group will know who to turn to for advice. Most people are comfortable

*Figure 2. BA Roles Categorized by Scope (project to enterprise)*
*and Focus (generalist, specialist, hybrid)[1]*

## Focus Context Within the Organization

| | | Project/Process/Service Continuous Improvement | Department/Business Function Transition | Enterprise |
|---|---|---|---|---|
| **Role Category** | **Generalist** | Business Analyst<br>Management Consultant<br>BA Project Lead | Business Consultant<br>Business Relationship Manager<br>Management Consultant<br>Portfolio Manager<br>BA Program Lead | Business Architect<br>Business Relationship Manager<br>Strategic Business Analyst<br>Management Consultant<br>Strategic Planner<br>BA Practice Leader |
| | **Specialist** | Agile Business Analyst<br>Application Domain Expert (SME)<br>Business Intelligence Analyst<br>Business Rules Analyst<br>Business Systems Analyst<br>Business Process Analyst<br>Data Analyst<br>Product Owner<br>Requirements Engineer/ Manager<br>Service Request Analyst<br>Systems Analyst | Business Intelligence Analyst<br>Business Domain Expert (SME)<br>Functional Business Analyst<br>Process Owner/Steward<br>Product Manager (Marketing)<br>Service Owner<br>Systems/Solution Architect<br>Functional Business Analyst | Industry Domain Expert (SME)<br>IT Strategist<br>Process Architect |
| | **Hybrid** | BA/PM<br>BA/Tester<br>BA/Developer<br>BA/User Experience<br>Database Analyst<br>Information Architect<br>Product Manager (Marketing)<br>Programmer/Analyst<br>Project Manager<br>QA Analyst<br>Usability/UXP | Middle-to-Senior Management<br>Product Manager (Marketing)<br>Solutions Architect<br>Systems Design Analyst | CXO<br>Enterprise Architect |

---

1    ©2011, International Institute of Business Analysis.

sharing positive results like this; if they are willing, ask them to publish a list of experts so anyone needing assistance can get help quickly. Since no one has to reveal a low competency—except to the mentor—this can help build a sense of control for the BAs in the group. It also provides recognition and helps BAs build a reputation for expertise with their peers and colleagues.

- *Building Baselines:* Individual results can also be compared to the overall competency of the CoP. To do this, all the individual results need to be aggregated into a *competency map*—an average of the assessment data—filtered into meaningful groups and combined with a variety of contextual data. In some CoPs, most BAs have similar responsibilities so they can compare themselves to a competency map describing the average for the whole CoP. If the BA role varies substantially (by organizational unit, for example), each unit should have a competency map. It may be worthwhile to aggregate results based on categories of BA (see Figure 1).

Competency maps can take many forms, depending on the assessment tool that you use. It may be enough to use a simple spreadsheet that calculates the average competency scores across the CoP. Since the model is aligned to the *BABOK® Guide*, the results can be structured to show competency in each Knowledge Area, Task, and Technique.

### Adding Perspective to the Current State Competency Map

At this point, your CoP has collected and analyzed the first set of data for the current state competency map: you can describe how the BAs see themselves. Unfortunately, you have no idea how confident you should be about these self-assessments. They are not likely to match up with the way that stakeholders perceive BAs because humans over-and under-estimate our own competency.

A stakeholder-focused 360° is one way to make the self-assessment data more meaningful. An ideal 360° is a short, evidence-based competency survey that is rigorously aligned to the BA self-assessment tool and *BABOK® Guide*. Each BA asks several colleagues to complete the assessment, including managers, project participants, and other BAs. Some competency assessment tools include this capability. If yours does not, you may be able to create this kind of 360° by choosing a limited set of behavioural indicators from the self-assessment—perhaps using the strongest and weakest competencies of the group. Make sure the behaviours are described in ways that a non-BA can recognize.

Be prepared to facilitate a discussion with CoP members about any significant discrepancies between the self-assessment and the stakeholder assessment. Investigate these differences before discussing them, to make sure they are the result of something related to BA competency rather than something like a poorly worded question.

### How Managers Can Support Competency Assessments

As a manager, you have access to resources that you can use to sponsor the licensing and use of a competency model. Be prepared to spend some money buying a good model, and commit non-billable time for your CoP to use it.

Your tangible commitment will help build trust and commitment in your CoP members; this, in turn, makes it easier to ask them to provide aggregated results describing the overall competency of the organization.

# Organizational Maturity and BA Practice Maturity

A mature organization has the capability to consistently achieve desired outcomes, in repeatable ways. One of the best-known models of organizational maturity is CMMI (Capability Maturity Model Integrated) created by SEI (Software Engineering Institute) from Carnegie Mellon.[6] As an organization matures, it gets better at achieving good outcomes. Performance increases occur because institutional barriers are removed and organizational supports are created.

Communities of Practice have a role in improving organizational maturity, with particular focus on using data gathered from competency assessments as a foundation for change and helping to manage that change. We discuss this, along with key aspects of organizational maturity, starting with a bottom-up approach. We take the perspective of a manager with a small team of BAs and build on the competency map you have already created.

## Define Organizational Context

At this point, your current state competency map has two data sets that allow you to assess how closely the competencies in your CoP match the standards set in the *BABOK® Guide*. For individual BAs, this is very useful information. From an organizational perspective this result is interesting but that is all: the results may not have a significant impact on the performance of your group. To see why, consider a group that is weak in Business Analysis Planning and Monitoring (BAPM), Enterprise Analysis (EA), and Solution Assessment and Validation (SAV)—the Knowledge Areas (KAs) more focus on the enterprise level or the transition between the project and the enterprise. If the BAs in this group work on tiny enhancement projects—two or three days total effort—these low scores in these KAs may be appropriate; they won't limit the performance of the group. BAs can deliver relevant services with an appropriate degree of competency.

To plan for performance improvement, compare three things:

- Service Level Map, describing who delivers BA services for every Task in the *BABOK® Guide* (your group or other groups)
- Current state competency map
- *BABOK® Guide* Tasks, describing the full scope of the BA role

---

6   SEI describes CMMI as "a process improvement approach that provides organizations with the essential elements of effective processes that ultimately improve their performance." Maturity is ranked from "incomplete" at level 0, with "a general failure to attain the purpose of the process," to "optimizing" at level 5, where "performance of the process is optimized to meet current and future business needs, and the process achieves repeatability in meeting its defined business goals."

Since your competency model is already aligned to the *BABOK° Guide*, it makes sense to describe your BA services in terms of the *BABOK° Guide* as well.

To create your Service Level Map, walk through the Tasks in the *BABOK° Guide* with your CoP, considering the BA services your group provides. Mark each Task as work you deliver, or don't. As you do, answer two questions:

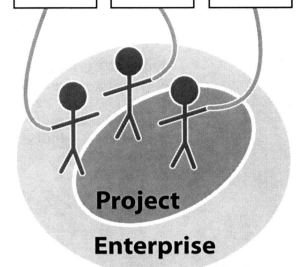

| Enterprise BAs | Transition BAs | Project BAs |
|---|---|---|
| most work is done outside of projects | work bridges project and enterprise | most work is done inside of projects |

**Project BAs** work primarily within projects. They focus on Elicitation, Requirements Analysis and Requirements Management and Communication.

**Transition BAs** straddle the boundary between the project and the enterprise. They have significant responsibilities in Business Analysis Planning and Monitoring and Solution Assessment and Validation—KAs that describe the BA's role in implementing the solution in the enterprise.

**Enterprise BAs** are the most concerned with Enterprise Analysis. They help determine which projects should be run in the first place.

- *Who delivers BA services that you don't deliver?* In almost all cases, every Task in the *BABOK° Guide* is being performed by someone somewhere in the organization because project success depends all of the tasks in the *BABOK° Guide* being fulfilled to some degree.[7] The work may be done formally as part of the mandate of a group or it may be done informally because it is necessary to do it for projects to succeed. If your group doesn't deliver a service, it will see these other groups as providing inputs to your work or using the outputs of the BA services you do provide. For example, an Enterprise Architecture group may complete Task *5.5 Define Business Case*, which your group needs for Tasks in the *Requirements Analysis* KA (6.1–6.6). If you don't know who is doing this work, you will need to find out. If no one is doing it, you will need to find a way to have the work done—by your team or by another.

- *For services you provide with no matching Task in the BABOK° Guide, why do you do this work?* Your group may be made up of hybrid practitioners, who

---

7　As long as there is a clean, efficient hand-off of the work from one team to another, responsibilities for the various tasks can be distributed through your organization in whatever way makes sense. Poor hand-offs and 'missed' tasks often manifest as rework. See *BABOK° Guide*, Version 2, 1.4 Knowledge Areas and 1.5 Tasks. Complete business analysis is necessary for project success but it is not sufficient; there is a lot of other work to be done.

provide services that are inputs or outputs to BA Tasks. For example, your group may use requirements packages (Task 4.4) to create solution designs or create plans for solution testing.

Your Service Level Map now describes where your group fits in the overall delivery of BA services and identifies hand-offs between other groups and your own. It gives your CoP perspective and may point to opportunities for improvement at an organizational level—something you can negotiate with other managers.

## Analyze Performance Gaps

Now it is time to compare the current state competency assessment to the Service Level Map. The comparison will allow you and your CoP to uncover organizational roadblocks that limit the performance of CoP members. We will use a simple example with a few stakeholders to describe this process but the analytical approach can be applied to each stakeholder in all four categories.

Consider a group where competency in the *Plan Business Analysis Approach* task of BAPM appears to be sufficient but your Service Level Map shows that they are not delivering this service regularly (Figure 3). CoP members report significant resistance from two places: Project Managers who think this is PM work and 'old school' BAs who agree with them. When BAs do try to share and validate an approach, PMs won't take the time to review it and complain about having to fund BA time to develop it at all. The resulting lack of coordination between team members increases the timeline and cost for projects. Symptoms include:

* BAs have difficulty getting the time needed to do their jobs
* BAs have difficulty getting people needed in elicitation sessions
* Many avoidable change requests are raised
* BAs feel that they don't have the organizational support they need

To change this situation, you need to understand the factors that prevent the *Plan Business Analysis Approach* Task from being performed.

Four stakeholder groups can prevent BAs from performing this Task:

1. Practitioner stakeholders
2. Project Participant stakeholders
3. Practice Support stakeholders
4. Organizational stakeholders

In each case, the stakeholder group must understand and support the service the BAs deliver or the Task will be very difficult to complete. Senior BAs may be able to influence these organizational barriers but for most, the Tasks become impossible.

Whatever approach you take in your gap analysis, make sure your CoP is involved. Have them describe gaps from the perspective of each stakeholder, rather than creating a list of problems that other groups have imposed on them. This will help your CoP take a positive, compassionate approach to advocating for change, wherever it is needed.

## Define the Future State

*Figure 3. Example Tool to Compare the Current State Competency Map, Service Level Map, and Future State Competency Map*

| KA | | Task | Group Competency | | BA Service Delivered By | Anonymous Individual Competency Scores | | | | | | | |
|---|---|---|---|---|---|---|---|---|---|---|---|---|---|
| | | | Current State | Future State | | A | B | C | D | E | F | G | H |
| BAPM | 2.1 | Plan Business Analysis Approach | 0.00 | 2.50 | PMs | 0.0 | 0.0 | 0.0 | 0.0 | 0.0 | 0.0 | 0.0 | 0.0 |
| | 2.2 | Conduct Stakeholder Analysis | 2.70 | 3.00 | US | 4.5 | 0.9 | 2.3 | 2.5 | 3.4 | 4.4 | 3.4 | 0.2 |
| | 2.3 | Plan BA Activities | 3.51 | 4.00 | US | 1.9 | 2.5 | 3.3 | 4.9 | 2.6 | 4.4 | 4.4 | 4.1 |
| | 2.4 | Plan BA Communication | 2.84 | 4.25 | US | 3.4 | 2.6 | 3.7 | 4.6 | 3.6 | 1.2 | 2.0 | 1.6 |
| | 2.5 | Plan Requirements Management Process | 2.35 | 3.00 | US | 4.7 | 0.4 | 3.7 | 4.7 | 2.3 | 0.4 | 2.5 | 0.1 |
| | 2.6 | Manage BA Performance | 0.00 | 2.00 | Unknown | 0.0 | 0.0 | 0.0 | 0.0 | 0.0 | 0.0 | 0.0 | 0.0 |

Now that you know where you stand and why your group is there, you can figure out where you want to be. This future state will describe the capabilities your group needs to:

- Deliver new BA services (filling in gaps in the current state)
- Increase the value of BA services it delivers today
- Increase the quality of the BA services it delivers today
- Decrease wasted effort in service delivery
- Increase efficiency in service delivery

*Figure 4. Example Worksheet for Recording Stakeholder Resistance Analysis*

| Stakeholder | | | Task | | Commitment | | Comments, Notes and Possible Remedies |
|---|---|---|---|---|---|---|---|
| Category | Group | ID | Name | | Understand | Support | |
| Practioners | New Hires | 2.1 | Plan Business Analysis Approach | | No | — | Update BA 101 Course |
| | Old Guard | 2.1 | Plan Business Analysis Approach | | Yes | No | Create pilots and 1-on-1 support |
| Project Participants | Project Managers | 2.1 | Plan Business Analysis Approach | | Yes | No | Create pilots and 1-on-1 support |
| | | 2.6 | Manage Business Analysis Performance | | No | — | Present purpose, benefits to PMO |
| | | 5.4 | Define Solution Scope | | Yes | No | Create pilots and 1-on-1 support |
| | Business Partner Leaders | 5.4 | Define Solution Scope | | No | — | Introduce via Manager Forum |
| | | 5.5 | Define Solution Scope | | No | Yes | Introduce via Manager Forum |
| | | 7.6 | Evaluate Solution Performance | | Yes | No | Discuss BA/Business Partnership |

Each component of your future state should be defined in measureable terms. Measures are powerful/dangerous and have an opportunity cost. For example, the effort expended measuring progress could be directed to billable work. Measures are worse than useless when they waste resources. They can:

- Actively promote undesirable behaviours in people being measured
- Not provide information needed by stakeholders to make decisions
- Provide information that causes stakeholders to make bad decisions

Measures will depend on your organization and your goals but a few examples include:

- BA career ladder established, over 1 year
- Hundred percent adoption rate for a new template or practice, in six months
- Twenty-five percent increase in hours spent performing a Task, over six months
- 0.75-point increase in competency in the CoP for a Task, over 1 year
- Twenty percent improvement in agreement between individual competency self assessments and 360° competency assessments
- Ten percent decrease in the duration of projects using a new technique

Many measures will be *leading indicators*—indirect assessments that should predict the *key performance indicators (KPI)* (the direct benefits). The first five examples listed above are leading indicators. The last is a KPI. Some measures—such as a career ladder—may be organizational in nature and outside of your direct control. Because the future state goes beyond the CoP and your group, defining these capabilities and measures means going beyond the gap analysis. Work with you CoP, peers, and Leaders to understand the value your group can deliver to the organization (the value *can* deliver is not always based on the what the organization expects of you today). You can think of the future state as a business rationale for filling or keeping gaps between the BA services you provide and the ones defined in the *BABOK° Guide* Tasks.

The future state vision should be delivered to stakeholder groups in whatever format will be most compelling to them; presentations are common but not always the best choice. You may create the foundation for describing and tracking the future state in a spreadsheet (as in our examples) but translate it into user stories delivered during lunch-and-learn sessions. Work with your CoP to develop and deliver this measurable vision to your stakeholders.

## Plan to Create the Future State

Before you take the final step in driving organizational maturity with your CoP—executing your plan—you need to define that plan. For a small team, this could be a simple roadmap with milestones and tasks. Larger change initiatives may need more significant project planning. The actions needed will vary widely between organizations and may include:

- Training for BAs
- Development and delivery of education sessions to BAs and other CoP stakeholders
- Developing and implementing new or changed BA techniques, processes, and templates
- Alterations to processes that provide inputs to BA services or that use outputs of BA services

Make certain that all stakeholder groups are involved in creating and validating your plans—especially stakeholders who you can influence but do not control. If your plan begins with establishing a limited set of standard techniques and templates, give Project Participants an opportunity to provide feedback. In Organizational stakeholder groups outside your control (such as human resources or finance), you may use your analysis to negotiate, build political capital, or create a business case for change. Engage them directly to discuss your plans and ensure that you and your CoP deliver the same message.

Your future state and transition plans are only realistic if they include the cost and effort of data collection and report generation as a recurring cost, not a project expense. Be wary of deferring these to 'phase 2'. Reports can become exponentially more expensive when delayed because the processes for data collection must be retrofitted into a poorly understood in-flight process instead of being built into the day-to-day process of doing business.

Take time creating your plan but don't let planning become a substitute for action. As your CoP grows, you will learn more about what works and what does not, and should adjust your plan accordingly. Ask your CoP members to think of each step as an experiment: build on successes, learn from failures, and keep driving toward your goals.

## Execute the Future State Plan

Making changes to the way your group works is not a trivial exercise. The work you have done with your CoP should make it much easier but it will likely be a messy affair with failures along with successes. Think of the plan as an experiment—something to learn from, whether you get the results you expect or not. "Failure" is the discovery of something that doesn't work, not the end of the world. Encourage CoP members to approach these changes the same way. The plan should be reviewed regularly and revised at each stage.

## Summary of Performance Improvement Planning Steps

This section took the perspective of a single manager building a CoP with the BAs that report to him or her. A CoP spanning many functional groups can still use this approach but managers and the CoP will need the guidance and leadership of a Practice Support group to coordinate their work and look for larger patterns across the organization. For example, the future states for different managers should not conflict by the time you begin to execute the future state plan.

### High Level Performance Improvement Steps

1. Increase individual competency
   a. Perform competency assessments
   b. Aggregate CoP results
   c. Assess validity of results
   d. Plan individual development
2. Increase organizational maturity
   a. Define organizational context
   b. Analyze performance gaps
   c. Define the future state
   d. Plan to create the future state
3. Execute the Future State Plan

## CoP Integration Scenarios

The relationship between organizational maturity and performance implies that, as much as possible, you should integrate your CoP into the operations of the organization. An integrated CoP should be able to influence or direct changes that increase organizational maturity, where a stand-alone CoP can only affect BAs. The degree of integration desired or possible will vary from organization to organization but the relationship between a CoP and stakeholders is always critical. The scenarios below show how good interactions between a CoP and stakeholders can help improve the way the organization operates. This is not a comprehensive list; it is a sample to guide you and your CoP in creating useful plans for managing stakeholders.

### Process, Tools, and Techniques

One key role of a CoP is to review and recommend updates to BA processes, tools, and techniques. BA teams drawn from across the organization can review process and tool standards established by Practice Support groups. CoP members can form a peer advisory team, available to provide high-level recommendations to BAs on the documents they produce and the techniques they use. If the peer advisory team is made up of senior BAs representing most parts of the organization, it can also provide insight to Practice Support and Organizational stakeholders on common challenges faced by BAs—feeding the process of continuous improvement.

One way or another, all Project Participants are concerned with these aspects of the BA role. Regular engagements with Project Participant stakeholders can help everyone directly involved in the Solution Development Life Cycle (SDLC) can discuss, understand, and coordinate updates and improvements. For example, if your organization has a PM CoP or council, a member of the BA CoP should sit as a representative at some of their meetings—and a PM should do the same with the BA CoP.

### Curriculum

A CoP can help improve the quality and impact of the BA curriculum in your organization by maintaining an index of the courses taken by CoP members. The index could include individual course evaluations and recommendations for BAs and managers who are considering BA Development plans. Recommendations could even be based on changes in competency measured before and after a course is taken. Practice Support groups can also consult with the CoP on the quality of training providers.

### Hiring and Career Planning

A strong CoP can support interview processes across the organization—assigning senior BAs to participate in panel interviews, for example. A CoP with strong ties to HR and managers could review—or even develop—a bank of question banks for hiring managers to use when interviewing BAs.

A CoP can also provide many useful insights to organizational stakeholders. For example, they can work with HR to review current career paths for BAs and recommend changes that will help BAs increase performance.

### Accreditation

A very mature CoP can establish a peer review board to formally evaluate the performance of BAs based on the documents they produce, attestations from stakeholders, and other observations of their work. If these evaluations are part of an accreditation program, managers can use this performance information as part of the annual performance review cycle.

### Resource Strategy and Planning

Whether your organization has a formal resource strategy or not, a CoP can offer insight and expertise on the competencies that BAs need in your organization and in your market. The leaders in a CoP can formally represent their peers in the strategic planning process, using competency assessment data, accreditation data, and so on to help the organization make useful long term plans.

If a CoP holds competency records in confidence, it can also help management discover opportunities to reallocate BAs from group to group. For example, managers can ask a CoP to help find candidates with competencies that complement the needs of the manager's group. Managers are still responsible for interviews, transfers and so on; a CoP acts as a trusted advisor to managers and trusted custodian of the records of individual BAs.

# Which CoP is right for me?

The rest of this chapter looks at the components of a CoP and how to utilize a CoP to drive individual competence and organizational maturity. In this section, we describe example CoPs that:

- Have a dozen, up to a hundred, or up to a thousand BAs
- Operate in consulting shops that supply BAs to other organizations
- Are made of mostly external consultants and global resources

Each scenario assumes that the CoP is mature, integrated into the organization, and has useful sponsorship. Several variations are also discussed.

## Up to Twelve BAs: Manage a Local Team

This small group provides services to a project organization with dozens of employees. All BAs participate directly in the CoP. Their local manager gives them autonomy in how they operate, while guiding them to focus on practical objectives instead of administration. Together, they develop milestones for the group, such as completing competency self-assessments, group competency mapping, and standardizing techniques. Members review each other's project work and recommend improvements.

### Variation: BA Office

The BAs in this group provide BA services to other groups in the organization. Like consultants, most of these BAs are generalists with experience and flexibility.

### Variation: Hybrid BAs

These BAs have responsibilities for non-BA work like project management or production work. The team rapidly handles many small projects. As a result, the CoP represents the whole SDLC, with sub-teams responsible for business analysis and the other disciplines represented in the group.

### Variation: Small Group in a Large Organization

This CoP is one of many. Managers are responsible for small groups of BAs with little coordination: some CoPs have generalists; others are specialized in a domain, such as industry knowledge or a methodology like Agile. The leadership team wants to copy the success of your CoP into other groups, with the intention to bring the groups together for larger scale work in the future. Other teams have started using the same competency model you piloted, so different group structures should not interfere with larger scale coordination of reports.

# Up to One Hundred BAs:
# Manage a Group with Local Teams

This CoP is made up of BAs providing services to a project organization with hundreds or thousands of employees, in several locations—and possibly several time zones. BAs are involved in dozens of projects, ranging from small updates to major implementations. Some BAs are senior resources, focused on enterprise analysis and reporting to Leaders. CoP members have chosen a few Champions, who represent BAs to the various stakeholder groups, coordinate the work of smaller CoP teams, and work with managers to define and implement CoP goals.

### Variation: BA Office

One senior manager runs a BA Office with functional responsibility for all the BAs in a large division or the whole organization. BAs report up though lower-level team-leads or managers. Champions and managers work together to set goals for BA competency development, process improvement, and so on. Managers provide administrative support to help make these goals realistic.

### Variation: Many BA Teams

One manager is responsible for the CoP but BAs work in groups of up to a dozen and report into managers all across the organization. The senior manager coordinates the overall direction of the CoP and manages the relationship to managers of BAs.

# Hundreds to Thousands of BAs:
# Lead Many Groups

This CoP is made up of BAs providing services to a project organization with thousands or tens of thousands of employees, in many locations and time zones. BAs are employed in many lines of business and may report into BA Offices or local managers. BAs are involved in almost all projects—not just technology projects. They have a clear career ladder that extends to the most senior levels of the organization.

A Practice Support group, such as a Centre of Competency (COC) works with a Practitioner Champion Group (PCG) to set goals and improve performance. Almost all groups have delegated a Champion to represent them on the PCG. The PCG works with the COC and CoP to:

- Manage relationships with CoP stakeholders
- Establish standards for competency measures, processes, tools, and techniques
- Create long-term strategic initiatives to improve BA performance at an organizational level

### Variation: Multinational Organization

The size and complexity of the organization makes it very difficult to establish standards across all groups. The CoP is fragmented in many senses: by geography, time zone, language, and culture, to name a few. The COC and PCG rely heavily on communication technologies such as forums, email, conference calls (video and audio), and instant messenger.

## All BAs: Consulting Houses

The CoP is made up of BAs providing services to external clients. Many consultants are hybrid practitioners, and may have other specializations such as industry subject matter expertise. The CoP is focused on improving individual BA competency and making it easy for BAs to get advice and mentor each other. Effective use of communication technologies is particularly important.

The impact of billable/non-billable time is exaggerated since all revenue is directly related to billable time. This restricts the time available for a CoP but many of the drivers for a CoP are not as severe: most projects follow the standards of the client organization, instead of the standards of the consulting house.

## External BAs: Global Resources and Consultants

This organization has outsourced a substantial part of the business—IT, production, or something else—so the number of BAs employed in the organization is relatively small. Many of these BAs are senior, hybrid practitioners, who work with the external BAs to make sure the solutions delivered are the solutions needed. Internal BAs spend more time on enterprise analysis, BA planning and monitoring, and solution assessment and validation; external BAs do more elicitation, requirements analysis, and requirement management and communication.

### Variation: Internal-Only CoP

The CoP works much like the 'Up to Twelve BAs' or 'Up to One Hundred BAs' CoP, with similar benefits and characteristics. Managing relationships with external BAs is a major topic of discussion for the CoP.

### Variation: Internal and External CoP

Competency assessments are managed by the CoP and are a significant component in performance management of external BAs. The CoP is also a forum for maintaining a smooth, effective relationship between internal and external BAs.

# Conclusion

At the start of this chapter we described a manager who was not sure how to make best use of BAs to drive performance. To answer this, we considered a CoP as a team, integrated into the operations of the organization. Together, these BAs work to improve both organizational maturity and individual competency. This integrated CoP affects organizational performance in measurable ways by provoking organizational and individual change, and by helping manage that change in positive ways.

Building this kind of CoP is not a trivial task. We explored ways for a manager to work with a CoP to drive performance gains, though many of these benefits are not directly in the control of the manager or CoP. To succeed, they must work together to influence the organization, following a long-term plan. Clear objectives and bite-sized packages of work—each with demonstrable benefits to BAs and to the organization—build momentum and credibility in the CoP and the manager.

There is no 'one-size-fits-all' community of practice: the best CoP is the one that you structure to fit through performance challenges of your organization. Learn from your BAs and CoP as it grows. Challenge them to improve, adapt, and innovate—and give them the resources they need to become an integrated, self-sustaining, and continuously improving business analysis community of practice.

# About the Author

Julian Sammy has a passion for the intersection of technology, behaviour and information. He is develop ing a science-based theory and approach to business analysis, which has lead to popular and provocative seminars such as The Dangerous Question and Gold From Garbage: Harnessing Human Irrationality. Julian is currently Enterprise BA for IIBA and the IIBA Head of New Media. He has fourteen years experience in IT, as a Project, Transition and Enterprise BA, Chief Architect, developer, designer, manager, strategist,

and Manager of a BA Centre of Competency. He proud to be a member of the BABOK® Guide v3 Core Team.

Find out more at theDangerousQuestion.com.

CPSIA information can be obtained at www.ICGtesting.com
Printed in the USA
BVOW051211021211

277471BV00003B/5/P